JOURNAL FOR THE STUDY OF THE OLD TESTAMENT SUPPLEMENT SERIES
137

JSOT Press
Sheffield

Professor Benjamin Uffenheimer

Justice

and

Righteousness

Biblical Themes and their Influence

Edited by
Henning Graf Reventlow
and
Yair Hoffman

Journal for the Study of the Old Testament
Supplement Series 137

Copyright © 1992 Sheffield Academic Press

Published by JSOT Press
JSOT Press is an imprint of
Sheffield Academic Press Ltd
The University of Sheffield
343 Fulwood Road
Sheffield S10 3BP
England

Typeset by Sheffield Academic Press
and
Printed on acid-free paper in Great Britain
by Billing & Sons Ltd
Worcester

British Library Cataloguing in Publication Data

Justice and Righteousness: Biblical Themes
and Their Influence. —(JSOT Supplement
Series, ISSN 0309-0787; No. 137)
I. Reventlow, Henning Graf
II. Hoffman, Yair III. Series
221.6

ISBN 1-85075-339-3

CONTENTS

In 1985 an informal partnership was founded between the Department of Bible, University of Tel Aviv, Israel, and the Faculties of Evangelical and Catholic Theology, University of the Ruhr, Bochum, Germany. It came to life in a first meeting in Tel Aviv. The papers read at this conference have been published in the volume *Creative Biblical Exegesis* that appeared in the JSOT Supplement Series.[1]

We are glad to deliver to the public a new volume containing the contributions of a second symposium held in Bochum, 19-21 June, 1990. It was attended by participants from Tel Aviv, Jerusalem, Beersheva and Bochum. The general aims were the same: to show that the closer cooperation of Jewish and Christian Bible scholars can help both sides to a deeper understanding of the common biblical heritage. Both the exegesis of the Bible itself and the study of the history of its influence were again the theme of our conference. This time we focused our discussions on the topic 'Justice and Righteousness', because we expected to be guided by these keywords to one of the central ideas of the Bible which has had an immense impact on the thinking of the modern world, be it Christian, Jewish or secular. The benevolent reader may judge himself if this expectation has been fulfilled. Most of the contributions were dedicated to biblical exegesis, problems and institutions, but some, and especially the concluding panel discussion, made visible how important justice and righteousness are for human life and society today. Social justice and human rights—are they thinkable without their biblical origins?

The volume is also a Festschrift for Benjamin Uffenheimer on his 70th birthday. Without his initiative our meetings would not have taken place, and he is already engaged in preparing a further one in Tel Aviv. The books he has published in Hebrew are well known: *The Visions of Zechariah* (Jerusalem, 1961) and *Ancient Prophecy in*

---

1. JSOTSup, 59; Sheffield: JSOT Press, 1988.

Israel (Jerusalem, 1973). The editors, one of whom is a student of Benjamin Uffenheimer, while the other has enjoyed his friendship for several years, together with all contributors to this volume, wish him God's blessing and that he may gather in further rich fruit of his scholarly work, in a land of Israel living in peace. Being a Festschrift, the volume also contains a contribution by Rivka Schatz-Uffenheimer as a gift to her husband, although she unfortunately could not herself be present at the conference. As all contributors regret deeply, she passed away in February, 1992. Blessed be her memory. The paper of Gershon Brin, who was prevented from coming at the last moment, has also been included.

We want to thank all who helped during the conference in catering for the participants, offering accommodation and other services. Our special thanks are directed to the Evangelical Church of Westfalia which by a generous grant made possible our coming together over so large a distance without financial problems.

We also thank the Editors of the JSOT Supplement Series for their friendly offer to publish the congress volume.

Henning Graf Reventlow
Yair Hoffman

ABBREVIATIONS

AfO	*Archiv für Orientforschung*
ASTI	*Annual of the Swedish Theological Institute*
ATD	Das Alte Testament Deutsch
BA	*Biblical Archaeologist*
BK	*Bibel und Kirche*
BSO(A)S	*Bulletin of the School of Oriental (and African) Studies*
BZAW	Beihefte zur ZAW
CAD	Assyrian Dictionary of the Oriental Institute of the University of Chicago
CAH	*Cambridge Ancient History*
CIS	*Corpus inscriptionum semiticarum*
CTA	A. Herdner, *Corpus des tablettes en cunéiformes alphabétiques de Ras Shamra*
EvT	*Evangelische Theologie*
EWNT	Exegetisches Wörterbuch zum Neuen Testament
FRLANT	Forschungen zur Religion und Literatur des Alten und Neuen Testaments
GTA	Göttinger theologische Arbeiten
HAT	Handbuch zum Alten Testament
HKAT	Handkommentar zum Alten Testament
HNT	Handbuch zum Neuen Testament
HTR	*Harvard Theological Review*
HUT	Hermeneutische Untersuchungen zur Theologie
ICC	International Critical Commentary
JANESCU	*Journal of the Ancient Near Eastern Society of Columbia University*
JAOS	*Journal of the American Oriental Society*
JHS	*Journal of Hellenic Studies*
JJS	*Journal of Jewish Studies*
JQR	*Jewish Quarterly Review*
JSS	*Journal of Semitic Studies*
KAI	H. Donner and W. Röllig, *Kanaanäische und aramäische Inschriften*
KAT	Kommentar zum Alten Testament
KeH	KurzgeFasstes exegetisches Handbuch
LCL	Loeb Classical Library
MGWJ	*Monatsschrift für Geschichte und Wissenschaft des Judentums*
OTL	Old Testament Library
PAAJR	*Proceedings of the American Academy of Jewish Research*

RA	*Revue d'assyriologie et d'archéologie orientale*
RGG	*Religion in Geschichte und Gegenwart*
RHR	*Revue de l'histoire des religions*
RS	Ras Samra Texts
SUNT	Studien zum Umwelt des Neuen Testaments
TBü	Theologische Bücherei
TDOT	*Theological Dictionary of the Old Testament*
TLZ	*Theologische Literaturzeitung*
TRE	*Theologische Realenzyklopädie*
TWNT	G. Kittel and G. Friedrich (eds.), *Theologisches Wörterbuch zum Neuen Testament*
UF	*Ugarit-Forschungen*
USQR	*Union Seminary Quarterly Review*
VT	*Vetus Testamentum*
VTSup	*Vetus Testamentum*, Supplements
WMANT	Wissenschaftliche Monographien zum Alten und Neuen Testament
WUNT	Wissenschaftliche Untersuchungen zum Neuen Testament
ZAW	*Zeitschrift für die alttestamentliche Wissenschaft*
ZEE	*Zeitschrift für Evangelische Ethik*
ZNW	*Zeitschrift für die neutestamentliche Wissenschaft*
ZTK	*Zeitschrift für Theologie und Kirche*

LAND AND JUSTICE

Shmuel Aḥituv

The allotment of the Land of Canaan to the tribes of Israel is described in the books of Numbers and Joshua. In the book of Numbers the rules for the distribution of the tribal territories are established and in the book of Joshua we are given a description of the distribution as it is purported to have taken place. These two accounts seem to complement each other, and as such were they understood by the rabbis. However, the scriptural descriptions pose some problems within their own contexts, as well as with regard to historical realities.

I

The book of Numbers connects the verses dealing with the tribal allotments to the report of the census after the plague caused by the sin of the Israelites at Baal Peor (ch. 26). The main issue dealt with in this section is the fair distribution of the territories among the tribes, in relation to their respective sizes. As an appendix, we are told of the case of the daughters of Zelophehad, which is a part and parcel of the tribal inheritance system. Is there any integral connection between the reports of the census and the plague at Baal Peor on the one hand, and the verses dealing with the allocation of the tribal allotments on the other?

The allocation of the tribal territories is discussed further in the book of Numbers in relation to the settlement of the land and its borders. In ch. 35 Moses commands the Israelites to destroy the Canaanites, their idols and cultic sites and installations. Verse 54 interrupts the account and mentions the principle of proportional allocation of the tribal allotments, in almost the same words as Num. 26.52-56.

Numbers 34 connects the description of the borders of the Land of

Canaan with the names of the tribal princes (נשׂיאים) of Israel who are commissioned with the distribution of the land to nine-and-a-half Cisjordanian tribes. However, v. 13 does not neglect the opportunity to remark that the division of the land should be by lot.

Naturally, the book of Joshua deals in much detail with the distribution of the tribal allotments. Phrases and terms used in connection with the division of the land are already encountered in the accounts of the completion of the conquest (11.23; 12.7), and they become much more prominent beginning with ch. 13. From this point onward the book deals with the distribution of the land proper. The account given there raises some questions: was the land distributed by lot or by a system in which the respective sizes of the tribes played a role? Were some tribes awarded their territories other than by lot, and, if so, why? I shall address myself to these questions later. However, we should not forget that the most concentrated and programmatic portion dealing with the allocation of the tribal allotments is Josh. 18.1-11.

After the description of the evidence given above, we may turn to the problems arising from the scriptural accounts. Following the order of Scriptures, I shall begin with the interconnection of the census of Numbers 26, the account of the plague at Baal Peor, and the principle of the allocation of the tribal allotments of Num. 26.52-56.

Num. 26.1-2 reads: 'When the plague was over, the LORD said to Moses and to Elazar son of Aaron the priest, "Take a census of the whole Israelite community. . . " ' Verse 1a thus connects the account of the plague to that of the census chronologically. The rabbis connected these two accounts, the plague and the census, in the following manner: 'Whenever they [Israel] fell they needed to be counted. It can be compared to a situation where a wolf enters a flock. The owner of the flock must count them in order to know how many are missing' (*Tanhuma*, *ad. loc.*). The Masoretes, however, insisted on having a space in the middle of v. 1 (פסקא באמצע הפסוק), after the word 'plague', as if to separate the two events. However, the date of the census is essential for the account of this census, just as it was for the first census of the Israelites in Num. 1.1, 'On the first day of the second month, in the second year following the exodus from the land of Egypt', and in v. 18: 'And on the first day of the second month they convoked the whole community who were registered by the clan of their ancestral houses—the names of those aged twenty years and over being listed head by head'.

The accounts of the two censuses are very similar, in context as well as in terminology. In both, all those who were liable for military service, from twenty years old upward, were counted. The first census was of those who had left Egypt, that is, the desert generation, which was condemned to die in the wilderness. The second census was carried out at the end of the wandering period 'on the steppes of Moab, at the Jordan near Jericho' (Num. 26.3). This was the new generation on the eve of its entrance into the Promised Land. But while in the first census Scripture did not bother to mention the subdivisions of the tribes, the second census takes care to name the clans too.

After summing up the total number of the Israelites, the chapter proceeds with the principles for allocating the land to the tribes (Num. 26.52-56). The rules seem to be contradictory. According to one of them the land should be distributed in proportion to the size of each tribe: 'With larger groups increase the share, with smaller groups reduce the share. Each is to be assigned its share according to its enrollment' (Num. 26.54). On the other hand, v. 56 has it: 'Each portion shall be assigned by lot, whether for larger or smaller groups'.

The rabbis, followed by the mediaeval Jewish commentators, were aware of this contradiction, and suggested a compromise to harmonize these two contradictory rules laid down by the Bible: the distribution of the land in proportion to the sizes of the tribes, and a distribution arrived at by lottery. The matter is discussed in the Babylonian Talmud (*b. B. Bat.* 121b-122a): 'The question was raised: Was the Land of Israel divided according to the [number of the] tribes [each tribe taking a twelfth of the land, and then subdividing it to its members], or was it perhaps divided according to the [number of the] head[s] of men [the entire land being divided into as many shares as there were men]?' Rashi (1040–1105), the greatest mediaeval commentator on the Torah and Talmud, comments there: 'Each tribe took the portion of the lot assigned it, whether a great parcel, i.e., a small tribe, or smaller part, i.e., a large tribe. For as all the tribes share equally, the greater tribe like the smaller one, then the shares of the members of the smaller tribe would be greater than those of the larger (tribe).'[1]

Rashi's comment reveals the complexity of the problems inherent in Scripture. His explanation is, of course, unacceptable, since it contradicts v. 54 which states unequivocally, 'With larger groups increase the share, with smaller groups reduce the share. Each is to be assigned its share according to its enrollment.'

The most expressive opposition to Rashi-style explanations of the contradiction is to be found in Don Isaac Abrabanel's commentary on the Torah (beginning v. 52):

> It was difficult for the former sages [to decide] in which manner the Land of Israel was distributed. Was it distributed to the twelve tribes equally, a tribe with a large population having the same parcel as a tribe having fewer in population? This would have been, of course, an injustice [perpetrated] by the law of [the] divine justice, and is contrary to what He [God] commanded here: 'Among these shall the land be apportioned as shares, according to the listed names: with larger groups increase the share, with smaller groups reduce the share. Each is to be assigned its share according to its enrollment' (Num. 26.53-54).[2]

However, a detailed examination of the description of the census of Numbers 26 reveals that there is no contradiction in vv. 52-56. As I have already pointed out, the thrust of the account of this census is the reference to the subdivision of the tribes into clans. This reference is of significance regarding the system of the distribution of the land to the tribes by lot in vv. 52-56. Verses 53-55 deal with the allotment of the land to the tribes according to their respective size: 'Among these shall the land be apportioned as shares, according to the listed names', that is, the names of the people registered in the census. Verse 55a adds 'The land, moreover, is to be apportioned by lot'. What, then, is the novelty introduced by v. 56: 'Each portion shall be assigned by lot, whether for larger or smaller groups'?

It might be argued that the verses suffer from verbosity. This seems to be the case in v. 55a, which does not seem to add anything new to what had already been written in v. 54b. However, taken as a whole, v. 55 does add a novelty when saying 'The land, moreover, is to be

1. *The Babylonian Talmud. Nezikin*, II (ed. I. Epstein; London: Soncino, 1935), pp. 501-502.

2. Warsaw 1862 edition (repr. Jerusalem n.d.) Pinhas, p. 4b = Jerusalem 1964 edition, p. 130.

apportioned by lot', but 'And the allotment shall be made according to the listings of their ancestral tribes',[1] that is, according to the names of the families registered in the census lists. Verse 56 adds: 'Each portion shall be assigned by lot', the 'portion' (נחלה) of each tribe shall be divided among the clans/families which were mentioned—and counted—before. The principle of equality should be applied not only in the distribution of the land to the tribes of Israel, but also in the distribution of the territory of each tribe to its clans.

One might ask, is v. 56 an integral part of the chapter or an addition, as might be suggested by its very place at the end of the section? However, this is the verse which gives the enumeration of the families in the account of the census its *raison d'être*. It is worthwhile to quote one of the later Jewish commentators, R. Hayim Ben-Atar of Morocco (1696–1743), who wrote a longish homiletic popular commentary on the Torah, *'Or ha-Hayim* (published in some *Miqra'oth Gedoloth* editions). In v. 52 he comments on the words במספר שמות ('according to the listed names'): 'To wit, that the distribution [of the land] shall be to the aforementioned families [i.e. clans], being 57. That means that the land shall be divided to 57 families, and to each family according to its size.'

It seems, therefore, that the census accounts for the subdivision of the tribes into clans/families, and accordingly v. 56 establishes the principle that the tribal allotments should be subdivided and distributed to the clans on the same principle; proportional to their size, and by lot.

Such subdivision is reflected in the description of the territory of Manasseh. Josh. 17.5 states, with reference to the inheritance of the daughters of Zelophehad, 'Ten districts fell to Manasseh' (ויפלו חבלי מנשה עשרה). These were the ten Cisjordanian clans of the tribe of Manasseh.

The census of the Israelites in Numbers 26 was of the twelve tribes of Israel. Numbers 34 describes a different situation. The Israelites had already conquered the Transjordanian kingdoms of Sihon and Og. Two-and-a-half tribes were given their territories in Transjordan. There remained only nine-and-a-half tribes to inherit 'the Land of Canaan with its various boundaries' as described in vv. 1-12.

---

1. Ancestral tribes—as in Num. 1.16 נשיאי מטות אבותם, 'the chieftains of their ancestral tribes'. Translations of biblical verses follow the Jewish Publication Society of America; *The Torah* (Philadelphia, 1967), *The Prophets* (Philadelphia, 1978).

Accordingly only ten tribal princes were commissioned with the distribution of the land (vv. 16-19). Here, too, the author does not neglect to mention that the land should be divided by lot (v. 13).

The distribution of the land by lot is constantly stressed in the book of Joshua. The verses dealing with it there are closely related to the verses dealing with the same matter in Numbers, and resemble them. They use the same terminology. The differences between them are only those arising from the circumstances. While in Numbers the distribution of the tribal allotments is a matter for the future, Joshua 14 describes it as already taking place. Joshua deals with the same nine-and-a-half tribes and refers to the same ten tribal princes as Numbers 34. The phrase אבות המטות ('the heads of the ancestral houses of the Israelite tribes') is coined after Num. 26.55 מטות אבותם ('their ancestral tribes'). Notwithstanding the dependency of Joshua on Numbers, I do not believe that the same author wrote both of them, since the account in Joshua raises some new points which do not exist in Numbers, as well as some new phrases.

The most important novelty in Joshua is presented in 18.1-10. There were seven tribes that did not take possession of their territories, after Judah and the house of Joseph had already taken theirs, as described in chs. 14–17. Josh. 18.1-10 describes in detail the system employed for the distribution of the land by a committee of surveyors, consisting of the representatives of these seven tribes. It was a committee of 21 members, three for each of the tribes. Like the ten tribal princes of Numbers 24 representing their tribes, this committee comprised only members of the tribes directly involved. The impression given is that it was no longer a matter of national interest, but of the parties involved. The ten tribal princes who were commissioned with the distribution of the land of Numbers 34 and Josh. 14.1 disappeared. Nothing is said of the identity of the committee members, in contrast to the pains taken in Numbers 34 to identify the ten tribal princes by name and patronym. It seems that another author, although of the same priestly school, elaborated the account of the distribution of the land to the remaining seven tribes and introduced the concept of the survey committee. The description of the distribution of the land to the seven Cisjordanian tribes in Josh. 18.1-10 reveals the mechanism.

It had two dimensions: the principle of parcels proportional to the size of the tribal units, and the work of the lottery. The first stage was the 'writing' of the land, that is, measuring it and recording the findings in a written document, which eventually will be brought back to Shilo, to Joshua. The results of the committee's work needed the approval of the lot. I shall return to this point later.

Why were Judah and the house of Joseph exempted from the decisions of the lot? Or did the author believe that they too were awarded their territories by the lot? Indeed the word גורל (lot) is also mentioned in the descriptions of the allotments of Judah and the tribes of Joseph—Ephraim and half-Manasseh—in Josh. 14.1-2, which deals with the nine-and-a-half tribes, as well as in the descriptions of the distinctive allotments of Judah, Ephraim and half-Manasseh.[1]

It has been argued[2] that the phrase גורל which fits well in the description of the allotments of the seven tribes which, according to Josh. 18.1-10, took their inheritance by the lot, does not suit the tribes of Judah, Ephraim and half-Manasseh. It is even argued that the original reading was גבול (border) as it is in the Septuagint to 14.2, 15.1, 16.1 and 17.1. Only in a later phrase, after the split of the *Urtext* into the Hebrew pre-Septuagint and pre-Masoretic forerunners, did the latter change גבול to גורל in order to subject all tribes to the same process which involved ratification of their allotments by the divine lot.

I suspect the validity of this argument. The word גורל in the descriptions of the allotments had already lost its initial meaning and became a synonym for נחלה ('estate'), which originally had been allocated by lot. The compound phrase בגורל נחלתם ('the portions that fell to them by lot') in Josh. 14.2 supports this contention.[3] The compound

---

1. Josh. 14.1-2: 'And these are the portions that the Israelites acquired in the land of Canaan, that were assigned to them by the priest Elazar, by Joshua son of Nun, and by the heads of the ancestral houses of the Israelite tribes, the portions that fell to them by lot, as the LORD had commanded through Moses for the nine and a half tribes'. Josh. 15.1: 'The portion that fell by lot to the various clans of the tribe of Judah . . . ' Josh. 16.1: 'The portion that fell by lot to the Josephites ran from the Jordan at Jericho. . . . ' Josh. 17.1: 'And this is the portion that fell by lot to the tribe of Manasseh. . . . ' Similar formulae using verbal derivations of עפ״ה or יצ״א with גורל are used for the remaining seven tribes (18.11; 19.1, 10, 17, 24, 32, 40).

2. A.G. Auld, 'Textual and Literary Studies in the Book of Joshua', *ZAW* 90 (1978), pp. 416-17.

3. This phrase is quite unique and the Septuagint has another version which probably goes back to the Hebrew בגורל נחלו אותם, 'by the lot they gave them their inheritance'. But if בגורל נחלתם is read not where it stands now in the beginning of v. 2, but at the end of v. 1, there will be no need of emendation.

phrase גורל נחלה goes back to the story of the daughters of Zelophehad in Num. 26.3, where the heads of the families of Gilead approach Moses complaining that if the daughters of Zelophehad should marry out of their tribe, 'Their share will be cut off from our ancestral portion... thus our allotted portion will be diminished'. The phrase גורל נחלה is a tight compound phrase with the same meaning of נחלה ('estate', 'possession').

Similarly, every גורל (lot) in the description of the tribal allotments is no more than a fossil-phrase with the original meaning of an allotted land in its background, just as the term חבל נחלה was coined after a parcel of land measured with a line. Thus we have in Josh. 19.9 חבל referring to the inheritance of Simeon: מחבל בני יהודה נחלת בני שמעון, 'The portion [literally 'line'] of the Simeonites was part of the territory of the Judites'. In the description of the territory of Benjamin we are told: ויהי גבול גורלם, 'The territory which fell to their lot lay...' (18.11). The house of Joseph complained to Joshua: מדוע נתתה לי וחבל נחלה גורל אחד אחד, 'Why have you assigned as our portion a single allotment and a single district' (17.14).

The complete removal of the term גורל from its initial meaning is best exemplified in Judg. 1.3: 'Judah then said to their brother-tribe Simeon, come up with us to our allotted territory (עלה אתי בגרלי), and let us attack the Canaanites, and then we will go with you to our allotted territory (והלכתי גם אני אתך בגרלך).'

The same development of the term 'lot' took place in other languages. In Akkadian *pūru* is the lot itself, the dice used in lot-casting, a lot as an allotment, a piece of land acquired by lot, and later any piece of land. In Greek *klēros* means lot and allotment. The same goes for European languages, such as the English 'lot'. Thus the Hebrew גורל is a pebble used in the casting of lots (Palestinian Arabic *ḡarl*, *ḡar'al*), a lot and allotment.

Although the word גורל lost its meaning in the description of the allotment, literacy (and colloquial) usage still kept many phrases derived from its etymology: נפל גורל, עלה גורל, יצא גורל (and likewise נפ״ל + נחלה, shortened from פלה נחלה בגורל 'possession which was acquired through lot').

In conclusion: the word גורל ('lot') used in the account of the allotments of Judah and the house of Joseph does not refer to the method by which they were awarded their territories. They got them otherwise, and we still have to explain why they were exempted from the decision of the lot.[1]

II

How did the lot function? How can we harmonize the contradiction between the registration of the land by the survey committees and its allocation by the lot? Obviously, the land should be distributed by rational means, such as described in Josh. 18.1-10. The lot, however, is by no means blind. The lot only confirms, being a divine confirmation of the just decisions of the survey committee. It was unthinkable that the lot should not confirm them. The ancients knew how to ensure the proper working of the lot.

Scripture does not describe how the lot functioned. The verbs used in connection with the lot, עָל"ה, יר"ה, יָצ"א (הִשְׁלִיךְ) שָׁל"ךְ ,נָפ"ל (come up, come out, and three verbs used for casting lots) allude to two practices: (1) that of casting lots, like casting dice; (2) some vessel from which the lot emerges (יָצ"א) or comes up (עָל"ה). This is described in *Mishnah Yoma*, pertaining to the choice by lot of the scapegoat on the Day of Atonement (3.9; 4.1): 'And an urn[2] was there with two lots in it. . . He [the high priest] shook the urn and brought out two lots—one had written on it "for the [divine] Name" and on the other was written "for Azazel".'

A more detailed description of the lot process—although quite imaginary—is found in the Babylonian Talmud (*b. B. Bat.* 122a) concerning the distribution of the land to the tribes. The rabbis were faced with the problem of harmonizing the lot with the principle of fair distribution as prescribed in Numbers 26. Thus it is described:

> Elazar was wearing the *Urim and Tumim*, while Joshua and all Israel stood before him. A urn [containing the names] of the tribes and a urn [containing descriptions] of the boundaries/zones were placed before him.

---

1. It must be admitted that the phrase ויצא הגורל in Josh. 16.1 does not fit well into the context. If we emend ויצא הגבול, it will be smooth enough, but then this will be the only case where a description of a tribal allotment fails to mention the word גורל in its very beginning. As it is phrased now, the word גבול is missing. Perhaps an emendation is called for. It is possible that we have here a case of omission by haplography of ויצא הגבול ויצא הגורל.

2. קלפי = *kalpē* is an urn; however, it might already have been applied even then to other vessels for the same use.

> Animated by the Holy Spirit, he gave directions, exclaiming: Zebulun is coming up and boundary lines of Acco are coming up with it. [Thereupon,] he shook the urn of the tribes and Zebulun came up in his hand, [likewise] he shook well the urn of the boundaries, and the boundary lines of Acco came up in his hand. . .

Thus, nothing was left to mere chance. The lot was directed by divine forces. The concept that the lot is a vehicle for divine decisions was quite clear (cf. Plato's comment in the *Laws* [5.741b]: 'the lot which is divine'). The book of Joshua states clearly that lots should be cast 'before the LORD' (לפני ה') (18.6, 8, 10).

The importance attached to the distribution of the tribal allotments by lot is evident also in the account of the Levitical cities. According to the book of Joshua, these, too, were allocated by lot: 'The [first] lot among the Levites fell to the Kohathite clans. To the descendants of the priest Aaron, there fell by lot thirteen towns from the tribe of Judah, the tribe of Simeon, and the tribe of Benjamin' (21.4). Similarly v. 8: 'The Israelites assigned those towns with their pastures by lot to the Levites—as the LORD had commanded through Moses'.

III

The account of the distribution of the tribal and sub-tribal allotments according to the size of the tribal units involved, as well as by lot, is, of course, unrealistic. It is a fictitious idealization of the past. Clearly, the tribal territories were not awarded by lot, or according to the respective sizes of the tribal units. The crystallization of the tribal units in their territories, and the size of the territories, which changed in the course of history, are long and complicated historical processes. Scripture depicts a schematic idealistic picture of the division of the land to the tribes of Israel, perhaps in a period in which the tribes had already—partially at least—vanished. The picture we have before us is utopian.

An interpretation of this utopia emerges from M. Greenberg's discussion of 'Idealism and Practicality in Numbers 35.4-5 and Ezekiel 48',[1] especially in Chapter II, 'Ezekiel's Allocation of Tribal Territory' (pp. 64-65). Greenberg stresses the utopian schematization of Ezekiel's description of the division of the Land of Israel to the twelve tribes of Israel in the future. A better understanding of this

---

1. In *E.A. Speiser Memorial Volume* (JAOS, 88; 1968), pp. 59-66.

utopia may be gleaned from M. Weinfeld in articles discussing the pattern of the Israelite settlement. In these studies, Weinfeld draws attention to the similarity between what he thinks was the actual Israelite settlement pattern and that of the Greeks.[1]

The following are the novelties in Ezekiel's plan as given in Ezek. 47.13–48.29:

1. All the tribes will take their allotments west of the Jordan. Ezekiel totally ignored the realities of the period of the First Temple. His schematic map draws latitudinal segments in the Land of Israel, one for each tribe. The central segment will include Jerusalem—which is not mentioned by name—and it is dedicated for the temple, the priests and the prince (נשיא). This segment separates the territories of the tribe of Judah and its northern neighbours (Ephraim, Manasseh, Naphtali, Asher and Dan) from those of Benjamin and his southern brethren (Simeon, Issachar, Zebulun and Gad). Thus, Ezekiel divided the land into 13 allotments; compare the *baraitha* (external *mishnah*) in *B. Bat.* 122a: 'It has been taught: In the time to come the Land of Israel shall be divided among thirteen tribes.'

2. All the allotments will be of equal size: 'And you shall share the rest equally' (47.14), and according to the proportional principle of Numbers 26.

3. The aliens (גרים) will have shares in the land equal to those of the other members of the tribe amongst which they reside:

> You shall allot it as a heritage for yourselves and for the strangers who reside among you, who have begotten children with you. You shall treat them as Israelite citizens; they shall receive allotments along with you among the tribes of Israel. You shall give the stranger allotment within the tribe where he resides (47.22-23).

4. Ezekiel ignores the agrarian committee of surveyors of Joshua 18. His proposed division of the land will be by the Lord himself: 'Thus said the Lord God: This shall be the boundaries of the land that you shall allot. . . ' (47.13-14).

5. Ezekiel ignores the role of the lot as described in Numbers and Joshua. Only fossilized phrases of the allotting terminology survive in

---

1. 'The Extent of the Promised Land—The Status of Trans-Jordan', in *Das Land Israel in biblischer Zeit* (Jerusalem Symposium 1981 der Hebräischen Universität und der Georg-August Universität, herausgegeben von G. Strecker; Tübingen: Mohr, 1983), pp. 59-77. 'The Pattern of the Israelite Settlement in Canaan', in *Congress Volume, Jerusalem 1986* (VTSup, 40; Leiden: Brill, 1988), pp. 270-83.

his vocabulary. Ezekiel locates each tribe in its allotment. These tribal allotments are arranged so that they have not even the slightest resemblance to the allotments of the First Temple period (only Dan retains his former position in the north).

6. As the lot plays no role in Ezekiel's vision of the new arrangement of the tribal territories, so Jerusalem—instead of Shilo—has no part in it.

IV

Greenberg compares Ezekiel's imaginary vision of the division of the land with the reform of Cleisthenes of Athens (end of sixth century BCE). Cleisthenes divided Athens and its land into ten units, which he named tribes (*phyle*). Each tribal unit consisted of three parts: one in the city, one on the shore and one inland. However, the comparison is untenable. Cleisthenes' reform worked because it was an artificial system which was purely political and it did not interfere with the Athenian economic structure and life. Ezekiel's plan had no basis whatsoever, it was entirely imaginary.

Although Ezekiel does not give any explanation for his division of the land, it is quite obvious that it was his idea of a just and equal distribution of the tribal, as well as personal, allotments. However, it would be going too far to interpret his division of the land into latitudinal segments as meaning that he wanted each allotment to include all the sorts of soil in the Land of Israel, as though each portion can include valley, mountain and plain lands. We cannot treat Ezekiel as if he had studied the talmudic portion on the division of the land in the messianic age:

> And the division in the world to come will not be like the division in this world. [In] this world, [if] a man possesses a cornfield [lit. 'a field of white'], he does not possess an orchard, [if he possesses] an orchard, he does not possess a cornfield, [but] in the world to come there will be no single individual who will not possess [land] in mountain, lowland and valley' (*B. Bat.* 122a).

Ezekiel's plan is the vision of a man who succeeded in disassociating himself from reality, and indulged in imaginary schematizations. Therefore he could envisage a city with twelve gates, three on each side, each of them named after a tribe (48.30ff.). Any resemblance between Ezekiel's plan of the divided Land of Israel and the reform of Cleisthenes in Athens is only incidental.

In the period around the destruction of the Second Temple and in the periods of the Mishnah and Talmud there was a current view that Joshua divided the land to the children of Israel according to its worth, that is, according to its fertility measured by its monetary value. Thus Josephus (*Ant.* 5.76-79):

> (76) Having delivered his speech and won the assent of the people thereto, Joshua sent out men to measure the country, attaching to them certain expert surveyors, from whom by reason of their skill the truth would not be hid, instructions being given them to assess separately the extent of the favoured land and that which was less fertile. (77) For the nature of the Land of Canaan is such that one may see plains, of great areas, fully fitted for bearing crops, and which compared with another district might be deemed altogether blest, yet when set beside the regions of the people of Jericho and Jerusalem would appear as nought. (78) Aye, though the territory of these folk happens to be quite diminutive and for the most part mountainous, yet for its extraordinary productiveness of crops and for beauty it yields to no other. And that was why Joshua held that the allotments should be fixed by the valuation rather than by measurement, a single *plethora* being often worth as much as a thousand. (79) So the men who had been sent, ten in number, having compassed the land and valued it, in the seventh month returned to him to the City of Silo, where the tabernacle had been set up.[1]

It should be noted that Josephus ignored the committee of 21 surveyors of Joshua 18. He attributes the description of the procedure of this committee to the ten tribal princes of Num. 34.16ff. and Josh. 14.1-2. Or perhaps he turned the surveyors into the princes' professional aids. He did not mention that Judah and the house of Joseph took their shares in the land before any valuation was made by the surveyors.

The view that the land was divided according to its value was shared by the rabbis. Their view is expressed in a *baraitha* in *Sifre* (a halakhic midrash) on Num. 26.56 (par. 131):[2]

> [This verse] tells us that the Land of Israel was only divided but by evaluation. R. Judah said: a *kur*-size portion for a *s'ea*-size one, and a *se'a*-size portion for a *kur*-size one.

1. H.StJ. Thackeray (ed.), *Josephus* (LCL; Cambridge, MA: Harvard University Press, 1934), pp. 36-37.

2. Ed. H.S. Horowitz; Lipsia, 1917 (repr. Jerusalem, 1966), p. 175.

A slightly different version of the *baraitha* is found in the Talmud (*B. Bat.* 122a):

> And it was only divided according to monetary [value], as it is written,
> ' . . . whether many or few'. R. Judah said: A *sea'*-size [portion] in
> Judea is worth of five *se'a*-size [portions] in the Galilee.

That the evaluation of land according to its productivity was a universal custom can be inferred from the description of the distribution of land in newly established Greek colonies. According to Plato's *Laws* (5.745b-c), 'The city and the land must be divided into twelve portions which are made equal by decreasing the size of the portions which contain good land, and increasing the size of those whose land is of inferior quality'.[1] Distribution of land on equal terms was vital for Greek colonization. The evidence from Greece is from the Classical Period; nothing pertaining to the system of land-distribution[2] is known of Greek colonization in the Archaic Period. However the term *klēros* for the settler's land-shares testifies to the use of the lottery for the distribution of colonial lands, perhaps on equal terms.

The search for a just and equitable system by which to divide land is a widespread one. We do not have to look for any influence of one society on another in this area. The same holds true for the distribution of the land by lots—it was used by various, totally unconnected societies.

Another matter is the question of whether there was any influence, direct or indirect, of the Greek idea of valuation of the land according to its fertility on Jewish thinkers in the period of the Second Temple. It is quite possible that Josephus and the rabbis were influenced by such ideas as reflected in the Platonic 'law' of equal sharing in the land. But they might just as well have arrived at it independently, by elaborating on the principle of just and equal distribution of the land so much emphasized in Scripture. Logically, such an attitude does not differ from their deduction that 'an eye for an eye' means monetary compensation. In a society which had already developed a money-

1. R.G. Bury (ed.), *Plato* (LCL; Cambridge, MA: Harvard University Press, 1926), pp. 380-81.

2. Cf. A.J. Graham, 'The Colonial Expansion of Greece', in *CAH*.III.3. *The Expansion of the Greek World, Eight to Sixth Centuries B.C.* (ed. J. Boardman and N.G.L. Hammond; Cambridge: Cambridge University Press, 2nd edn, 1982), p. 151; *idem, Colony and Mother City in Ancient Greece* (Manchester, 1964), p. 59.

based economy, there is no objective criterion other than money.

Although the principle of equality seems to be inherent in both the Greek colonization system and the biblical settlement accounts, they stemmed from different outlooks. The Greek principle is rooted in Greek democratic ideas and on the need to win colonists. In the Bible, however, there is no reference to individuals; it is the tribe and the family which are prominent. Equality, too, concerns the tribal system in theory, as is demonstrated by the story of the daughters of Zelophehad.

V

We can now turn to the realistic background of the description of the distribution of the land to the tribes of Israel. I have already mentioned that the distribution of land by lot is a universal custom which is not restricted to specific societies or to specific periods, although, of course, is not found in modern societies. It might seem curious that except for the description of the distribution of the land to the tribes, there are no references to the casting of lots in land-distribution in the Bible. However, there is one exception. Micah prophesied against those who 'covet fields and seize them; Houses and take them away. They defraud men of their homes, and people of their land [נחלתו]' (2.2); the prophet says: לכן לא יהיה לך משליך חבל בגורל בקהל ה', 'Truly, none of you shall cast a lot cord in the assembly of the LORD' (v. 5). To what is the prophet referring—a line (חבל) or a lot (גורל)? If casting a line is a phrase for measuring a field, then lot (גורל) must mean an allotment. But the scene is better understood if the lot (גורל) is cast for the חבל, a land possession measured usually by a line (cf. Amos 7.17: 'Your land be parcelled out by measuring line [בחבל]'). The verb 'to cast' suits a lot (גורל) more than a line (חבל). Nowhere in the Bible is 'to cast a line' (להשליך חבל) used for measuring. The prophet used phrases which were already anachronistic,[1] but he was referring to measuring land with a line and then casting lots for its parcels. The phrase בקהל ה', 'in the assembly of the LORD', might refer to the publicity of the act (but it may as well be meant to remind the reader of the same usage in Deut. 23.2-9).

It is possible that casting lots over parcels of land took place when dividing up an inheritance among the heirs. The biblical laws of

---

1. Cf. also Ps. 78.55: ויפילם בחבל נחלה, 'Allotting them their portion by the line'.

inheritance deal only with a special case of a man who has heirs by two women, a beloved one and an unbeloved one. If the firstborn is the son of the unbeloved woman, the father cannot disinherit him from his double share in the inheritance (Deut. 21.15-17). But there is not even the slightest hint in Scriptures for the system of dividing up an inheritance. In this case I refer to the Middle Assyrian Laws which deal with inheritance (Tablet B, par. 1):

> Any cultivated land and all [the produce of their labours], the younger son shall divide into shares. The eldest son shall choose and take one portion, and shall cast lots with his brothers for his second portion.[1]

If a similar procedure can be applied to Israel, it illustrates an opportunity for lot-casting in distributing land. It might explain also why Judah and Joseph took their shares in the Land of Canaan before their brothers, and without reference to the lot—by virtue of their prime status in Israel, notwithstanding the fact that neither was the firstborn.

Weinfeld has pointed to a fascinating similarity between the survey committee of Joshua 18 and the account of the establishment of the Athenian colony of Brea in Thracea (*stela* dating to 445 BCE). The relevant portion reads as follows: '*Geōnomoi* shall be elected [ten in number] from each tribe. These are to distribute [the land].'[2] The installation of the land surveyors, the *gēonomoi*, resembles the surveyors' committee of Joshua 18, while the nomination of one per tribe reminds us of the nomination of the ten tribal princes who were commissioned with the distribution of the land in Numbers 34 (it is a mere coincidence that in both cases there were ten). Such a survey committee as described in Joshua 18 can be appointed only by a highly centralized authority, not by any loose tribal system. The same holds true for censuses. In Israel it can reflect only acts taken by monarchical governments.

Distribution of common lands (*muša'*) was still effective in Ottoman Palestine at the beginning of this century. *muša'*-land is the common property of a village or a tribe, each family having in it an undefined share (*sahm*). *muša'*-land was divided every few years among the families. In many cases a family got a share proportional to

---

1. G.R. Driver and J.C. Miles, *The Assyrian Laws* (Oxford: Oxford University Press, 1935), pp. 426-27.

2. C.W. Fornara, *Archaic Times to the End of the Peloponnesian War* (Translated Documents of Greece and Rome, 1; Baltimore, 1977), p. 22.

its size and its ability to cultivate it. The shares were not continuous fields, but consisted of various long parcels of fertile and unfertile fields.

According to A. Musil,[1] certain tribes were accustomed to make an annual distribution of their common lands. This was done by lot. The land was measured by lines and divided into equal shares. Every head of a family gave his lot (being a *ǧarl*, a small stone, or something else) into a covered vessel which was carried by a small boy into the field. The procession stopped at each parcel of land and the boy, or the *sheikh*, took a lot from the pot. The family whose lot came up was entitled to that parcel.[2]

According to experts in Ottoman Palestine, *muša'* was not a relic of an ancient primitive social system, but a system employed by the Ottoman Empire to exact taxes from the communities, making them responsible for the taxes, as the authorities were unable to deal with each villager or tribal member. However, even if this is so, not all the details of the system depended upon the authorities. The equal distribution of the common land and the use of lots were devices used by the community itself.

VI

While the biblical description of the allotment of the Land of Canaan to the tribes of Israel is not a historical account, it reflects historical situations and cultural and social concepts. Its historical and social background is the tribal-communal organization of the Judahite–Israelite peasantry. Even after the system collapsed with the destruction of the kingdoms of Israel and Judah, its ideas were still fostered. It is possible that it assumed a utopian form when it was no longer implemented in reality. Its principles of justice and equality were projected backwards to the forefathers in the heroic period, to Moses and Joshua, at the very beginning of the national history. Let me suggest that by projecting these ideas back to the venerated past, the

---

1. *Arabia Petraea*, III (Vienna, 1908), pp. 293-94.
2. *En passant*, in 1909 the first plots of land in the new quarter of Jaffa, Aḥuzat Bait, the first houses of the future Tel Aviv were distributed by lot. The lots were sea-shells inscribed on their inner side. But the founding fathers of Tel Aviv knew their Bible and had had good Jewish educations.

authors had in mind not only the past, but also, without articulating it, the future, as was done by Ezekiel.

MEASURE FOR MEASURE IN TALMUDIC LITERATURE AND IN THE WISDOM OF SOLOMON

Yehoshua Amir

The most remarkable contribution of rabbinical Judaism to the topic of divine providence seems to be comprised in the formula מידה כנגד מידה[1] frequently occurring in midrashic texts, which I provisionally translate as 'measure for measure'. As a full sentence, this principle is formulated in the following form: 'With what measure a man metes, with it will one mete to him', 'one' being a reverent circumlocution for God.[2] (In New Testament Greek the impersonal verb is replaced by the passive form: μετρηθήσεται.[3]) In this essay I shall first establish the meaning of this formula according to the rabbis, and afterwards turn to the transformations it underwent in the peculiar intellectual climate of Hellenistic Jewry in the apocryphal Wisdom of Solomon. The seeming inversion of chronological sequence involved in my order of proceeding may be justified by the fact that the later rabbinical concept is essentially already present in biblical Judaism.

Concerning these biblical origins and their continuations in talmudic literature, very astute scholarly work has been done by Benno Jacob in *Auge um Auge*.[4] As far as the rabbinic material goes, I profited greatly from the important study *The Methods of Aggadah*[5] by my late teacher Isaac Heinemann, which not only provides an excellent approach to the understanding of rabbinical hermeneutics in general but also devotes special attention to the explication of the special

---

1. E.g. *Ber.R.* 9, 10.
2. *M. Sot.* 1.7.
3. Mt. 7.2; Mk 4.24; Lk. 6.38.
4. B. Jacob, *Auge um Auge* (Berlin: Philo Verlag, 1929).
5. I. Heinemann, *The Methods of Aggadah* (Jerusalem: Magnes, 1949) (Hebrew).

formula which is the subject of this paper.[1] For the relevant text from Wisdom of Solomon I had at my disposal an illuminating paper by Edmund Stein,[2] a very promising Jewish scholar who was murdered in the holocaust.

The sages were well aware of the fact that for their doctrine of God's meting out 'measure for measure' there exists a full-fledged biblical precedent in Num. 14.34. The Israelites, after hearing the spies' report, despair of conquering the Land of Israel and thereby rebel against God and Moses. In consequence, they are condemned to wander in the wilderness for 40 years, till the whole generation of the exodus will pass away. The reason for this punishment is given in the following verse: 'After the number of the days in which ye searched the land, even forty days, each day for a year, shall ye bear your iniquities, even forty days'. Now, it must be noticed that this calculation of the punishment is by far less rational than *prima facie* it may seen to be. Even the transmutation of days into years is quite arbitrary. Much more serious is that those 40 days during which the spies were on their way do not constitute the crime that is to be punished but are only connected to it by association. The repeated number 40, which comes to accentuate the parallelism between human sin and divine retribution, as the pathos of the biblical text makes clear, does not function here by virtue of its arithmetical qualities. Here is at work a way of thinking that is termed by Ernst Cassirer in his *Philosophy of Symbolic Forms*[3] as 'mythical thought'. One of the characteristics of this kind of thought is defined by this author as follows: 'In mythical thinking any similarity of sensuous manifestation suffices to group the entities in which it appears into a single mythical "genus". Any characteristic, however external, is as good as another.'[4] Among such characteristics number occupies a prominent place, but its function in this context must be properly understood: 'While in scientific thinking number appears as the great instrument of *explanation*, in mythical thinking it appears as a vehicle of religious

---

1. Heinemann, *Aggadah*, pp. 64-68.

2. E. Stein, 'Ein jüdisch-hellenistischer Midrasch über den Auszug aus Ägypten', *MGWJ* 78 (1934), pp. 558-75 (missing in the table of contents of the volume).

3. E. Cassirer, *The Philosophy of Symbolic Forms*. II. *Mythical Thought* (New Haven: Yale University Press, 1955).

4. Cassirer, *Philosophy*, p. 67.

signification.[1] Such indeed is surely so concerning the function of the number 40 in our case. Heinemann, when investigating this type of midrashic thought, does not label it as 'mythical thought' but uses the more obscure term 'organic thinking'. I cannot enter here into the questions of principle involved in this discussion but in any case I see no need to avoid using the term 'mythical'.

At any rate, if number includes—to use Cassirer's words— 'whatever partakes of that number in any way',[2] the question that should be crucial for rational thinking, that is, does the penalty fit the crime, becomes pointless. In the atmosphere of this kind of thought the correspondence in number stands for a kind of correlation that cannot be calculated beforehand but can nevertheless be retrospectively experienced as meaningful.

I

If we wish to trace throughout Jewish spiritual history this motif which we find at work for the first time in a biblical passage, it would be advisable to neglect the chronological sequence and to skip over immediately to rabbinic literature. Meaningful coordination of two topics is a habit of rabbinical thought; Heinemann termed it 'analogical thinking'.[3] The rabbis were living within a large network of relationships, the one between sin and punishment being just one of them. Numerical equality is only one of the many means—although a much favoured one—for creating such relationships. So, for example, it is held to be a sign of a blessed life if a person dies on the same date on which he was born: 'The Holy One, Blessed be He, sits and fills the years of the righteous, day for day and month for month'.[4] Yet such a line of thought, once set in motion, can take on even cosmic dimensions:

> Everything created by the Holy One, Blessed be He, exists for the sake of the twelve tribes (of Israel). You find twelve months in the year, twelve constellations in heaven (in the zodiac), twelve hours in the day, and twelve hours in the night. The Holy One, Blessed be He, says: Even the Upper Ones and the Lower Ones (the heavenly and the earthly creatures) I

1. Cassirer, *Philosophy*, p. 137.
2. Cassirer, *Philosophy*, p. 137.
3. Heinemann, *Aggadah*, pp. 62ff.
4. *Bibliotheca Rerum Historicarum* 11a.

have only created because of the merit of the tribes, for so it is written: '*All those* have my hands created' (Isa. 66.2); for the merit of '*All those* are the tribes of Israel, twelve they are' (Gen. 49.28). So that is why I created the twelve constellations.[1]

The words 'all those' occurring in both of the verses create a relationship of meaning between them, and the mention of the number twelve indicates that whatever carries this number in heaven and on earth is derivative of the primordial creature, that is, of Israel with its twelve tribes. Concatenation between the scriptural verses is achieved by a vocable common to both—just as Cassirer had it—any vocable, however external, and this procedure is ubiquitous in rabbinic literature. But once this connection is established, its content is comprised in the number twelve, identified with the twelve tribes of Israel as the focus of significance of the world order.

The correlation between two entities which makes them into a significant whole is expressed in the language of haggadah by the preposition כנגד, which might be most adequately translated as 'corresponding to (a thing, an event)'. Such being the case, it is only logical that in a traditional list of the exegetical categories of the haggadah[2] we find the category of כנגד illustrated by the biblical example of the narrative of the spies.

This preposition is used, for instance, in a midrash which works out the correspondence between heaven and earth. God's earthly throne (meaning the temple) is said there[3] to be arranged correlatively to his heavenly throne. The same is attested to—through the use of appropriate scriptural verses—concerning the Holy Hall, the Cherubim, etc. It should be noticed that the temple with its vessels is here not seen as an imitation of a heavenly original but rather as its earthly counterpart, so granting an equality of sorts between the upper and lower worlds.

Such a counterpoising antithesis can be carried through in almost any other dimension. Take, for example, the comparison that the midrash draws between the lives of Jacob and Joseph, tiring the reader with an immense wealth of detail and finding no less than 23 common traits in both men's biographies: both were hated by their brother(s),

---

1. *Pes. R.* 4.1.

2. *Mishnat R. Eliezer* (ed. H.G. Enelow; New York, 1933), rule 27, p. 37.

3. *Mek.Y.* (ed. Hor-Rab; Jerusalem, 2nd edn, 1960), p. 150; *Shem. R.* 33.4.

both went abroad, etc.[1] If we ask ourselves, what is expected to be the outcome of such a round-up of similarities, we get the impression that such a network of well-knit interrelationships is experienced as a guarantee for a well-ordered world. All-pervading correspondence makes one sure of meaningfulness; ultimately, of course, behind this well-disposed world order stands God himself, who guides his world according to wise rules, repeating themselves until eternity. Lines of thought of this sort are not abstractly formulated, let alone systematized, yet they shine through the untiring exegetical endeavours of the rabbis.

We had to adumbrate this broader context in order to reach a deeper understanding of the Sages' use of the preposition כנגד, the medium term of our formula מידה כנגד מידה. We shall now be very hesitant to translate it 'measure for measure', especially after we have learnt that מידה is not adequately understood as a numerical equivalence but that it indicates a kind of correlation not simply resulting from arithmetical manipulations, but rather irresistibly imposing itself upon mythological thought. No exact measuring instrument will be helpful in determining this 'measure', but by being embedded in an all-pervading network of correspondences it partakes of the accepted legitimacy of the whole, and is even one of the major components of this whole. Only in this light can it be understood how the Hebrew word מידה, originally 'measure', especially longitudinal size, comes to denote moral attributes of a person that determine his attitude toward other persons. When considering all these facts, we come close to a loose translation of מידה כנגד מידה as 'God's behaviour as correlated to man's behaviour', if we understand this correlation as being marked out by a tangible distinctness. To make it visible to all is the aim of rabbinical exegesis.

The *locus classicus* of our problem in the Mishnah—and in close parallel to it in the Tosefta—is the tractate *Sota* whose subject-matter is the ordeal of the woman suspected of adultery, as described in Num. 5.11-31. This archaic piece of divine judgment with a magical overtone was bound to be strange to the rabbinic mind, such that an explanatory theological approach was certainly in order. The Mishnah[2] provides such an explanation assuming that adultery has actually been committed. The exposition opens with a statement of

1. *Ber. R.* 84.6.
2. *M. Sot.* 1.7-9.

principle: 'With what measure a man mete, with it will one mete to him' and applies this to the present case: 'She adorned herself for sin. Therefore God makes her ugly', where we have to notice that the ritual acts of the priest are designated not as human acts but as divine deeds. The parallelization continues:

> She laid herself bare for sin; God uncovers her. She began her sin with her loin and afterwards with her belly; therefore her loin is smitten first (by the effects of the cursed water) and afterward her belly, and the rest of her body does not come out unharmed either.

The parallel text of the Tosefta[1] supplements some further details in the same vein, as each point is proved there by a biblical verse. But in both sources the underlying idea is further expanded by examples taken from different subject-matters. So in the Mishnah:[2] 'Samson went after his eyes [= was seduced by his eyes; cf. Num. 15.39]; therefore the Philistines gouged out his eyes'. Here we should take notice of the word 'therefore' which contains the gist of the whole idea; it returns in the following examples: 'Absalom was proud of his hair; therefore he died by being hung by his hair. Because he lay with the ten concubines of his father, he was pierced through by ten spears.' We have already become acquainted with the fact that the points of congruence are usually merely incidental. The same applies to the supplementary example about Samson given in the Tosefta:[3] 'As his misconduct began in Gaza, He was punished in Gaza'. Again the Tosefta has far more examples than the Mishnah. One of them[4] is related to the exodus from Egypt, a theme we shall return to later on:

> There is nothing the Egyptians were proud of against God like the water, as it says: 'And Pharaoh charged all his people, saying, Every son that is born ye shall cast into the river'; *therefore* it says later on: 'Pharaoh's chariots and his host he hath cast into the sea'.

The same correlation between the Egyptian catastrophe in the Red Sea and the drowning of the children in the Nile we find in another midrashic source.[5] There the principle of divine retribution, illustrated by a wealth of examples, is formulated:

1. *T. Sot.* 3–4.
2. *M. Sot.* 1.8.
3. *T. Sot.* 3.15.
4. *T. Sot.* 3.13.
5. *Mek.Y.* (ed. Hor-Rab), p. 110.

The wheel will turn upon them and their criminal intention will turn itself against them. With the same device which they thought to use in order to destroy Israel, I shall judge them. They intended to destroy Israel with water; so I shall punish them with none other than water, as it says (Ps. 7.16): 'He has made a pit and has dug it out, and has fallen into the ditch which he made' and further (17): 'His mischief shall return upon his own head'.

In this source follow nine quotations of similar verses, of which I wish to quote only two: 'I will measure their former work into their bosom' (Isa. 65.7), and secondly Jethro's declaration, after hearing of Israel's redemption from Egypt, freely paraphrased from Exod. 18.11:

I had already known him beforehand but now even more so has his name become great in the world, for with the very same object by which they intended to destroy Israel he visited upon them, as it says (in that verse); 'for by that which they plotted (were they punished)'.

Here just this correspondence between sin and punishment is held to be the proof of God's greatness. So here is stated incidentally that which we shall see later on in a systematized form, that is, that for a human spectator this is the most convincing show of divine power. To this idea we shall return in another context.

The tractate *Sota*, both in the Mishnah and in the Tosefta, takes a further step in developing the idea of the correlation between man's actions and God's meting out of justice. After the texts quoted already the Mishnah goes on:[1] 'The same applies to the good deed'. Again, the Tosefta[2] is more verbose:

So far as to the measure (*midda*) of punishment. Yet whence do I know that it is so for the measure of the good too? What do you say, is the measure of the good greater or is the measure of the punishment greater? The measure of the good is five hundred times greater than the measure of punishment. Concerning the measure of punishment it says (Exod. 20.5): 'He visits the iniquity of the fathers upon the children unto the third and fourth generations' while concerning the measure of good it is written (ibid): 'He shows mercy unto thousands (that is, at least two thousand)', so it is five hundred times as much.

The Mishnah continues and adduces examples for this positive side of the correlation: 'Miriam waited for Moses one hour (while watching

1. *M. Sot.* 1.9.
2. *T. Sot.* 4.1.

him as a baby) (Exod. 2.4); *therefore* Israel lingered for her sake seven days in the desert (Num. 12.15)'. A second example follows:

> Joseph was privileged to bury his father, and he was then the greatest of the brothers, and none other than Moses tended to (his bones). Moses was privileged (to tend) to the bones of Joseph, and there was none other in Israel greater than Moses. . . and none other than God himself tended to (his burial).

All these motifs are further elaborated upon in the Tosefta. The Tosefta also adds a number of stories concerning good deeds of Abraham whose reward is paid to his descendants, that is, to Israel in the wilderness, the parallels always being documented by certain words recurring in the biblical text. Cases like these serve incidentally to substantiate the promise that God will recompense good deeds even in far-removed generations.

These examples may suffice to characterize the rabbinic concept of מידה כנגד מידה and to determine its place within an all-embracing picture of the rabbinic world.

II

I should now like to go back in time from the world of the Sages to the apocryphal book Wisdom of Solomon which stems from the first century BCE or the first century CE; in doing so I am acting on the assumption that, concerning the concept under discussion, there is a continuous line of thought connecting biblical and rabbinic Judaism, and that the essence of what I presented as the rabbinic doctrine was already part and parcel of the traditional Jewish *weltanschauung* by the time of the composition of the Greek book. We have seen that the rabbis did not need to reinterpret biblical material in order to adapt it to their opinions. For that reason I did not concern myself with questions of the dating of the sources used in the foregoing part. Therefore, if we find in the apocryphal book some peculiar trends in the development of our motif, we are entitled to see them as an outcome of the fact that here Jewish-traditional thought is exposed to the influence of Hellenistic culture. For the scholar who wants to trace this influence, this book is especially attractive because its author is a Jew in whose mind the inherited world of Jewish faith on the one hand, and the new philosophical erudition on the other hand—the latter not yet fully digested—form a very interesting amalgam.[1] It should be mentioned that my assumption throughout is that the book comprises a single literary unit and that Greek is its original language. I am of course aware that both of these theses are not uncontested—the case for upholding them I have made elsewhere.[2]

I should like to call this work a reflective book. What I mean by this designation finds its first expression in the book's first verse where it says, 'Think of God in the good way'.[3] Such a phrase 'to think of God' is never found in the Hebrew Bible. In accordance with the tradition of Wisdom literature to which the book belongs, its main topic is the struggle between the 'good' and the 'wicked'. The good are distinguished by their connection with the divine figure of Wisdom, while to the evil—whose way of life is portrayed as it is in the Psalms—the author lends an ideology strangely concocted through a combination of Kohelet[4] and scraps of Epicurean philosophy.[5] Further on we shall return to this ideology. Yet in the last part of the book these universal moral entities are replaced by concrete historical figures, Israel on the one hand, and the biblical Egyptians on the other hand. This form of presentation leads the author to the narration of the ten plagues of Egypt and to a theological discussion centring around them. To the plagues the author opposes the many instances of God's graciousness to Israel in the desert.

The discussion of the ten plagues is clearly oriented around the principle which we are dealing with. This is actually stated in so many words: 'By what things a man sins, thereby is he punished',[6] where the

---

1. This amalgam I tried to characterize in the opening section (pp. 154-56) of my article, 'The Figure of Death in the "Book of Wisdom"', *JSS* 30 (1979), pp. 154-78. For English translations from the book I used, where not stated otherwise, see J. Reider, *The Book of Wisdom*, in *Jewish Apocryphal Literature* (New York: Dropsie College, 1957).

2. In my article, quoted in the previous note, I brought some arguments for this opinion.

3. Wis. 1.1; this seems to me an adequate translation of the Greek words.

4. Concerning this (not undisputed) point cf. my article, 'Figure', p. 175 n. 72.

5. This influence seems to be to have been proven by A. Dupont-Sommer, 'Les impies du L. de S. sont-ils des Epicuriens?', *RHR* 3 (1945), pp. 90-109. Of course, only a superficial reception of Epicureanism could be expected from those half-educated people in question; as to the practical conclusions drawn by them, neither Kohelet nor Epicurus can be held responsible.

6. Wis. 11.16.

context makes it clear that not human but divine punishment is meant. But by closer reading we can discover certain important nuances of our author's approach which clearly distinguish it from that of the rabbis. First, we have to consider what exactly is the kind of wickedness which calls for divine punishment. Men are punished, says the foregoing verse, ἀντὶ λογισμῶν ἀσυνέτων ἀδικίας αὐτῶν, 'for the foolish reasonings of their unrighteousness'.[1] What exactly these foolish reasonings are we shall soon see. But first we must note that our author is not concerned with wicked deeds *per se*, but rather with the wicked thoughts which underlie them. These are what constitute the real crime—and this is in line with the character of our book. 'Being wicked' for this author means 'having wicked thoughts'. Even more important seems to be another peculiarity of our book, one which logically develops from the previous point. If the punishment is to be adequate to the crime, it has to hit upon the wicked man's thought, and this is expressed in the opening words of the verse just quoted, which I withheld until now. The full verse reads: 'That they might know (ἵνα γνῶσιν) that by what things a man sins, thereby is he punished'. If we compare this sentence with what we found in rabbinic literature, we begin to become aware of the fact that a shift in the point of gravity has occurred here. What is at stake, when punishment is assessed, is not so much the equilibrium in the order of the world which might be restored by the correspondence between sin and penalty, but rather the wicked man's consciousness which is forced to internalize the experience of this correspondence. This understanding is meant to bring the sinner to an acknowledgment of divine justice. That a human spectator may become aware of God's greatness through the experience of the correspondence between sin and punishment we have already found in the Torah in the declaration of Jethro quoted above. Yet now such a one-time experience is not only generalized but also— and this is what is decisive—it is made into the *aim* of divine retribution. Among the rabbis we found an untiring endeavour to identify as many divine deeds as possible which follow the pattern of מידה כנגד מידה, while here this very procedure is made the object of religious reflection. For the Wisdom of Solomon it is not sufficient to state that God acts this way with man, but it claims even to know why or, to be even more precise, for what purpose God acts in this

---

1. Wis. 11.15.

manner. This is the meaning of the word ἵνα (in order that) that opens the sentence.

For this reason it cannot be enough for our author simply to find, like the rabbis in the midrashim we reviewed, points of correspondence between human acts and the divine response, both concerning reward as well as punishment. For him the crucial point must be that the culprits themselves be made aware of the relation between their wrongdoing and the tribulations they suffer. To this end he invents, when telling about the death of the Egyptian firstborn, horrid dreams and visions presaging the victims' terrible fate 'that they might not perish without knowing why they were afflicted'.[1] The author needs this cruel detail for, without it, the punishment becomes pointless. In order for the punishment to have its proper effect it must be understood.

In a similar way the author treats the various plagues effected through the agency of the animal kingdom. These are explained as the divine reaction to the specific Egyptian sin of the adoration of animals as gods. For the Jewish Egyptian author this topic carries such a weight that he introduces into his book a whole excursus of three chapters (13–15) dedicated to the origin of religious aberration.[2] The condemnation of Gentile idolatry as a cardinal sin never occurs in the Hebrew Bible, and appears for the first time in Hellenistic Judaism. It now becomes clear that these are the 'foolish reasonings' of the wicked mentioned before. For the Egyptians this means specifically a punishment for their theriolatry. What effect must the plagues have had on the minds of the Egyptians? The answer is unequivocal. 'Being punished by those very creatures whom they esteemed gods, knowing him whom before they refused to know,[3] they recognized the true God'.[4] So here we are clearly told just how the concatenation of sin and punishment brings man, even against his will, to the recognition of the true God.

We have seen that the continued speculation concerning divine

1. Wis. 18.19.

2. The disquisitions of these chapters work with the materials of Hellenistic, especially Stoic, theology and psychology of religion. Yet that which in these theories is meant as an explanation of religious conscience in general is used by the Jewish author as an explanation of false religion and wrong forms of worship.

3. Clearly an allusion to Pharaoh's saying: 'I don't know the Lord' (Exod. 5.2).

4. Wis. 12.27.

retribution has come to a conclusion concerning its pedagogical function. It may have been this shift of emphasis that led the author to a
further elaboration of the network of correlations here under discussion. But before we consider this addition to the system, we must
anticipate an unexpected twist which occurred in the concept of
'measure' when it was transplanted into a Greek context. Of course,
when the Jewish author spoke of μέτρον, he was just translating the
Hebrew מידה that seems to have been already the usual word for correlation between human acts and divine reactions. But in one place in
his book the word takes on a new connotation originating from quite
another source.

When telling about the plagues effected through the agency of
various animals, our author raises the question of why God sent only
lowly creatures against the Egyptians.[1] With an impressive display of
rhetoric he conjures up images of wild beasts and even fabulous creatures that God could have mobilized against the sinners, if he had so
wanted.[2] His answer is that—for pedagogical reasons to be discussed
later on—God decided to hold back from employing his 'strongest
weapons' and, for the time being, to content himself with 'ludicrous'[3]
means. It befits, as it were, the unlimited greatness of God that he
should not give free play to his omnipotence. Rather, just the opposite
is the case: 'Thou didst order all things by measure and number and
weight'.[4] Now, the formula here used, μέτρῳ καὶ ἀριθμῷ καὶ
σταθμῷ has a long history in Greek literature,[5] from Greek tragedy
until late antiquity. Originally it denoted the idea of exact science, but
it came also to express the just partition of political power in the *polis*.
Since Plato opposed the old sophist declaration that man is the measure of all things with his antithesis that God is the measure of all

---

1. Wis. 11.15. Here, this point is more hinted at than actually expressed, but
through a comparison to the parallel passage in Philo (*Vit. Mos.* 1.109) we may
assume that our author, too, had this point in mind.

2. Concerning this point, the similarity to the passage in Philo is so striking that
we may assume that here we have an exegetical tradition current in Hellenistic
Judaism.

3. Wis. 12.26. I prefer this translation to Reider's 'mockeries', implying an
offensive note I do not find in the Greek original.

4. Wis. 11.20.

5. This history has been outlined by F. Heinemann, 'Mass, Gewicht und Zahl',
Museum Helveticum 32 (1975), pp. 181-296.

things,[1] the ground was prepared for Philo's paraphrase to the effect
that God is the measure, number and weight of all things.[2] Therefore,
when Plato says on another occasion[3] that God formed the entire
cosmos by ideas and numbers, it is only natural that from late
antiquity[4] we have an echo of this statement too, wherein 'ideas and
numbers' are replaced by our tripartite formula. So it may well be
that our author took this phrase describing acting in the world from
some previously existing literary source.[5] His own use of it shows that
for him, 'measure' involves moderation too.

After this digression we return to the special elaboration of the
network of correspondences found in Wisdom of Solomon, which I
mentioned earlier. If God's deeds must be made understandable to the
human objects of those deeds in order that they may fulfil their pedagogical purpose, then the web of connections must be worked out
much more densely than we are accustomed to in the rabbinic
midrashim. In a book which has the contest between the good and the
wicked as its central topic, a doctrine which keeps asunder the punishment for bad deeds and the reward for good ones in two separate
accounts is not at all satisfactory. There must be, as it were, an
interrelation between the two categories. And this is the new idea
introduced by our book. It is even the starting point for its whole
argument. After a survey of the providential guidance of Wisdom in
the prehistory of biblical Israel, we come to the exodus from Egypt
and the children of Israel's thirsting in the desert.[6] They call upon
God, and water is miraculously brought forth out of the hard stone.
And then our author writes: 'For by those things whereby their
enemies were punished, by these they in their need were benefited'.[7]
This refers to the first plague with which God afflicted the Egyptians,

1. Plato, *Legg.* 717c.
2. Philo, *Somn.* 2.193.
3. Plato, *Tim.* 53b.
4. Plut. *Quaest. Conv.* 83. = 720b.
5. The use of the tripartite formula by our author—from whatever source he may
have derived it—had a completely unexpected afterlife. As his book was incorporated
as part of the Septuagint, St Augustine found it as part of his Bible. Such being the
case, the verse in question served him as a scriptural authority that aided him in his
theological endeavour to penetrate the intricacies of the Christian dogma of the Holy
Trinity. This chapter must, of course, remain outside the scope of this essay.
6. Wis. 11.
7. Wis. 11.5.

when their 'everflowing river' had been made 'turbid with gory blood'—a punishment that in turn was wrought upon them 'in rebuke of the decree for the slaying of the babes'. It is not expressly mentioned that the crime against the babes was committed by water too, but perhaps we are entitled to supplement this detail as a well-known fact. If so, the punishment itself is already interpreted as retribution of like by like. But now this chain is expanded by an additional link. By providing plenty of water to the parched Israelites, God 'shows through their thirst at the time how he punished their adversaries'.[1] This sentence makes a mental connection between the water-plague of Egypt and the water-miracle of Israel. But that is not all. The salient point is that Israel itself has to be aware of this connection. The Israelites are to experience the miracle that is done for them against the backdrop of the Egyptian plague, and by virtue of the present miracle to come to a deeper understanding of the past Egyptian plague. The author even insists on the other side of this connection, too. He assumes—artificially enough—that the news of the water-miracle that was performed for Israel in the desert reached the ears of the Egyptians and that its significance was grasped by them. He insists that 'they heard that by their own punishments the others were being benefited',[2] and that this caused them a 'double grief'. Furthermore, this matter had for the Egyptians—so our author claims—a much more far-reaching consequence: in comprehending the correlation here at work 'they learned to know the Lord' (ἤσθοντο τοῦ κυρίου). Here we have to notice that a mental procedure that has been vilified by some scholars as a piece of idle sophistry is meant by the author as no less than a sort of subjective proof of the existence of God. This is the pedagogical twist that our author gives to the motif מידה כנגד מידה.

Yet the Israelites too have to learn their lesson from the connection between their water-miracle and the water-plague suffered by the Egyptians. After all, the thirst they had to endure was a sort of plague also. It is not at all our author's opinion that the good, or the Israelites in this case, are free from suffering. God 'tries',[3] he 'educates' Israel—and here it is proper to remember that in the verse that in the

---

1. Wis. 11.8.
2. Wis. 11.13.
3. Wis. 11.9.

authorized version reads, 'As a man chasteth his son',[1] the Septuagint has παιδεύει (educates). But here there is a distinction to be made: God acts with Israel 'as a father' and with the Egyptians as a 'stern king',[2] with Israel 'in mercy' and with the Egyptians 'in anger'.[3] Israel discovers this difference by comparing its own suffering with that of the Egyptians. Even during difficult times Israel must be ever cognizant of God's mercy and this awareness is acquired by remembering the sufferings of the Egyptians, which are comparable but essentially different.

We find another variation of the same topic in the narration of the death of the firstborn.[4] This plague too is associated with an Israelite counterpart, but whereas the counterpart of the water-plague of Egypt was God's gracious provision of water to Israel in the desert, the death of the Egyptian firstborn is associated not with a beneficial act but rather with a terrible punishment which is brought upon Israel, viz. the pestilence which befell them after the rebellion of Korah.[5] This is an 'experience of death' touching the 'righteous'[6] and exposing them to stern judgment. Nevertheless, there exists a difference even here: 'The wrath not for long remained' for 'the mere experience of wrath was sufficient'.[7] What made for this difference was the fact that the Israelites had on their side a champion, Aharon the High Priest who interceded and succeeded in checking the raging divine wrath.[8] By saying words of prayer he 'subdued the chastiser', reminding him of 'the oaths and covenants of the fathers'. All this is told in a language very close to that of the biblical text. It is true, this time there is missing any reference—in other cases so diligently emphasized—to the victims of the plague being aware of that meaningful difference between their own situation and that of the Egyptians during the tenth plague. Only by closely comparing their own limited calamity with the devastating death-blow visited upon the Egyptian firstborn should they have been able to discern the component of mercy even in their

1. Deut. 8.5.
2. Wis. 11.10.
3. Wis. 11.9.
4. Wis. 18.
5. Wis. 18.20ff.
6. Wis. 18.20.
7. Wis. 18.25.
8. Wis. 18.22.

present disaster, but I must confess that this time the author failed to make this point.

The motif of graded punishments sent by God can take on, according to our author, an additional form too, not easily harmonized with what we have seen till now. Sometimes the idea prevails that God is essentially clement and his wish 'to spare all'[1] does not altogether exclude even the wicked. The author's way of setting forth this idea is somewhat complicated by the fact that this time the wicked are historically represented not by the Egyptians but by the primordial inhabitants of Canaan. When those are to be punished for their godless deeds, God does not annihilate them immediately but as a first step he sends wasps against them,[2] and by this troublesome but not yet pernicious visitation he gives them a warning, 'giving them time and place to change from their wickedness'.[3] Such an opportunity God grants even to the enemies of his people. Only after they have failed to pay heed to his warning does he condemn them to destruction. According to the same scheme, it seems, we have to interpret the animal plagues visited upon the Egyptians as a sort of warning signal. Before striking the main blow, viz. the death of the firstborn, God chooses milder forms of chastisement that may possibly make the severest one superfluous. This is what seems to be meant by the designation of the first punishment as 'ludicrous'.

This time the line of argument does not make it necessary that the victim be aware of the relation between the former, milder punishment and the final, decisive one. Yet it is God's pedagogical intention that we should understand this providential connection, reflect on it, and learn a practical lesson from it. The object is that man will imitate God's ways: 'By such works did thou teach thy people that the righteous must needs be a lover of men (φιλάνθρωποι), and madest thy sons to be of good hope that thou grantest repentance for sins'.[4] This is the last step in the shifting of the faith in the reciprocity of God's acting with men to the pedagogical level.

1. Wis. 12.16.
2. Wis. 12.18 according to Deut. 7.20.
3. Wis. 12.20.
4. Wis. 12.19.

III

After my analysis of the last part of our author's book, it seems worthwhile to have a retrospective look upon its first part, where, if I understand correctly, the author held vaguely the same ideas concerning God's behaviour towards men, although at the time of the writing of the first chapters[1] he may not yet have been able to give it so clear-cut a formulation as we found in the historical part.

As I said above, in the first part of the book 'the good' and 'the wicked' are abstract entities, not yet embedded in any historical setting. The wickedness of the wicked is in their 'reasoning not aright' (λογισάμενοι οὐκ ὀρθῶς),[2] the crux of their error being their conviction that death is the end of everything.[3] When man dies, so they hold, his soul is 'dispersed as thin air'.[4] This dissipation of the soul is depicted with a wealth of similes: the soul is like a fugitive shadow, like mist chased by the sun's rays, etc. The author, with his staunch faith in immortality, sees in this unbelief the source of all evil. He describes the majestic appearance of the pious in the hereafter and imagines a re-encounter between the wicked and the pious that brings the wicked to utter despair. In the end, they avow the futility of their life.[5] They admit that they were 'as a ship that passes through billowy water, of whose passage there is no trace to be found. . . or as a bird . . . or as an arrow. . . as smoke'.[6] There is a striking similarity between their own confession concerning their former lives on the one hand, and their doctrine, developed before, of the extinction of the soul after death on the other hand, a similarity that in some cases takes the form of verbal concordance.[7] What is the inner significance of this similarity? The doctrine of the future extinction of the soul, as

1. Although the many parallels and cross-references between the different parts of the book seem to prove its literary unity, it is a tempting assumption that the author wrote the different parts of the book during different periods of his inner intellectual development.
2. Wis. 2.1.
3. Wis. 2.2.
4. Wis. 2.3.
5. Wis. 5.6ff.
6. Wis. 5.10ff.
7. I have collected a number of such concordances in my essay 'Figure', p. 177 nn. 76-78.

held by the wicked during their lives, is expressly declared by the
author to be wrong.[1] But now it emerges that the wicked's own souls
are bound to suffer an end which is strikingly similar to that which
they held to be the destiny of all souls. Of course, in this general form
their tenet is strongly denied by the author, but what he has to tell
about the wicked's own soul is not so far away from it. We may therefore say that the eternal punishment of the wrongdoers is—paradoxically enough—in their false philosophy coming true.

Indeed, our author does not put it in such a clear-cut formulation.
But he seems to be going in this direction when he states, 'Just as they
reasoned, the impious will have their punishment' (οἱ δὲ ἀσεβεῖς
καθὰ ἐλογίσαντο ἕξουσιν ἐπιτιμίαν).[2] If my reading is correct, and
in this vague statement the author hints to the above-mentioned mate-
rialization of the erroneous imaginings of the evildoers, then what we
have here is an application of the highest level of the principle מידה
כנגד מידה .

1. Wis. 5.15.
2. Wis. 3.10.

THE JUBILEE LAW—AN ATTEMPT AT INSTITUTING SOCIAL JUSTICE

Yairah Amit

I

The perception of material values as the source of injustice and the corruption of morality is already present in the story of the Garden of Eden. In the long introduction, which describes in detail the conditions which existed in the Garden before man's sin (Gen. 2.4b-25), the narrator is at pains to point out that gold and precious stones, which are a manifestation of material values, were not present in the Garden. They are to be found in the land of Havilah which is located outside the Garden. As it is written:

> A river issues from Eden to water the garden, and it then divides and becomes four branches. The name of the first is Pishon, the one that winds through the whole land of Havilah, where the gold is. The gold of that land is good; bdellium is there, and lapis lazuli. . . (Gen. 2.10-12).[1]

In the setting of life in the Garden, man did not need to struggle for his existence. Only after being damned did economic values such as land in its various forms, the labour invested, work tools, etc. become the object of his desires, since,

> cursed be the ground because of you; by toil shall you eat of it all the days of your life; thorns and thistles shall it sprout for you; but your food shall be the grasses of the field; by the sweat of your brow shall you get bread to eat. . . (Gen. 3.17b-19).

In modern terms we might say that in life outside the Garden, the means of production, which can ease confrontation with accursed reality and afford their owners economic-existential security, became the object of the aspirations of society as a whole as well as of each

---

1. See my article, 'Biblical Utopianism—A Mapmaker's Guide to Eden', *USQR* 44 (1990), pp. 11-17.

individual within it. The exigencies of life outside the utopian Garden introduced man to the new experience of resources and means of production and taught him to appreciate the advantages afforded by capital, which is to say, economic power. The result was that economic control became the source of social injustice.

In the world of biblical thought, therefore, there is a realistic recognition that the Garden of Eden has been taken away from man irrevocably and that life outside the Garden is driven by economic struggle and economic forces. Such struggle is perceived as accursed or as an evil sickness which characterizes human existence since the banishment from protected hothouse conditions. It is in the nature of things that in this conceptual world, any limitation or reduction in the economic struggle for existence may be understood as a blessing or a benevolence. It should be noted that this perception is not consistent with the conceptual world of the ancient Middle East. Thus, for example, in the wondrous garden of the goddess Siduri, to which Utnapishtim comes on his way to achieving eternal life, there are precious stones on the trees.[1] In other words, Utnapishtim finds in Siduri's garden the fulfilment of aspirations which are far beyond man's reach in daily life. Its advantage and its uniqueness lie in the facility with which material values can be attained within it. In the ancient Middle East, the Garden of Hopes was perceived simply as a place to satisfy needs which could not easily be met in everyday life, but the biblical perception protests and rebels against reality, and sets as its ideal a significant change in what exists. It should be noted too that biblical realism is also shown in the recognition that the pursuit of substantive change in what exists is in constant conflict with the deeprooted impulses of man's heart. For it is only because of man's inability to master his impulses and not touch the fruit of the forbidden tree that he is banished from the Garden. In other words, because of its realistic and critical perception of what exists, we find in the Bible not only the utopian perception of what is desirable but also the comprehension that it is essentially not possible to bridge the gap between these two extremes. Still, knowing what is desirable serves as a challenge or as an instrument of guidance and education.

---

1. *The Epic of Gilgamesh*, Assyrian Version, tablet IX, cols. v, vi.

II

In this essay I should like to examine whether knowledge of that ideal—removal of the threat of the curse—played some part in biblical legislation. Unlike the laws of science which describe regularities, the legal, religious, or moral systems are prescriptive and are intended to goad, to dictate and even to compel behaviour. That is to say, as with any legal system which strives for improvement and for justice for those under its jurisdiction, the biblical legal system too takes as its starting point an actual situation and strives to improve it. Thus, it is appropriate to ask whether the ideal objective which I have described—the removal of the pressure of economic struggle—finds expression in the system of biblical law and justice.

I do not direct this question to classical prophecy. This is not only because the activity of the prophets may be seen as a reaction with limited ability to change reality (and there is no point in describing the meagre influence of the prophets on their contemporaries), but primarily since, although protest is to be found in their prophecies, there is no real attempt to solve the problem. From the second half of the eighth century BCE, Amos and Isaiah, as well as those who followed, voiced prophecies of severe chastisement against the rich and those who dominated society and who were interested in exploiting the poor and in perpetuating their deprivation.[1] However, in their prophecies—including the prophecies of the end of days—we do not find any attempt to solve the problem of the gap between the classes through the proposal of a new and different socioeconomic order.

The situation is different when we examine what exists in the biblical legal system. This framework includes morality and religion as well, and thus does not limit itself to such values as stability and security, but rather deals with an additional complex of happiness, freedom, aspiration for equality, striving for perfection, respect for the character and uniqueness of others, etc. Some of these spheres are characterized only by recommendations which are not necessarily accompanied by a system of punishments whose purpose is to prevent instances of violation. It is in the nature of things that these recommendations do not in all cases become compulsory law, and as we shall see, this is the situation in the case of the jubilee law as well.

---

1. As, for example, see Amos 2.6-8; 4.1; 5.11; Isa. 5.8; 10.1; 11.4.

The jubilee law, according to Benjamin Uffenheimer, is part of a time cycle which includes the sabbath and the sabbatical year and is characterized by the typological number, seven. Choice of the number seven is arbitrary and divorced from the cycle of seasons of the year. In his opinion, it moulds the rhythm of life in Israel into

> three concentric circles, intended to gradually realize the idea of equality in the society of ancient Israel. . . their purpose being to base interpersonal relations and the social structure on social principles which guarantee the greatest possible social equality as well as ecological balance between man and his environment. . . [1]

It is only natural that the implementation of laws which have an arbitrary aspect and are likely to interfere with immediate profit encounters opposition which is related to the materialistic instinct of man.

And indeed, from available biblical evidence we see that enforcement of those laws which contain an arbitrary aspect met with opposition. Thus, for example, despite the fact that the sabbath was an integral part of life in Israel during the days of the First Temple (see Hos. 2.13; Isa. 1.13; 2 Kgs 11.5-9; 16.8; etc.), it was often not kept (Amos 8.5; Jer. 17.21-22; Ezek. 20.12-24; 22.8; 23.38). Furthermore, the struggle for its observance was no less difficult at the beginning of the days of the Second Temple, as may be learned from the prophecies of Third Isaiah (56.2, 4, 6; 58.13) and from the story of Nehemiah (10.32, 34; 13.15-21). It is only reasonable to assume that enforcement of such laws as leaving land fallow (Exod. 23.10-11), debt moratorium (Deut. 15.1-11), and freeing slaves (Exod. 21.1-6; Deut. 15.12-18) would be very difficult. It was only in the covenant signed during the time of Nehemiah that the people pledged that in addition to keeping the sabbath and holy days, they would forgo agricultural labour during the seventh year and forgive those debts owed them: 'we will not buy from them on the sabbath or a holy day. We will forgo [the produce of] the seventh year and every outstanding debt' (Neh. 10.32). The difficulty of enforcing the law of debt moratorium, interpreted as meaning the cancellation of the debt, is seen in the special declaration enacted by Hillel at a later date (*prosbol*, Seventh

---

1. B. Uffenheimer, 'Sabbath–Sabbatical–Jubilee', in *Beth-Mikra* 100.1 (1985), pp. 28-40 (Hebrew), esp. pp. 28-29. See also that author's 'Utopia and Reality in Biblical Thought', in *Shnaton—An Annual for Biblical and Ancient Near Eastern Studies*, IV (ed. M. Weinfeld; Jerusalem-Tel-Aviv, 1980), pp. 10-26 (Hebrew).

Mishnah 3, 10) which was nothing other than an attempt to circum-
vent the law which had come to be seen as a decree the people could
not live with and, as Rofe says, to return to it its original meaning.[1]
The excessive protection provided by Nehemiah to debtors proved to
be their undoing, since the lenders stopped lending.

In the light of this reality, the jubilee law is even more perplexing.
According to this law, after seven sabbatical years, that is, after 49
years, there would be a jubilee year:

> and you shall hallow the fiftieth year. You shall proclaim release through-
> out the land for all its inhabitants. It shall be a jubilee for you; each of you
> shall return to his holding, and each of you shall return to his
> family. . . (Lev. 25.10).

The principle behind the definition and evolution of the jubilee law is
'But the land must not be sold beyond reclaim, for the land is Mine;
you are but strangers resident with Me' (Lev. 25.23). Along with this
principle, there is another: 'For it is to Me that the Israelites are
servants; they are My servants, whom I freed from the land of
Egypt. . . ' (Lev. 25.55). And in addition, one is enjoined not to
demand excessive interest from a brother (Lev. 25.35-37). This
system of laws indicates an attempt to diminish the gaps between the
members of the society of Israel: loans which do not entail usurious
interest lessen the potential for slaves; regarding the Hebrew slave as a
wage labourer and resident who must not be sold as a slave, and who
in any case, would be redeemed along with his children in the jubilee
year (Lev. 25.39-42) gives the institution of slavery a new meaning;
likewise, regarding all sales of land as *a priori* not being in force
beyond the 49th year—all these demonstrate an attempt to struggle,
through the framework of the law, against the phenomenon of
economic inequality and against the domination and exploitation of
one part of society by another. The jubilee law is an astonishing
attempt to forestall the possibility that any Israelite would find himself
a slave, lacking everything.

It is common practice to compare this law to the Mesopotamian

---

1. For the interpretation of Deut. 15.1-15 as debt moratorium and not cancellation
of debts, see A. Rofe, 'Methodological Aspects of the Study of Biblical Law', in
Jewish Law Association Studies—The Jerusalem Conference Volume (ed. B.S.
Jackson; Atlanta: Scholars Press, 1986), pp. 1-16. Rofe explains Nehemiah's
mistaken understanding of Deut. 15.1-11.

institutions of *misarum* (ancient Babylonian) or *anduraru(m)* (Assyrian), which were administrative edicts involving cancellation of taxes and forgiving of debts, freeing slaves, and returning fields to their owners, issued upon the assumption of power by a new king, or when any king decided to activate this decree because the economic situation had become untenable. But the outstanding difference between the jubilee and the edict mentioned above is that the jubilee became a sacred cyclical law, which operated without any connection to the will or decree of the king. The force of the Babylonian edict lay wholly in its power of surprise. It acted like an amnesty, which could not be predicted in advance, since otherwise those wielding the economic power in the society would have organized to lessen the expected economic damage. In contrast, the jubilee law shows a desire to free men and property from the social interests of any king, by presenting them as belonging to God. The law of the Torah therefore emphasizes that the source of power is God and not the king. As Greenberg writes, 'The Divine regime embodied in the Tora entails spreading social power among the members of society and preventing the accumulation of power in human foci'.[1] In the law which emphasizes that the land belongs to God, and all the people alike are his slaves, any sale is understood *a priori* as leasing, and all bondage as hired labour. In this way divine dominion over the land and the people serves as a platform for a programme of wide-ranging agrarian and social reform, whose apparent purpose is the rehabilitation of a social class whose economic status has been undermined.

The jubilee law includes clarifications which amount to economic reorganization and the assignment of different economic values to means of production: 'the more such years, the higher the price you pay; the fewer such years, the lower the price; for what he is selling you is a number of harvests' (Lev. 25.16). This new economic perception is intended to moderate and blunt the sharpness of the economic extremes. The jubilee law may therefore be described as having fundamentally socialistic characteristics. This applies when the term socialism is taken to denote a system of social conceptions chiefly characterized by the attempt to prevent instances of materialism which perpetuate discrimination against the weak classes; the aspiration to build a just society, marked by its concern for the welfare and support

---

1. M. Greenberg, 'The Attitude toward Power in the Torah and in the Prophets', in *Hasegulah vehakoach* (Oranim, 1985), pp. 29-47 (Hebrew) (esp. p. 32).

of all who belong to it; the desire to lessen the causes for social conflict, which makes relations inhuman; and the attempt to decrease the inequality of opportunity. It seems to me that the jubilee law, along with its appendices—the subject of loans and slavery—expresses the desire to create a different society in which once every 50 years there are again opportunities, in which ever-increasing gaps are not perpetuated, in which there is an attempt to explain that not only does man not have control over his fellow man but also that he does not even have full control over the land; in other words, a society in which the competitive race for achievement is arrested every 50 years, so that each member gains a new cycle of opportunities.

III

Any attempt to consider this law in terms of application leads to a number of problems both as a result of phrasing which is not sufficiently clear and also as a result of inattention to many difficulties which may be created in the process of its enforcement. Thus, for example, the first question which arises upon reading the wording of the law is: is the fiftieth year an additional sabbatical year? From the argument between R. Yehuda and the rabbis (*Ned.* 61.6; *Erub.* 24.2) we learn that the jubilee comes after the seventh sabbatical year; thus two consecutive sabbatical years are to be observed. However, they disagree as to how the following years are to be counted. According to the rabbis, the jubilee year ends the jubilee period, so that the next sabbatical year would be the seventh year after the jubilee (= 57th); whereas according to R. Yehuda the jubilee year should be counted as the first year of the new jubilee, so that the next sabbatical year would be six years later (= 56th). It is no wonder that researchers regard the two consecutive sabbatical years as a decree which the public would be unable to abide, and in their opinion, the fiftieth year should be considered the first year of the new cycle. Thus, according to them, and in accordance with the count in the *Book of Jubilees* (4.29; 10.16), the jubilee year is the forty-ninth year, and the jubilee is a cycle of 49 rather than 50 years.

The reasoning of many researchers, that if the jubilee takes place in the forty-ninth year it makes of the law a decree which the public is able to live with, seems strange to me, since it ignores the substantive problem—the relationship of the individual to his property. Actually, the difficulty in applying the jubilee law does not lie in counting the years and in the observance of a fallow year on the land but rather in the ability, or more precisely, the inability of human beings to control their appetite for ownership and property. For the same reason, it is also difficult to accept the solution proffered by North.[1] According to him, the jubilee law is a realistic law, which existed on a personal and not a national level. His suggestion, that each land-sale had its own jubilee and that we cannot speak of an application of the law to all the lands of the state, does away with the illogical possibility of two consecutive sabbatical years. However, not only does it run counter to the appetites of individuals to acquire property, it also opens up any number of breaches in applying the law. Loewenstamm[2] concludes, from the existence of the limitation which completely removes residences in walled cities from the purview of the law, that 'Jubilee law was customarily followed in Israel in ancient times in both theory and in practice'. This conclusion is based on the argument that although 'social and economic development could bring about a change in existing law, this is not true in the case of Utopian law which reflects a socio-religious ideal unrelated to reality and is therefore not in need of amendments or changes'. In his opinion, the changes in the jubilee law reflect the disintegration of the tribal and family organization along with the consolidation of urbanization and commerce. Weinfeld also emphasizes that 'there is no doubt that the roots of the jubilee institution are to be found in an ancient patriarchial trend whose goal is to preserve the land patrimony and the framework of the ancestral family, a tendency very characteristic of the nomadic Semitic society'.[3] However, on the other hand, an exegete whose starting point, no less legitimate, is that the jubilee law is a late occurrence may argue that those limitations which appear in it are an integral part of the rhetorical strategy of representing it as a law capable of being applied, a kind of extensive itemization characteristic of the genre of

---

1. R. North, *Sociology of the Biblical Jubilee* (Rome: Pontifical Biblical Institute, 1954).

2. S.E. Loewenstamm, 'Jubilee (2)', *Encyclopaedia Biblica*, III (Jerusalem: Magnes Press, 1958), pp. 578-82 (Hebrew).

3. M. Weinfeld, *Justice and Righteousness in Israel and the Nations—Equality and Freedom in Ancient Israel in Light of Social Justice in the Ancient Near East* (Jerusalem: Magnes, 1985), p. 104. See also pp. 105-106 (Hebrew).

utopian writings.[1] According to this school of thought, the jubilee law was never practised in Israel and may thus be considered utopian law, reflecting a social ideal. The legislator, being aware of the difficulties in its application and being interested in it serving as a formative factor, itemized various real details in order to emphasize the possibility of its application. Thus the apparently realistic presentation of the law does not indicate a real situation.

IV

The examination of the jubilee law shows that it is an editorial combination of some well-known subjects—fallow year, levitical cities, redemption, slavery and loans—to which a new interpretation was given. Therefore, although Reventlow[2] has taught us that the connection between similar laws is not necessarily interdependent, it seems more logical to me that in our case the detail which exists in the jubilee law results from a dependence on laws which preceded it, and the tradition of their violation, and from the ideological desire to enforce the new combination. In other words, a legislator who was aware of the problems inherent in implementing the sabbatical year, of the nullification of the debt moratorium, and of the tendency not to free slaves during the seventh year, attempted, by means of the jubilee law, to find a solution to these problems. Of three laws, he found two already existing in the Book of the Covenant (the laws of the slave and the bond-woman and the law of fallow lands), and two of the three— debt moratorium and freeing the slaves—consecutively in Deut. 15.1-18. For his part, he strengthened the connection between the three, presented them as a model which resolves the discrepancies that existed in previous legal collections, and even made use of the system of justification which he found there. Thus, for example, the discrepancy between the laws of the slave and the bond-woman in Exodus and those in Deuteronomy was resolved by means of repealing slavery between Israelites: 'Such male and female slaves as you may have—it is from the nations round about you that you may acquire male and

---

1. See, for example, Thomas More, *De Optimo Reipublicae statu deque nova Insula Utopia libellus*, 1516; Tomaso Campanella, *Le Citta del Sole*, 1602; and others.

2. H.G. Reventlow, *Das Heiligkeitsgesetz formgeschichtlich untersucht* (WMANT, 6; Neukirchen–Vluyn: Neukirchener Verlag, 1961).

female slaves' (Lev. 25.44). He took the idea that an Israelite who needs to sell himself has the status of a hired labourer and a resident from Deut. 15.18: 'When you do set him free, do not feel aggrieved; for in the six years he has given you double the service of a hired man . . . 'Likewise, the calculation that the value of the land decreases as the jubilee year approaches is based on the admonition in Deuteronomy against not granting loans before the sabbatical year. Therefore, the divine commitment, 'I will ordain My blessing for you in the sixth year, so that it shall yield a crop sufficient for three years' in Lev. 25.21 is reminiscent of the promise in Deuteronomy that the lender will be blessed and there will not be paupers in Israel.[1]

I have used these examples to express my opinion that the jubilee law came after the other laws which I have mentioned. It should be added that this conclusion is supported by the increasing tendency of research to regard the Law of Holiness (= H Lev. 17–26), or the writings of the 'School of Holiness', as late, at least later than those of the Priestly Code.[2] In the spirit of this explanation, which I accept, I argue that the legislator who shaped the jubilee law was aware not only of the different mentioned laws, but also of the reality of their violation. Through his shaping of these earlier laws, he indeed tried to fashion a new and just social reality. I would even dare to say that because of his experience, this legislator took into consideration the habitual violation of the earlier laws and therefore stressed the idea that the jubilee year must begin on the Day of Atonement. Thus the fiftieth year is assigned the task of atoning for all previous violations and begins a new cycle. In other words, it seems to me that he knew that the problem of two consecutive sabbatical years was only

1. S. Japhet thinks otherwise in 'Laws concerning Freeing the Slaves and the Relationship between Collections of Laws in the Torah', in S.E. Loewenstamm, *Studies in the Bible and the Ancient Near East* (ed. Y. Avishur and J. Blau), pp. 231-50 (Hebrew). The linguistic–stylistic arguments which she sets forth can support both sides of the argument at the same time. Weinfeld (*Justice*, pp. 94-95) notes the linguistic connection between Deut. 15.2 and Lev. 25.10. From his explanation, it is possible to understand the language in Deuteronomy, in Jer. 34.8, 15, 17, and in Isa. 61.1-2 as taken from Lev. 25, but there is no doubt that this conclusion depends upon the antecedence of the *misarum* and *anduraru(m)* in Mesopotamia and upon his basic assumption concerning the nomadic and ancient background of law in Israel.

2. I. Knohl, 'The Conception of God and Cult, in the Priestly Torah and in the Holiness School' (thesis, Hebrew University, Jerusalem, 1988).

theoretical, therefore he explained that God would ordain his blessing for only three years and not for four. However, like his predecessors, he too created a law which was unenforceable, since it contradicted human nature. This conclusion explains, on the one hand, why we find no hint of the jubilee law in other collections of laws, and on the other hand, why we have no evidence of its violation during the days of the First Temple and even of the Second Temple period.[1]

In this last part of my essay, I would like to pay attention to some facts which can throw more light on the question of when and why this law was formulated. First of all, it is pertinent to consider the fact that the jubilee law describes the strange situation of a return to the conditions which existed after the conquest of the land and after Joshua apportioned it by lot into patrimonies. As our knowledge concerning the period of the conquest and settlement grows, I am increasingly convinced that the land was conquered by a process of creeping settlement, so that the model of division by lot, which in the earliest period allocated to each man of Israel a plot of land within the framework of the tribal patrimony, is artificial and unrealistic.[2] The question to be asked is: what society would be interested in representing the tribal period as a territorial ideal which should be revived in 50-year cycles? It would not seem that the period of the united kingdom, in which there was an attempt to blur the tribal situation (see 2 Kgs 4), suits the application of this ideology. It also would not appear that this was the official ideal during the period of the divided kingdom, when Israel and Judaea were two separate kingdoms, each governed by a king who would certainly not countenance limitation of his power. It is more likely that the jubilee law represents a position which is critical of the monarchy and presents the tribal period as the model to be adopted for imitation. It would seem that affording recognition to such an ideology would be appropriate for the end of the First Temple period, or the period of the Babylonian Diaspora, or

1. See Weinfeld, *Justice*, pp. 101-104. The exegesis of Josephus in *Ant.* 3.12c is not consistent with the Bible and is not even hinted at in the Mishnah and the Talmud. Even the allusion in 1 Macc. 6.49, 53 is not proof that this law was observed.

2. See the recent study of I. Finkelstein, *The Archeology of the Period of Settlement and Judges* (Tel Aviv: Israel Exploration Society, 1986) (Hebrew); N. Na'aman and I. Finkelstein (eds.), *From Nomadism to Monarchy: Archaeological and Historical Aspects of Early Israel* (Jerusalem, 1990) (Hebrew).

even the beginning of the Second Temple period. During these periods there was great disappointment with the leadership of the kings, and when they returned home, the area of Israel shrank to the region of lesser Judaea, the economic situation was difficult, and the hopes of the exiles evaporated.[1] In this setting there was a reason to cling to the idea of settlement, which hints at a broader territorial entity, and to plan for a better social reality. The jubilee law was a means to realize these goals. I must admit that this conclusion is very similar to Kuenen's from 1886: 'this scheme could never have arisen while the national existence flowed on without a break, but when it had been violently interrupted, and a new beginning was to be made, the introduction of a new social order might be conceived'.[2] It should also be noted that the tribal ideal is not to be interpreted as indicating equality, since there is not even a hint that during the tribal period of the division of the land plots was equal. The ideal is, therefore, that every citizen should possess some parcel of land, which would represent the minimal amount of property needed to conduct life as a free man. In order to maintain this situation, the struggle for existence must be halted and the situation revert to its starting point to enable each clan a renewed opportunity.

Secondly, it is interesting to note that the jubilee law is not a part of the covenant undertaken in the days of Nehemiah and that the debt moratorium is not described in connection with this law.

It would appear, therefore, that the jubilee law is a relatively late law, legislated under the influence of the violation of laws which preceded it and in the hope of shaping a different reality. Since human monarchy was criticized, and since the society of Israel had known and experienced the Mesopotamian *misarum* or *anduraru(m)*,[3] the cyclical compromise was created: instead of monarchical amnesty, there would be cyclical amnesties not arbitrarily dependent on the goodness of heart of human kings. In actuality, the jubilee law was

---

1. See the book of Kings and other writings of the Deuteronomic School and also the literature from the early days of the Second Temple: Haggai, Zechariah and Ezra.

2. A. Kuenen, *An Historico-Critical Inquiry into the Origin and Composition of the Hexateuch* (London, 1886), p. 298.

3. According to Weinfeld (*Justice*, p. 56), the fact that Jehoiachin, king of Judah, was released from his captivity by Evil-merodach, king of Babylon, in the year that he began to reign, is one of the proofs to the existence of the *anduraru(m)* in the first millenium and not only in earlier periods.

intended to prevent the emergence of the very social situation which confronted Nehemiah. However, since this law too was not observed, Nehemiah interpreted the debt moratorium as meaning the cancellation of debt and concluded his covenant in intentional disregard of the utopian jubilee law. When the public was not able to live with the debt cancellation, Hillel issued the *prosbol*.

The jubilee law is, therefore, an attempt by means of legislation to impose divine justice upon the society and, beyond this, to impose society's own will to ensure the right of every one of its members to live honourably, with a guaranteed minimum of economic means, and thereby overcome the curse of banishment from the Garden of Eden.

Gershon Brin

The different views of the collections regarding certain laws are a result of different positions of the law. The collections are a product of certain periods and locations. Therefore the differences between them, even regarding the same laws, sometimes are a result of differences in time or location, and of ideology.

It is generally agreed that the most ancient collection of laws in the Bible is the Book of the Covenant.[1] I would like to show that even this ancient codex has undergone inner developments and changes prior to its present state. This is true for the relations *between* laws as well as for the laws themselves.

The main aim of my paper is to show that by examining some laws in the collection, stages of development can be discovered. I will start with a preliminary example in order to demonstrate relations between the laws within the Book of the Covenant. The law in Exod. 21.16 depicts the case of a pregnant woman who is struck by a quarrelling group of people. If she dies the punishment is death[2] ('soul for soul') although her death was a result of unintended action. However, this contradicts another law of the same collection: (Exod. 21.13) 'But if he did not lie in wait for him, but God let him fall into his hand, then I will appoint for you a place where he may flee'. According to this law a killer who did not have any intention to kill the victim is not put to death, but will be punished in a less severe manner. This law is

---

1. Regarding the early date of the Book of the Covenant see, *inter alia*, S.M. Paul, *Studies in the Book of the Covenant in the Light of the Cuneiform and Biblical Law* (VTSup, 18; Leiden: Brill, 1970), pp. 42-45.

2. Any other explanation of the form 'soul for soul' does not suit the plain meaning of the law. On the other hand the rabbis, as well as the Jewish commentators of the Middle Ages, interpret the form as referring to a payment and not to a death penalty.

completed by v. 14 which deals with a murderer (by intention) whose punishment is, of course, death. The contradiction can be solved by the explanation that the Book of the Covenant is a composition which consists of different sections stemming from different authors and periods.

Next I would like to show that even within a single section, one can sometimes find a text which is the result of a complicated history of development. This shows that the borderlines exist not only between different laws, but also within the laws themselves.

We will start our discussion with the law concerning kidnapping. Exod. 21.16 reads, 'Whoever steals a man and (then) sells him and if he is found in possession of him shall be put to death'. This law is worded in the particip (which is a middle form between the casuistic and apodicdic forms).[1] It is worth noting that some other laws in this context are worded in the same manner: one who strikes another person to death (21.12); one who hits his father or mother (21.15); one who curses his father or mother (21.17). The law states that kidnapping a person and (then) selling him are forbidden, and that one who acts in such a way will be put to death. There is a difficulty with this simple explanation because of the phrase ונמצא בידו, for how can the situation be understood according to the wording of the law? The kidnapped person cannot be sold by the kidnapper and be found in his possession at the same time. On the other hand, could it be possible that this form refers merely to the procedure of proof, as in Rashi's explanation: 'that the witnesses saw him [= the kidnapped person] . . . in his [= the kidnapper's] possession prior to the act of the selling' (following the rabbis, as in *Mek. Exod.* 21.16 = *Mishpatim* section 5). Compare also Ibn Ezra: '(. . . the witnesses had seen him) . . . in the Market before being sold'. This means that although the kidnapped person is *now* in a third place, there is evidence which connects him with the kidnapper before the selling. This explanation, however, does not fit the usual manner of the law, because usually it does not include *procedural* elements like this. An ordinary law deals with the case itself without dealing with procedural issues such as the definition of the judge, the nature of proof, witnesses, etc.

Therefore ונמצא בידו means 'and he (the kidnapped) is found in his

---

1. See A. Alt's well-known study, *Die Ursprünge des israelitischen Rechts, Kleine Schriften*, I (München, 1953), pp. 278-332 (see esp. pp. 308, 311ff.).

hands'.[1] Thus, the law deals with the two cases: first, one who kidnaps and sells the victim; secondly, one who kidnaps a person, but continues to hold him (in his possession). In both cases the penalty is a death sentence.[2]

In favour of this explanation one can add the following proofs:

1. The *order* of the actions seems strange because of the fact that the act of selling is mentioned *before* the act of holding the victim in the kidnapper's possession (which is the immediate result of the kidnapping).

2. In the Bible there is a usage of the form ו (= 'and') which is especially used in judicial texts to mean או (= 'or') as in 'one who strikes his father *and* his mother', meaning 'or his mother'.[3]

From this and a parallel law in Deut. 24.7 (see below) it is clear that the law of Exod. 21.16 in its present wording intends to define as an absolute sin, the penalty for which is death, the kidnapping of a person regardless of his fate, whether he is sold to a third person or kept as a slave in the kidnapper's house.

This is not the whole picture. For if the intention of the legislator was to state that the kidnapper has to be put to death, why did he not define his law in the following form: 'One who kidnaps a person will be put to death' (like the neighbouring law 'One who causes a man to die will be put to death', Exod. 21.12).

Combining the items which I have dealt with previously, I find that I have to modify my earlier conclusion by saying that *in the beginning* the law dealt with the issue of the kidnapping of a person and selling him to a third person. At that stage the wording was 'one who kidnaps a person and sells him will be put to death'. Later on, when the authorities saw that there was a need, for various reasons, to make the

1. An additional proof in favour of this interpretation can be found in Exod. 22.3, 'if the stolen beast is found alive in his possession', etc.

2. Regarding this law and its meaning see, *inter alia*, S.R. Driver, *Exodus* (CB; Cambridge, 1911); B.S. Childs, *The Book of Exodus* (OTL; Philadelphia, 1974), *ad loc.* R. Westbrook (*Studies in Biblical and Cuneiform Law* [Paris: Gabalda, 1988], p. 119) explains the words ונמצא בידו as referring to the person who has bought the kidnapped from the kidnapper. However, I cannot accept this explanation either from the wording of the law nor from its content.

3. See my paper, 'The Uses of או (= or) in the Biblical Legal Texts', *Shnaton* 5–6 (1982), pp. 25-26 (Hebrew).

law more stringent they added at the end of the law ונמצא בידו ('or is found in possession of him').

Thus, I explain the strange wording and order of words by suggesting that they are a result of a growth of the law in *two* stages. However, as people in ancient times were not used to changing a *holy* text by erasing any item from it, but by adding a new item into it, they inserted in our case the words ונמצא בידו at the *end* of the text (as Daube's rule).[1] I have already mentioned that the law does not reflect the logical order of the acts of the sin, but the order of the *growth* of the law.

Another proof for the existence of a less stringent stage in which only one who kidnaps a person and sells him will be punished by death can be found in Deut. 24.7: 'If a man is found stealing one of his brethren, the people of Israel, and if he treats him as a slave[2] and sells him, then that thief shall die. So you shall purge the evil from the midst of you'.

There are several differences between the two laws, most of them stylistic. Only one difference between Exod. 21.16 and Deut. 24.7 is essential. That is that the law in Deut. 24.7 deals with a person who commits a sin consisting of two actions: kidnapping *and* selling. Therefore one can imagine that according to the opinion of the Deuteronomistic legislator, the punishment for a person who kidnaps another person, but does not sell him is *not* death, but a less severe penalty. That exact case is of course not mentioned in the book of Deuteronomy, but it is a reasonable conclusion to deduce.

I will now indicate the Deuteronomistic idioms which are mentioned in the law of Deut. 24.7:

1. מאחיו מבני ישראל   one of his brethren the people of Israel
2. והתעמר בו   if he treats him as a slave
3. ומת הגנב ההוא   then that thief shall die

---

1. D. Daube, *Studies in Biblical Law* (Cambridge, 1947), pp. 85-86.

2. The Hebrew reads here *hit<amer*; compare M. David, 'HIT 'ĀMĒR (Deut. XXI 14; XXIV 7)', *VT* 1 (1951), pp. 219-21 who regards the root *<mr* as referring to business matters, i.e., the law forbids the kidnapper from behaving towards the kidnapped person as if he is part of his goods. A. Alt points to some texts from Ugarit in which a similar usage of *<mr* is found; see his article 'Zu HIT 'ĀMMĒR',*VT* 2 (1952), pp. 153-59.

4.   ובערת הרע מקרבך   so you shall purge the evil from the midst
of you.

1 is a typical Deuteronomistic idiom, used to indicate the priorities of
its ideology. 2 is an idiom which is found only in the book of
Deuteronomy (here and in 21.14). 3 is the stylistic method for an
absolute penalty statement using the form וקטל (וּמֵת) instead of the
usual form יקטל (מות יומת) in the passive form. 4 is a motive clause
used by the Deuteronomist to encourage the people to obey the laws.[1]

One cannot question this hypothesis by saying, 'How could it be that
the more ancient codex of the two—the Book of the Covenant—
reflects a "modern" stage of the law of kidnapping, while the younger
parallel in the book of Deuteronomy does not?' We know that the
different collections have different routes of development depending,
inter alia, on local and ideological factors. Hence the change in the law
of kidnapping in order to make it more stringent did not have any
influence on other sources (such as Deut. 24.7 and others). The explanation which I have just given is based on the conception that the law
in Exod. 21.16 reflects the results of two stages of the law of kidnapping in which the later stage is depicted in the present law. This shows
the legislator's attitude toward this kind of sin.[2]

On the other hand there is a possibility of a variant explanation: my
previous description could be replaced by another one saying that the
two stages happened before the law was 'planted' into the Book of the
Covenant. That is to say, the author of the Book of the Covenant
borrowed the law as it was after it had undergone two rounds of
developments in its earlier history. This explanation does not change
anything regarding the creation of the law, but only its method of
arrival in the present Book of the Covenant. It does not even change
the explanation which I have given referring to the less stringent law
of Deut. 24.7.[3]

I pass on now to discuss another law which shows a similar
development: the law of the goring ox (Exod. 21.28-36). It reads:

1.   Regarding typical Deuteronomistic phrases see M. Weinfeld, *Deuteronomy and
the Deuteronomic School* (Oxford: Clarendon Press, 1972), *passim*.
2.   This conclusion follows Daube's short statement regarding the later stage
which ומצא בידו represents in the history of the law of kidnapping (*Studies*).
3.   The law allows the selling of a person in the case of a thief who cannot pay the
fine; see B. Baentsch, *Exodus* (HKAT; Göttingen: Vandenhoeck & Ruprecht, 1903),
p. 197.

(28) When an ox gores a man or a woman to death the ox shall be stoned, and his flesh shall not be eaten; but the owner of the ox shall be free of liability. (29) But if the ox has been known as goring in the past, and its owner has been warned but has not kept it under control, and it kills a man or a woman, the ox shall be stoned, and its owner also shall be put to death. (30) If a ransom is laid on him then he shall give for the redemption of his life whatever is laid upon him.

Verse 28 deals with the issue of an 'innocent' ox, which means an ox which has not yet gored any person. On the other hand v. 29 deals with an ox that already has a 'history' of goring persons. The main point which I intend to deal with is the relation between vv. 29 and 30. According to v. 29 the penalty for the owner of the ox is death along with his ox ('and its owner also shall be put to death'). Verse 30, however, mentions the possibility of avoiding the death penalty by paying ransom.[1] This change is worded in v. 30 in a conditional: 'If a ransom is laid on him then he shall give for the redemption of his life whatever is laid upon him'. The passive form יושת 'is laid . . . whatever is laid upon him' raises some difficulties.

1. If we suppose that the owner of the ox has an option to save his life by paying ransom, it is clear that anyone involved in such an incident would choose that option, although the ransom might be a very high amount. So anyone paying it would have to be a rich man. Therefore it is difficult to assume that the legislator would cause a discrimination in the law by offering different options which depend on a distinction between those who belong to different ranks. This opposes the judicial-ethical principle which is described, for instance, in Num. 15.16: 'One law and one ordinance shall be for you and for the stranger who sojourns with you'. One cannot solve this problem by saying that the idea of equality before the law is unique and is typical to the legislator of Numbers 15, because it is a general understanding in all parts of the Bible. Therefore any interpretation of a biblical law which stands against this principle should be rejected.[2]

In addition to this argument the above-mentioned explanation should be rejected for the reason that the text speaks about the ransom

1. According to Westbrook, *Studies*, pp. 60-61, there are examples of 'double laws', among which he includes the law of the goring ox. However, I cannot agree with him for this particular law for the reasons which I will mention in the following discussion.

2. The issue of slaves and the like is irrelevant to the present discussion.

as being 'laid upon him', which means that the owner does not have the power to decide for himself in this case.

2. Even if we suppose that the option of deciding which of the two kinds of punishments (v. 29 or v. 30) is to be effective lies in the hands of the victim's *family*,[1] the problem still remains. The reason for this is that if the victim's family is rich they will insist on the option of killing the owner of the ox. However, if they are poor, they will be forced to choose the option of payment, unless they choose to insist on demanding the killing of the owner of the ox, which caused, by his negligence, the death of one of their family. In both cases there is a clash with the principle of equality of persons before the law.

3. Even the solution that the choice between the two actions of punishment is in the hands of the judges is to be rejected for other reasons. According to the text of the law the differences in wording between v. 28 and v. 29 define the different status of the ox—does it have or does it not have a 'history' of goring any persons? Verse 29, as we have seen, deals with the case where it had gored some persons in the past, and although its owner was warned by the authorities, he did not keep it as had been ordered by them. From this description one can see that the judges do not have any role in deciding which of

---

1. This is the explanation of Paul, *Studies*, p. 82, who says that in this case the law allows the taking of ransom, because it is not a regular case of murder. Paul remarks that in the Bible there is no system of compensation, for only in a society with an economic system of thinking is there such a method. See also M. Greenberg, *Some Postulates of Biblical Criminal Law*, Y. *Kaufmann Jubilee Volume* (Jerusalem, 1960), pp. 5-28, esp. pp. 23-24 about the argument that ransom is allowed in this case since the ox-owner did not personally commit the homicide, nor did he intend or premeditate it. Compare also Greenberg in *Religion and Law* (Winona Lake: Eisenbraum, 1990), pp. 120-25; J. Finkelstein, *The Ox that Gored* (Philadelphia: Transactions of the American Philosophical Society, 1981), pp. 29-30. B.S. Jackson, on the other hand, thinks that ransom was allowed in the ancient biblical law as against the prohibition to do so in the later stage, which is represented in Num. 35.31. See B.S. Jackson, 'Reflections on Biblical Criminal Law', *JJS* 24 (1973), pp. 8-38, esp. 21-24 (reprinted in *Essays in Jewish and Comparative History* [Leiden: Brill, 1975], pp. 25-63, esp. 38-41). From my point of view, both Greenberg and Jackson are equal in seeing vv. 29-30 as belonging to the same stage of the law, while I see them as stemming from two stages. A. Phillips ('Another Look at Murder', *JJS* 28 [1977], pp. 115-16), on the other hand, sees in v. 30 a result of a later development, but v. 29 was still in existence at that stage, which means that both were in effect simultaneously. Phillips connects the creation of v. 30 with the cancellation of v. 12 as an independent law of homicide.

the two punishments is to be applied. If the case deals with an 'innocent' ox, then the judge must act according to v. 28, and if the ox did have a 'history' of goring people, then he does not have any choice and v. 29 is to be applied.

The issues of ולא ישמרנו and והועד בבעליו cannot be the basis for the decision between v. 29 and v. 30, but either for the choice between v. 28 or v. 29, or for a decision about the question if the owner is guilty or not, as in all judicial cases in which the judge is asked to search and find the truth. All this shows that the law does not give the judge the right to choose between v. 29 and v. 30 and the question returns to its original position: who will decide?

4. It is worth noting that (ancient and modern) legislators try hard to exclude wordings which give *choice* options for fulfilling a certain law. It is so because such a choice may give a way to disobey the law in general, and especially because of the fact that the authorities cannot check and try to find who has not fulfilled the law. Therefore it is not surprising that even in the Bible such 'double'-laws are rare. One exception to this is the law of tithe (Deut. 14.22-29). The law shows that there are two options for fulfilling it. These depend on the *distance* from 'the place that your God may choose' (= the city of the temple). Another case deals with the firstling of an ass (Exod. 13.13): 'The firstling of an ass you have to redeem by a sheep but if you do not redeem it you have to behead it'. As I have shown in a previous article the double punishments are a result of a growth in a law, whose original form was extended by the addition of a sanction in those cases where the original demand was not fulfilled.[1]

Another example of a 'double'-option is the law regarding the dedication to the temple (Lev. 27 דיני ערכים, Laws of Valuation). See, for example, in v. 10: 'He shall not substitute anything for it or exchange it, a good for a bad, or a bad for a good, and if he makes any exchange of beast for beast, then both it and for which it is exchanged shall be holy'.

One should mention also the law of levirate which says (Deut. 25.1-10): 'and one of them dies and has no son. . . her husband's brother shall go in to her. . . and if the man does not wish to take his brother's wife. . . and the name of his house shall be called in Israel. . . '[2] It is clear that the second option is used when the main

---

1. 'The Firstling of Unclean Animals', *JQR* 68 (1977), pp. 1-15.
2. I am involved now in preparing research regarding the formula 'if he does not'

one is not obeyed. The legislator knows that the ancient usage of levi-rate marriage had changed and that not all parts of the society fulfil the orders of the law. Therefore he agrees to the other option, but he shows his negative attitude toward it by defining it in a negative style.[1]

I return now to our case, the law of the goring ox. According to our discussion one can see that the real relation between v. 29 and v. 30 lies in a different direction. I mean that the real relation between the two kinds of punishments is not an option for an alterna-tive act, because it is just a 'cover' for the real solution of the prob-lem. Even the rabbis themselves and the Jewish mediaeval commenta-tors saw in the word 'if' (אם) in v. 30 a term which does not relate to an ordinary usage of a conditional sentence.

R. Abraham Ibn Ezra says regarding the phrase 'and its owner also shall be put to death': 'He is *worthy* to be killed, if he does not pay a ransom for his soul. . . as is the explanation of the phrase "an eye for an eye". . . (moreover) this is so because the text says יומת and not ימות'. This explanation follows the *Mek. Exod.* 21.30 (= *Mishpatim* section 10). Ibn Ezra's wording shows that he interprets the form 'if' (אם) as an *actual* law, not as the *theoretical* one. Therefore he sees in v. 29 (about the death penalty) not the actual punishment, but a theo-retical guideline. However, the truth is that we have to interpret the law in the same way as we have done regarding the law of kidnapping, i.e., here too we have to see a reflection of two stages that the law had undergone. In the earlier period the law of the goring ox was fulfilled according to the guideline of v. 29: 'and its owner shall also be put to death'. However, later on people started to doubt the justice of that system. They thought that it was not right to kill the owner of the ox for a deed which was done by his ox. The case is a severe one, but it is not a direct sin of the owner of the ox. At most he is guilty of carelessness.

At this stage an additional item (v. 30) was added to the law. By this addition the original death penalty was demoted, and it became a theoretical demand (compare Ibn Ezra's definition: 'He is *worthy* to be killed', etc.). So, the only actual penalty is that of v. 30: 'If a ransom is laid on him'.

___

referring to the refusal to obey the law, and the sanction which the lawgiver applies in those cases.

1.   These remarks cannot be seen as research on the subject of the 'double laws' in the Bible. I intend to deal with this issue in another place.

It may be that the date of that change parallels the change of the law of homicide, so that unintentional killing is to be punished different than murder (Exod. 21.13-14), while beforehand the punishment of any killer was death (21.12). As in earlier periods the change is achieved by adding some items to the holy text instead of erasing any item in it. With regard to our case—the law of the goring ox—the addition (v. 30) is defined as a condition, although this is just a fictitious one.

One has to assume that if they had worded the addition in a positive form, it might have caused even more difficulties, for how could one understand the relation between the two actions? Therefore they decided to r ɔe the unique usage of אם ('if'), but not for a real conditional.

Such is the usage even in Lev. 2.14: 'If you offer a cereal offering of first fruits to the Lord', etc. As there is a duty to bring the first fruits as a compulsory gift to the temple, we need to understand the form 'if' as meaning 'when' or 'as you bring', etc., and not as an ordinary 'if'. The rabbis in the *Mekilta* even say כל אם ואם שבתורה רשות חוץ מ-ג וכו. That is,

> All the 'ifs' in the Torah are 'free', except three: 'and if you make me an altar of stones' (Exod. 21.25); this 'if' means actually 'when' 'as soon as', etc.; 'If you offer a cereal offering of first fruits to the Lord' (Lev. 2.14); 'If you lend money to any of my people' (Exod. 22.25).

The explanation which I have suggested in this research can be proved by a group of laws from the Hittite laws. In these laws the existence of two stages is explicitly defined by their author, and is not just a product of a scholar's explanation as in the biblical law. In several items in the Hittite laws there is an explicit mention of the stage of the law prior to the present law. The wording is in this form: '*formerly* the punishment was x, but *now* it is y'.

In some of these laws the king is mentioned as the reformer of the law, that is, he initiated the change. One can see in all these laws explicit evidence of the fact that certain laws reflect in their present state a second stage in the history of the law, in which the previous stage was changed by the replacement of a different kind of punishment. See, for example, laws nos. 7, 9, 19, 59, 67, 91, etc.

It is worth noting that there are two cases in the Hittite laws in which a death penalty was replaced by a monetary punishment. This resembles perfectly our case of Exod. 21.29-30. The two laws are no. 121 and no. 123. Number 121 reads:

> If anyone, a free man, steals a plow and its owner finds it out, he shall put him upon the. . . and. . . Formerly they proceeded in this way, (but) now he shall give 6 shekels of silver and pledge his estate as security.

The same applies to no. 123: 'If anyone [steals a cart a. . . it was formerly considered] a capital crime. [Now. . .] he shall give three shekels of silver and pledge his estate as security'. In law no. 92 a physical punishment was replaced by a payment. It reads, 'If anyone steals two beehives or three beehives, formerly [it meant exposure to] bee-sting; now he shall give 6 shekels of silver', etc.[1]

All this shows that the replacement of capital punishment (or the like) by a payment was a common occurrence in the ancient Near East. Therefore my explanation regarding the phenomenon of 'double laws' can be justified by these Hittite laws.[2]

---

1. See E. Neufeld, *The Hittite Laws* (London, 1951), p. 117 and n. 11.
2. P. Artzi ('Mari document 17 [ARM XIV, 17]', *Shnaton* 4 [1980], pp. 270-72 [Hebrew]) points to a document from Mari in which capital punishment is replaced by a monetary one.

THEODICY IN THE BOOK OF QOHELET

Pin'has Carny

As is well known, the book of Qohelet seems to be the most problematic of the whole Hebrew Bible, as much for the theologian, the
exegete and the educator as for the plain reader. The attempts to
render it inoffensive by which Jewish and Christian hermeneutics has
tried to cope with its innumerable problems are also known, but not
always sufficiently. For the development in philological and literary
insight, as much as historical events together with the questions they
raised, forces us to deal with the book more than ever in a fair and
honest way. The most difficult problem then turns out to be the position of Qohelet regarding a central idea in the Bible and in dealing
with the Bible (that is practical theology): the question of theodicy. I
use the term 'theodicy' in the sense of 'the justification of God against
the objections which can be raised from the fact of the physical and
moral evils in the world against his wisdom, love and justice'.

Such a true and convincing theodicy can only rise and endure at the
turning point of the following statements of faith, which intersect with
one another.

1. God's providence is active in the world of man.
2. Human justice is not just in an absolute sense and does not say
   anything about divine justice. The latter is unconditional,
   higher and better than the former.
3. Therefore man has to fix his theological position upon God as
   person. God is one, a person who sees, hears and does what is
   right, sooner or later.
4. In the case of not finding divine activity in the immanent world
   the idea of retribution after the death of man arises. Although
   this idea is not distinctly expressed in the Hebrew Bible, it is

the 'logical' consequence of faith in absolute justice and can be regarded as rooted in the Bible.

These statements in their inner connection seem to represent the main material of the whole immanent biblical theology. But, as we know, this description is not absolutely unobjectionable. The dramatic encounter of this faith with the reality of human life inevitably leads to objections against the above-mentioned statements of faith. This contestation appears in all forms of biblical literature or, if not expressed verbatim, is present in a latent way to the eyes of the reader. Some examples are given below:

1. The idea of a just retribution presupposes the belief in human freedom to choose between good and evil. In the narrative of the ten plagues Pharaoh more than once decides to let the children of Israel go, but 'the Lord hardened his heart'. The problem is not outspoken, may be not even seen by the author, but the reader must be startled.

2. The question is expressedly raised above all in laments and prayers, as often in the Psalter. Cf. also Hab. 1.12-17; Jeremiah 12.

3. As a special example of a detailed contestation of the consensus of wisdom the dialogue between Job and his friends may be mentioned. In his doxology Eliphaz utters his standpoint concerning the picture of God:

> (God) . . . who does great deeds inscrutable,
> Marvels beyond number,
> Who gives rain to the earth,
> Sends water on the face of the field,
> Who exalts the lowly on high,
> Lifts the forlorn to safety (Job 5.9-11).

This means that God is the creator, a god of providence and lord of morals in human life. Job answers to this, it seems in ironic tone: 'Indeed, I know that this is so. . . These are the great things he does'. A terrible arbitrariness without any moral and legal basis; earthquake, flood, failure of sun and stars and a terrible human fate: these are the 'wonders' (Job

9.2-7). At last, this allows a modern theologian to speak of 'the
demonic in the picture of God!'[1]

As a last example to contest the sapiential concept of the harmony of
the world I refer to a case of redactional work in which the demonic
picture of God could originate from the approach of different
sources. In the first report about the vocation of Moses in the burning
bush God says, 'I have certainly seen the misery of my people and I
have heard their cry because of the overseers; I have *perceived* their
sufferings' (Exod. 3.7 according to Luther's translation). It seems that
the rabbinic midrash understood the verb ידע in another way and
better than the German translation. I cite *Exod. R.* 2.7 (freely):

> Why did the Lord appear from heaven and speak to Moses out of the
> burning bush: He should have spoken to him from the top of the moun-
> tains, from the heights of the earth and the cedars of Lebanon!. . . But as
> two twins: one feels headache, the other feels with him. As is written: 'I
> am with him in misery' (Ps. 91.15). So spoke the Lord to Moses: 'Don't
> you feel that I am in misery like Israel? Do know: at the place from which
> I am speaking to you, from the thorns, I am, so to speak, suffering with
> them.'

ידע, that is to say, not in a cognitive sense (I perceive, I know), but in
an emphatic sense (I am coming myself, I come to know). Compassion
not in the usual sense, but com-passion.

In the second report about the mission of Moses, the Bible says,
after the Lord has talked to Moses about different operative aspects of
this mission, 'And the Lord said to Moses: "When you return to
Egypt, see that you perform before Pharaoh all the marvels. . . For
my part I will harden his heart. . . Then you shall say to Pharaoh:
Thus says the Lord, Israel is my first-born son. . . " ' (Exod. 4.21-
22). Thus it is not just compassion, but a relation between father and
firstborn son. And here, in the transition from v. 23 to v. 24, suddenly the story of the blood-bridegroom comes in: 'Then it happened,
at an encampment on the way, the Lord met him and sought to kill
him' (Exod. 4.24). I cannot enter into the complex problems of this
narrative and am content with stressing the abrupt transition. The
reader has to put the unavoidable question to himself: 'Just now the
Lord has assured Moses of his love for the children of Israel and has
informed him in detail what will be asked from him, from Moses, in

---

1. P. Volz, *Das Dämonische in Jahwe* (Tübingen: Mohr, 1924).

speaking and acting. Now Moses goes to realize the word of God, and, behold! the Lord meets him and seeks to kill him!'

The examples given of a latent, indirect or directly outspoken contestation of divine righteousness, postulated as an axiom, may also serve as examples of the different ways of evading the problems which arise. These attempts by theologians, exegetes and the pious reader, one would call, in the main, rendering things harmless.

Such attempts often are superfluous because the context of the passage in question explains the problem from inside. When God is metaphorically described as a roaring, ripping lion and as a blood-thirsty she-bear (e.g. Hos. 5.14; 13.7-8), the offence of the elite of Israel stands in the background. The sense of the metaphor results from itself: it is not speaking of a demonic act of God, but of the just revenge on the wicked. The praying individual in the Psalter is con-scious of the dynamics between the feeling of God's nearness and the feeling of his distance (cf., e.g., the structure of Psalm 72 and the expression 'hiding of God's face' in Psalm 30 in its context. In any case the end of the wicked 'with terror' is sure, even if at the moment no pains torture them and their body is fat.)

The hardening of Pharaoh's heart can be explained by the reader as God's wish to punish him as an example, especially if he is not con-scious of the determinism that underlies his exegesis. In any case the belief in God's righteousness gets the upper hand.

More difficult is the embarrassment of the reader when confronted with the episode of the blood-bridegroom. The opinion that Moses himself should have known that he had to circumcise his son before travelling to Egypt unfortunately does not escape the sharp contrast between, on one side, the exact instructions with which the Lord provides Moses, and on the other side, the lack of such instruction concerning the circumcision. The method of source-division and of literary criticism can lead to the conclusion that from v. 24 on, a primitive conception of God is active. Such a conception, therefore, could be dropped by modern theologians, and thereby the strange, sudden transition from the witness of God's love and mercy to the report of his cruel arbitrariness would be rendered, partly or totally, harmless.

The dramatic exclamations of the prophets against the injustice pre-vailing in the system of social relations between the individual (mostly the widow, the orphan, the poor and the stranger) and (above all the judicial, but also the religious and secular) establishment are basically not a calling into question of divine justice or of God's activity in history and society. The presupposition of Jeremiah's complaint is 'Just art thou, O God, even if I wanted to dispute with thee. Yet I must ask thee: Why do the fortunes of wicked men prosper?' Likewise in Psalm 73 no lack of divine justice, but a lack of adaptation of human justice to the principles of divine justice is deplored. What did Isaiah say? 'Woe to those who decree iniquitous decrees and the writers who write unjust decisions' (Isa. 10.1). The whole legitimation of prophetic activity is based upon the certainty that human justice, as code of human laws, is not just, that is, it is a negation of divine justice. It should be the operative execution of divine justice in human being and acting.

Especially grave are the problems raised in the book of Job concerning God's just activity in human existence. In order to render these problems harmless, most theologians appeal, on one side, to the structure of the book as a whole (Job's temptations are embedded in the legend of a family story with a happy ending). On the other side this neutering is the result of endless exegeses of the theophany out of the whirlwind (chs. 38–41). Even if Job does not seem to be impressed by the first speech of the Lord (cf. 40.1-5), he declares himself 'guilty and repents in dust and ashes' (thus our questionable translation of 42.1-6) after the second speech. Does Job disavow the divine justice all in all or does he not understand it, in spite of his wrestling with himself in order to arrive at such an understanding? So the modern theologian can arrive at his conclusion: not a lack of trust, but a wrong trust upon God.[1] The 'wrong' in traditional wisdom, as represented by Job's friends, can be 'interpreted away' now with more or less ease. In this way (1) the composition of the book, (2) the understanding of the theophany, and (3) exegesis which aims on purpose at rendering the content harmless, make it possible to annul the contestation of the picture of God by the author.

The result of our considerations in connection with the examples given is the knowledge that the justification of all divine activity in secular reality is without doubt the all-comprising central belief in biblical theology. Is this the case also in the book of Qohelet? Can the

---

1. G. von Rad, *Weisheit in Israel* (Neukirchen–Vluyn: Neukirchener Verlag, 1970), p. 247 (= *Wisdom in Israel* [London: SCM Press, 1972]).

problems which the book raises be solved in the sense of the common biblical theodicy?

It is true that in the book itself some basic question are already rendered harmless, since it had circulated among the people. To these passages belong the bio-bibliographical annotations at the end of the book (12.9-14) and the pseudepigraphical remark which identifies the author with king Solomon (1.1, 12). Literary-critical examination has shown also that glosses with a disarming slant from the hand of pious readers, perhaps also from the first editors, do exist here and there. One of these first editors is probably also responsible for having inserted into the book traditional proverbs and parables which perhaps served the preacher Qohelet as didactic material in his earlier years (for instance ch. 7). Lastly may be remembered the interpretations and translations of many centuries which had the object of softening offensive passages for the respectful pious reader. To give one petty but decisive example: when Qohelet asks, 'How does a man benefit from all his toil which he has under the sun?' (2.22), the answer to this rhetorical question seems to be, 'Nothing is worth the toil, because all is an empty breath and a grasping at the wind' (1.14). But the rabbinic midrash, which has been repeated by nearly all the interpreters of the Middle Ages, says: '*Under* the sun man has no gain from his toil, but *over* the sun (in the other world) the gain waits for his acting' (*Qoh. R.* 1.4).

That these attempts at softening offensive material mentioned above are not all acceptable may have been felt by the rabbis who said, describing the work of king Solomon

> In his youth Solomon spoke songs [i.e. the Song of Songs], as an adult he spoke parables [i.e. the instructive and edifying proverbs], and in his old age he spoke vanity [I would translate הבל by 'nothingness'] (*Qoh. R.* 1.10).

After long and not always successful attempts at isolating the literary and rhetorical problems in the book and elucidating them, removing all endeavours at rendering them harmless, the following picture of God in the book remains. God is the creator of the phenomena in nature and in human life. 'He has made everything beautiful' (3.11). This statement stands at the end of the poem about the balance of events. 'Everything has its season and there is a proper time for every happening' (3.1). How beautiful would this statement sound, if sung by a psalmist, as the one of Psalm 104! But the composition of the poem shows that this 'harmonic' balance is attained by the periodic occurrence of good and evil, not, as with the psalmist, by the glory of the world as image of the glory of its creator. And the change between good and evil in creation, each at its time as a firm order of events, is actually not understandable to man. 'One may trouble therewith, one has no gain therefrom' (3.9). And this torment has God put into the heart of man (3.11—'Heart' is here, as in innumerable cases, the organ of knowledge in man). Thus we could detect here a first allusion to the tree of knowledge. If this is correct, we would have with Qohelet an interesting interpretation of this story. Cf. below. Thus: 'beautiful at *its* time', but not absolutely 'beautiful', incomprehensible for the thinker Qohelet and irrevocable also by the acts of man, for 'who could straighten what he has made bent?' (7.13; cf. 3.14-15).

At this point one could object that all this, from the restricted insight of man, could be argued away (as are God's discourses in the book of Job according to a certain interpretation). We would then have the traditional theological scheme: God is just, he acts in his creation according to a moral plan, and the alleged deviations of reality from this system man actually does not understand (8.16-17; 11.5)—being like cattle! If so, we would have also in Qohelet a representative of the classic theodicy, understandable and helpful for the theologian. Unfortunately this standpoint is, at best, a *pium desiderium*. Even if Qohelet started his examination of the picture of God and the world from the position of orthodox theodicy, his observations and experiences brought him to a sceptical position in the face of confessions of faith which were in contrast to reality, as he saw and understood it. God gives life to man (12.7), he destines the duration of it 'under the sun' (5.18; 8.15), he distributes to everybody his measure of trouble and torment (1.13; 3.10) and of good things (in the toil, 2.24; 3.13). But these pleasures can be taken from man, without taking regard of his moral worth (9.2). Success or failure in human acting is arbitrarily determined and is not based on justice (9.11-12; 6.10-12). There is no divine providence which is just. The free will of God is not disputed, but its enactment is arbitrary; that is already visible in the story of the Fall. God acts and walks with the good and the wicked, with the wise and the fool, and both have one fate (2.14-17; 7.15; 8.10, 14). Therewith, the idea of just retribution was also to provoke a deep crisis for our author. The theory of such retribution is rooted in the doctrine of divine providence and of free human will. This doctrine is fastened in the Bible by the experience of man with God as the principle of justice. And that is mediated, as often in the Psalter, and immediated, as with nearly all the prophets, in the history of the people (for instance in the covenant-faith) and even with Job: 'I had heard of you by hearsay, but now my own eyes have seen you' (Job 42.5).

These spiritual adventures and experiences are completely absent in the book of Qohelet, as in Wisdom literature overall. But the proverbs of Solomon and Wisdom psalms say at least theoretically something positive about God that is consonant with the biblical picture of God. Also Qohelet has his positive statements, but they are antithetically opposed to those. As already said, a faith not proven by empirical facts had no real worth for him; so he arrived at his sceptical position. The prophet thunders against human, unjust justice, because he starts from the conscience of the immanence of a divine justice. The prophetic paraenesis arose and endured in the focus of this dynamics (e.g. Deut. 1.17; 16.20). The psalmists pray for the realization of God's justice and mercy. Qohelet does not thunder and does not pray, but states simply: 'Another thing I observed under the sun: in the place of justice there is wickedness, and in the place of righteousness there is wickedness' (3.16).

Taken together, Qohelet's picture of God is conditioned by his belief in the creation, the negation of a ruling providence, of just retribution, of human freewill. The order of the world is a continuous up and down, to and fro, between poles which are fastened once for all, in its ineffability and 'Unaushörbarkeit'[1] withdrawn from human understanding. All this and other observations lead him to see in anguish and terror the only possible relation of man to God. Therefore also his counsel is to evade divine attention, because you cannot wish it.

The statements about the lack of just retribution must bewilder the reader most. Neither in this life (6.8b; 8.10, 14), nor after death (5.14-16; 6.6; 9.5-6, 10; 11.8) can it be expected, for there is no life after death (3.19-20; 6.4).

The Hebrew Bible expresses nothing about the belief in an existence after death or a possible resurrection (except in an esoteric verse in

1. Cf. W. Zimmerli, *Das Buch des Predigers Salomo* (ATD, 16.1; Göttingen: Vandenhoeck & Ruprecht, 1962) on Qoh. 1.6-9, p. 149.

Dan. 12.2). That is curious, as these questions are a central occupation of the human spirit. Two answers seem to be possible: (1) belief in and questioning of the events after death did not exist as far as late in the period of the Second Temple; (2) the biblical thinkers and authors have intentionally tried to suppress, by not mentioning them, such beliefs which very likely went around among the people. Israel was not hermetically separated from the cultic and cultural influences of its neighbours. And the intercourse with such a faith is expressly Gentile, in conscience and use. In the frame of our deliberations we must not reach a definite decision. In any case nothing is said *for* or *against* the belief in existence in the other world, so interpreters and theologians could arrive by allusions, metaphors, syllogistic techniques of interpretation at different decisions.[1]

Such a subterfuge is, in my opinion, not possible with the book of Qohelet, not only because in this book the belief in a life after death is neither thought about nor possible, but especially because Qohelet is the only book in the whole Bible (except perhaps for two or three statements in Job) which unmistakeably states the finiteness of man and postulates it as an axiom. Additionally to the passages cited above, some of many, I want to cite the decisive passage in 12.7:

> And the dust returns to the earth, as it has been and the רוח returns to God, who has given it.

If one translates רוח as 'spirit', all speculations are open. But this additional allusion of Qohelet to the creation story, verified by the connection between 'dust' and רוח, proves that it is here the breath of life (the same as in 3.19-20) which makes of the dust the 'living flesh', that is, a נפש[2] (cf. Gen. 2.7). When this רוח leaves the נפש, just the dust of the earth is left.

It may be added that the term רוח nowhere in the Hebrew Bible says anything about the essence or about a part of the essence of man. רוח denotes always the existential dependence of man on God, who is the 'God of all רוחח for the flesh'.[3] God moves and equips man with the

---

1. Especially important are the attempts of some rabbis to anchor the belief in another world and in resurrection in biblical statements whereas others criticize these attempts.

2. The translation of נפש by 'soul' leads the modern reader astray again.

3. Num. 16.22. Cf. the translation in the Septuagint: 'God of the spirit *and* all flesh', which again misleads.

breath of life, the spirit of jealousy, of foolishness, of deceit, of wisdom, of wickedness, of repentance, etc., as the wind (also denoted by the term רוח) moves the trees or dries up the ocean, always as an expression of divine influence on human acting and historical events. And all this at a certain time and from time to time. Man *is* נפש and *has* נפש, as long as God lends it to him, be it what it be. When it leaves man, nothing essential of him remains. And when the רוח, as a term for the breath of life, leaves it, the נפש decays to dust.

This means, not just that there is a lack of retribution, in this and in the other world, but also that there is an essential finality of man with his death. Lastly the scepticism of Qohelet in the face of all that happens under the sun can only be understood from his concept of death as the starting point of his philosophical considerations. Seen from such a final death, all the life and strife of man is null and void.[1]

As a final question, a possible one in the period of Qohelet, there is the notion of a hypostasis of evil. The Gentile faith, and above all the heathen cult, allows man to find his place in a certain system of the world and to be content with it. Many things can be explained by the seasons of nature, by the manifoldness and many-sidedness of divine powers. One can solve many problems by a belief in evil and good powers which are opposed to one another. Biblical monotheism at first did not allow such a subterfuge for the explanation of evil. But later on, new attitudes in many fields came through, among them the exteriorization of injustice and evil out of the person of God and its incorporation into the person of Satan. As late as about the end of the fifth century BC second Isaiah rose against this tendency (Isa. 45.5-7). It is certain that this process has come to its conclusion in the age of the Chronicler.[2] This possible way out of the grave questions which we have discussed was known to the author, or authors, of Qohelet. But he did not use it and probably refused it deliberately. For him God remains the only cause of all that exists in the cosmic and the human realm. And so it becomes impossible to him to open his mind to the idea of a theodicy. It seems that the thinker Qohelet could actually not digest the idea offered to him of a justification of God, because he could not integrate the nullity of human justice with the absence of God's justice from the starting point of death as finality of human existence.

1. Cf. also W. Zimmerli's reflections on 1.9.
2. Cf. to this question 2 Sam. 24.1 with 1 Chron. 21.1.

It seems that the lack of a 'classical' theodicy in the book Qohelet is a result of the following:

1. Qohelet's picture of God.
2. His denial of a just retribution in this world.
3. His deliberate denial of the belief in a life after death, that means, a retribution in the other world.
4. The rejection of the idea of a hypostasis and thereby of a possibility to justify God.

Many subordinate questions accompany the main problems. How was it possible that such peculiarities, measured on biblical piety, could be published for centuries and attain canonical rank? And that, though attempts to render the statements of the book harmless proved to be completely insufficient? Who is the man who had gathered and published such offensive material? Where were his roots? In the orthodox faith of his time or in a foreign country? What happened to his opinions and assumptions? Did they ooze through into an ideology of later times, or did they peter out? And so much more that awaits upon an answer. . .

LAW AND ETHICS IN THE HEBREW BIBLE

Ze'ev W. Falk

The topic of law and ethics in the Hebrew Bible has an urgent actuality. While *law* stands for the particular tradition of Israel, *ethics*, in this context, means the universal aspect of the biblical message. The question is whether beyond the historical tradition of the *chosen people* there exists in Scripture a kind of natural system applying to humanity in general. Indeed, the two aspects of the faith of Israel are symbolized by the forthcoming sabbath, which is also new moon. Although the sabbath in general is the creation of law and a historical symbol of creation, it also entails a universal idea of nature. The day represents the unique dignity of the universe, the limits of human interference, the respect due to the creator and the basic equality and freedom of all creatures. New moon, likewise, has a universal meaning beyond that of the historical tradition of the Bible. The day represents the cyclic aspect of life, renewal and hope, as well as the need for atonement and redemption. Both the sabbath and the new moon are institutions of Israelite religion having at the same time a universal message. Therefore, the pericope read in the synagogue on this forthcoming sabbath speaks to all mankind:

> And they shall bring all your brethren from all the nations as an offering to the Lord, upon horses, and in chariots, and in litters, and upon mules, and upon dromedaries, to my holy mountain Jerusalem, says the Lord, just as the Israelites bring their cereal offering in a clean vessel to the house of the Lord. And some of them also I will take for priests and for Levites, says the Lord. . . From new moon to new moon, and from sabbath to sabbath, all flesh shall come to worship before me, says the Lord (Isa. 66.20-23).

Thus the biblical teaching starts with the universal idea of creation, the unity of mankind, and leads towards the universal idea of human unity, equality and salvation. It shows the way from particularity to universality and from law to ethics.

In the following I will try to define the concept of justice both in the objective and the subjective senses, then proceed to treat the idea of ethics against the background of biblical theonomy. My interpretation of the text sometimes differs from the standard translations and I tend to follow the rabbinical interpretation as far as the literal meaning of the text permits it.

Justice can be understood as the goal and criterion of the legal process and of the legal system. Neither of them can be taken as a mere positivist phenomenon or as a mere heteronomous command. The legal process and the system of laws are a means to an end, viz. to administer justice. The judge is therefore called to fulfil his function 'in justice' (Lev. 19.15), which means that he must keep this warning constantly in his mind. The statutes and judgments of the Bible, likewise, are said to be righteous (Deut. 4.8), viz. to be means towards the realization of justice. Divine judgments are said to aim at the realization of justice (Ps. 94.15), which means that God himself submits to this concept of human reason.

However, justice is not the only end of the legal process and of legal rules; there are other values and goals which are mentioned together with those of justice. Samuel is said to have taught the people how to follow 'the good and just path' (1 Sam. 12.23), which means that justice is not enough but needs to be complemented by goodness. God is being lauded for being 'good and just' (Ps. 25.9), and human beings should also do 'what is good and just in the sight of God' (Deut. 12.28). The idea of *good* beside the *just* corresponds with the modern concepts of welfare, security or stability, which sometimes function as alternatives to justice. An attitude of pure justice is insufficient in certain cases where one has the feeling that *dura lex sed lex*. The people of Israel, likewise, are said to long for justice in the subjective sense and for 'salvation' as an alternative and corollary of justice (Isa. 62.1). This is the idea that one has to appeal to the grace of God and not claim any right. Salvation is the result of the goodness of God rather than of his justice.

The administration of justice is an activity within the framework of practical *wisdom*. Therefore, wisdom is credited with making 'kings rule and princes create statutes of justice' (Prov. 8.15). In other words, the right decision must be taken through the use of reason and by following the way of the wise. This is of course the attitude of Wisdom literature, and the question may be raised whether priestly circles or prophetic schools would define the judicial function in a different way. As to the former, they acknowledged certain rules which were independent of any particular tradition but followed from general principles of practical wisdom. Equality before the law, irrespective of descent and ethnic identity, for instance, was such a rule based on reason rather than on tradition. 'You shall have one law for the sojourner and for the native; for I am the Lord your God' (Lev. 24.22), though derived from the divine will, is also a rule of reason. The text, therefore, takes reason as a source of information about the will of God.

The attitude of the prophet did not differ from that of the wise in tracing just government in rules of wisdom: 'Behold a king will reign in righteousness, and princes will rule in justice' (Isa. 32.1), which is a clear quotation from the above-mentioned saying of Wisdom (Prov. 8.15).

If justice is a matter of reason, it can also be taken as a synonym of truthfulness. Hence the warning that judgments (i.e. judicial allocations), scales, weights and measures be *just* (Lev. 19.36), viz. truthful and correct. The same idea is behind the parallelism of 'speaking the truth in one's heart' and 'walking in integrity and acting justly' (Ps. 15.2). The just action is the realization of the true thought, such as justice is an application of the idea of truth. The same can be said of the opposite situation. 'He who speaks the truth gives just evidence, but a false witness utters deceit' (Prov. 12.17). By telling the truth the witness helps in the administration of justice, but a false witness practises the opposite of justice, that is, deceit.

Turning now to the definition of justice in the subjective sense, we may quote again the psalmist describing justice as a virtue: 'He who walks blamelessly, and does justice and speaks truth in his heart' (Ps. 15.2). *Doing justice* in this context does not mean the administration of justice but the attitude towards fellow human beings. It is a conscientious relation towards others taking care to give them their due. *A fortiori* the people administering justice on behalf of society are in need of this virtue. The judge is asked to fulfil his function *justly* (Lev. 19.15), which refers to his attitude rather than the objective contents of the decision.

Obviously, there exist other attitudes beside that of justice, as already said above. The motivation by love and the going beyond one's duty is called by an extended form of the same root, viz. *tsedaqah*. Thus Abraham's trust in God against all the odds was *more than justice* (Gen. 15.6). Likewise, in contradistinction to the Sodomites, Abraham and his family were said to observe *tsedaqah umishpat*, that is, to go beyond their duty and to follow the strict rule (Gen. 18.19). The same term is used with regard to the creditor who returns a pledge to the debtor needing it for the night (Deut. 24.13).

This idea is actually a form of *imitatio dei*. According to the list of divine attributes (Exod. 34.6), compassion, grace and forgiveness are said to mitigate the rigour of stern judgment. Petitionary prayer is made possible on this ground (Ps. 86.5). God is seen as being compassionate, merciful and just, and the same is expected of the righteous person. This is the basis for such a person's willingness to give more than his duty and to lend money to the needy (Ps. 112.4-5; cf. 37.21).

We may notice in Scripture the concept of distributive justice, especially what Professor Edmond Cahn of New York University called *The Sense of Injustice*.[1] It is expressed in the question why the speaker was discriminated against, such as found in the argument of the daughters of Zelophead (Num. 27.4), the counterclaim of the family (Num. 36.3) and the petition about the celebration of Passover (Num. 9.7). The Hebrew term in these cases is *gara'*, meaning to detract. It is a description of the sense of unequal treatment of equals. The positive aspect of distributive justice is mentioned as a principle of land allotment: 'To a large tribe you shall give a large inheritance, and to a small tribe you shall give a small inheritance; every tribe shall be given its inheritance according to its numbers' (Num. 26.54).

Likewise the concept of commutative justice is expressed both in the positive and the negative form.

> And if you sell to your neighbour or buy from your neighbour, you shall not wrong one another. According to the number of years after the Jubilee, you shall buy from your neighbour, and according to the number of years for crops he shall sell to you. If the years are many you shall increase the price, and if the years are few you shall diminish the price. . . (Lev. 25.14-16).

The classical term of commutative justice is the talionic formula *life for life* or *an eye for an eye* (e.g. Exod. 21.23-24). Although this is

---

1. New York, 1949.

not meant to be implemented but should be settled by payment (the exception being murder: Num. 35.31-32; cf. Exod. 21.30), it is a guideline for the assessment of a just equivalent. Commutative justice also plays an important role in biblical theology and theodicy. In rabbinical hermeneutics the concept of *measure for measure* can be found in connection with various laws and narratives describing divine providence (*m. Sot.* 1.7).[1]

Just as the application of the talionic principle would exaggerate the rule of justice, there are similar cases where a strict execution of the law would violate the idea of justice. There must be a certain discretion to decide against the routine in order to satisfy the wish of the legislator in a higher respect. This concept, which the Greek called *epieikeia* (reasonableness, equity), has its equivalent in biblical thought. It seems to be behind the argument of Aaron as to why he had not followed the rules of the sin offering (Lev. 10.17-20). In consideration of the fact of his bereavement, the argument went, there was need for an exception, and such an exception was indeed justified by Moses.[2]

The definition of ethics belonging to the framework of ethics, we must now speak of the latter concept in biblical thought. According to the teaching of Isaiah Leibowitz, 'ethics as an intrinsic value is indubitably an atheistic category'.[3] Biblical theonomy, in his view, does not permit human autonomy and does not refer any problem to the decision of human beings. Indeed, there are many indications that Scripture puts obedience to God at the top of all virtues. This does not, however, necessarily exclude human responsibility for the decision in exceptional situations or for a rational interpretation of theonomic sources. Beside the areas covered by expressions of divine will, there may be other areas without such guidance, left to the ruling of human decision. Theonomy may also, in certain cases, refer humankind to the guidance of conscience or reason. This justified the systematic attempt to provide rules of the second order to fill such empty spaces, and these rules amount to ethics.

As already mentioned, ethics is the theory of just and good

1. Cf. Y. Amir, above, pp. 29-46.
2. For other examples in biblical and rabbinical thought see my *Dat haNetsach weTsorkhey Sha 'ah* (Jerusalem: Mesharim Publishers, 1986), pp. 113-17.
3. A.A. Cohen and P. Mendes-Flohr, *Contemporary Jewish Religious Thought* (New York: Charles Scribner's Sons, 1987), p. 71.

behaviour. Ethics is therefore more comprehensive than justice and may sometimes formulate norms which are in conflict with the norm of pure justice. We spoke of the divine attributes of grace and compassion (Exod. 34.6; cf. Ps. 145.8-9) becoming also human virtues by way of *imitatio dei*. Having spoken of the various norms of theonomy, the text goes on demanding that a person should 'do what is just and good in the sight of God' (Deut. 6.18) or 'what is good and just in the sight of God' (Deut. 12.28). There is room for ethical discourse as to the meaning of these terms and their order, respectively.

That a tension is often felt between various values of morality appears in the following saying: 'Lovingkindness and truthfulness encounter each other, justice and peace kiss each other' (Ps. 85.11). This chiasm describes two dichotomies which are brought to a synthesis under the divine will. The same tension was on the mind of the prophet when calling for the observance of other moral values along with that of justice: 'Administer true justice and act with lovingkindness and compassion towards each other' (Zech. 7.9); or, 'Speak the truth to each other; the truth and the justice of peace administer in your gates' (Zech. 8.16).

The essence of theonomy is the trust in God and his guidance; the essence of ethics is the questioning of all authority and individual responsibility for the setting of norms. Neither custom, institutions and tradition, nor the authority of God himself can discharge the thinker from the personal responsibility to find the truth. He must be convinced through reason and experience that a certain norm of behaviour should be followed.

Nevertheless we find ethical discourse in biblical thought. Abraham is said to have used the insight of his conscience on behalf of Sodom. He dares to criticize the intention of God:

> Will you destroy and not forgive the place for the fifty righteous people living there? Far be it from You to do such a thing, to kill the righteous together with the evildoer, so that both be treated alike. Far be it from You, should the Judge of the whole earth not act justly? (Gen. 18.24-25).

Such an argument would not have been possible on the grounds of theonomy and in the absence of ethical discourse. It shows that there exists a rule of justice outside of the will of God and allowing him to be called to account.

Likewise, Moses is depicted at various occasions criticizing divine decisions by use of human moral concepts (Exod. 32.11-13; Num.

14.13-19). In a prayer on behalf of the congregation he questions the divine wish imposing vicarious liability: 'O God, God of spirits of all flesh, shall You be angry with the whole congregation for the sin of a single person?' (Num. 16.22). The fact that these arguments have been put on record and that God himself was said to have retracted from his initial intention is a clear justification of ethics.

The arguments of discrimination levelled against divine rules, as above-mentioned, are another example for the legitimacy of ethical thought. There could be only one meaning to these narratives: not to take anything for granted and to question authority.

Ethics is based on the recognition of human authority for the finding of moral rules. This is the underlying idea in Wisdom literature. The proverbs are meant to let the listener 'know wisdom and instruction. . . to receive the instruction of wisdom, justice, judgment and equity' (Prov. 1.2-3). In other words, moral insight can be gained from reason and experience and concepts like justice and judgment are developed by listening to the wise. No mention is made of revealed sources of law or of theonomy.

Experience is relied upon to teach virtue:

> I went by the field of a lazy man. . . and lo, it was all covered with thorns. . . Then I saw and turned my heart to it, I saw and received instruction: A little sleep, a little slumber. . . and your poverty comes. . . (Prov. 24.30-32).

But even prophets appeal to experience and reason, not only to the revealed word of God. Thus, the mere observation of the historical scene and the experience of other nations should have been taken as a warning to Israel (Zeph. 3.6-7). In the same way, the other nations were expected to use their experience with the fate of Israel as a guideline for their behaviour (Ezek. 5.6).

Reason is not the only source of information in moral questions; a person was also thought to receive intuition by his feeling. Thus, 'it came to pass afterwards, that David's heart smote him for having cut off the robe of Saul' (1 Sam. 24.5). God was praised for the counsel he had given to the psalmist and for the kidney which he had created and which admonished the psalmist at night (Ps. 16.7). Here a distinction is made between the direct instruction given by God in a dream and the insights received through certain bodily feeling, which we would call moral intuition.

The question must, however, be raised, why is there need for personal search of the truth, as demanded by Socrates and by Descartes, if God has already revealed the good and the just? Likewise, theonomic thinkers must have *a priori* to reject Kant's teaching of human autonomy, so that there would be no point in their engaging in ethical discourse. Indeed, the biblical idea of the servant and of absolute obedience (e.g. Deut. 10.12) could be used against the whole endeavour of moral philosophy. If a person should not go astray after his or her heart or eyes (Num. 15.39), it could be taken as a rejection of rationalism and autonomy.

Nevertheless, the biblical ideas of *imago dei*, of the covenant relationship, of moral monotheism and of the rationality of most of the teaching—all this points at a more differentiated reply. If humankind is expected to be godlike, it is expected to reason about the problems of justice and ethics. Unlike the attitude of the political subject towards his unfettered superior, the partner to the covenant is permitted to apply his personal concepts of right and wrong in criticism of divine sources. Once God was ascribed the attribute of justice, his behaviour, like that of every human being, became subject to ethical tests and evaluations. Although there are irrational elements in the religious tradition of Israel, this does not take away from the essential rationality of inter-human duties.

Worshipping God with one's whole heart (Deut. 6.5) certainly includes the need of interiorization and of using one's conscience in the service of God. Reason, freedom, dignity, even autonomy, are powers bestowed by God upon human beings and must therefore have a function in the divine economy. The proper use of these faculties is their engagement in ethics.

Two of the criteria of ethical discourse which can be found in biblical thought are universalizability and consistency. The former follows from the idea of equality and the latter from that of rationality, which can both be harmonized with the belief system of Israel.

Although the teaching of Moses addresses a particular group, the chosen people, there exists an aspect of universalism both at the beginning of the world and in the expectation of salvation at its goal. The first part of the book of Genesis, the story of early humankind and the Noachide Commandments (Gen. 9.1-7) represent the universalist aspects of Israelite religion and the generalizing tendency of Scripture. On the other hand, the messianic prophecies (e.g. Isa. 2.1-4), the book of Jonah and Wisdom literature address all mankind and thereby fulfil the criterion of ethics.

The principle of consistency, too, may be found in biblical thought. Moses' prayer on behalf of the people relies on the attributes of God as represented at an earlier occasion (Exod. 34.6-7), asking for the change of the stern judgment to prevent a contradiction:

> And now let the power of God overcome, as You have spoken: God is longsuffering and great in lovingkindness, forgiving sin and transgression, but not clearing the guilty, visiting the sin of the parents upon their children to the third and fourth generations. Forgive the sin of this people according to your great lovingkindness. . . (Num. 14.17-19).

Although God is free, goes the argument, he cannot contradict himself, at least not in the direction of exchanging leniency for strict punishment.

Another example of this principle is the discourse on the theodicy. The prophet starts with the assumption that God is righteous (cf. Ps. 145.17) as a basis for his argument: 'God, You are righteous if I wanted to contend with You. Yet I will present my case against You: Why does the way of the wicked lead to success. . . ?' (Jer. 12.1). God cannot, according to the argument, contradict himself.

In conclusion, a form of the singularity of Israel can be found in its theonomy which tolerates also ethical thought. Hence biblical faith can make a contribution to modern theology and to modern moral philosophy.

THE IMPACT OF THE BIBLICAL IDEA OF JUSTICE
ON PRESENT DISCUSSIONS OF SOCIAL JUSTICE

Christofer Frey

1. *Introduction*

Most preachers usually begin their reflections with the exegesis of a
biblical text; they sometimes continue with an attempt to bridge the
gap between the Bible and present social problems (assuming they are
at all able to recognize them). A theologian who engages in *ethical or
moral deliberations* should go the other way: he should identify and
analyse present-day problems and then point to the possibility of
dealing with them by devoting some attention to biblical conceptions.
However, some Protestant ethicists prefer to separate both aspects.
According to them, faith and the biblical tradition motivate action,
whereas reason governs the analysis of reality and dictates the necessary decisions.[1] Unfortunately, their statements are not very precise
when they try to explain the meaning of 'reason'.
Part of the confusion in Christian ethics depends on *the way the
Bible is interpreted*, in which connection at least four ways present
themselves.

1. The isolated *critical way* which deals with fragments of the
   biblical text by observing the most stringent scholarly methods.
2. The *cumulative interpretation*, in which connection especially
   Jewish exegesis, a tradition of many centuries, provides a mas-
   terful example. It presupposes a hidden systematic hermeneutics, one which, however, is hardly ever revealed.
3. The *eclectic approach* which has historically characterized
   Protestantism in particular, and which is currently popular; it

---

1. Cf. M. Honecker, *Sozialethik zwischen Tradition und Vernunft* (Tübingen:
Mohr [Paul Siebeck], 1977); G. Ebeling, *Zum Verhältnis von Dogmatik und Ethik*,
in *ZEE* 26 (1982), pp. 10-18.

entails the constant repetition of the metaphor of the exodus.

4. The *theological way*, that is, an attempt to express the core of the biblical message; this is not confined to isolated verses, but seeks rather to express a tendency inherent in the biblical message which could point the direction for today's decisions.[1] In connection with Christian ethics, biblical theology offers the only serious possibility to explore critically the connotations of the concept of justice.

2. *Problems of Defining 'Justice'*

'Justice' does not present a rigorously defined notion; it seems to be more or less a cluster of normative ideas combined in one fashion or another; their common basis and content, however, is continuously discussed.[2] Recent linguistic philosophy proposes both an extensional and an intentional understanding of concepts. If the extension includes a hierarchical ordering of all the essential elements of a definition, the case of justice seems to be somehow different. Is there any self-evident, all-embracing and general point of view which includes the further points hierarchically? Wittgenstein offered an alternative in the second period of his activity when he pointed to the so-called 'family similarities'.[3] The various members of a family are not subordinated to some single general type, of which they are only examples or variations; rather, family similarities permit us to discover and redefine the typical element of the family, in the event, for instance, that we meet a member of the family which has never been seen before. The typical element presents itself anew and in each new case in a different form.

Following the analogy of family similarities, justice may be considered as a *cluster of norms* which presents itself in continuously varied forms and which stimulates anyone who is concerned with it to iden-

1. Cf. M. Luther, *Assertio omnium articulorum*, in *Weimarer Ausgabe* (Graz: Akademische Druch-u. Verlagsanstalt, 1964ff.), VII, pp. 96-101; K. Barth, *Einführung in die evangelische Theologie* (Zürich: Zollikon, 1962), pp. 21-68.

2. See R. Hauser, H.K. Kohlenberger, F. Loos, H.-L. Schreiber, H. Walzel, 'Gerechtigkeit', in *Historisches Wörterbuch der Philosophie*, III (Basel: Schwabe, 1974), cols. 329-38.

3. Cf. L. Wittgenstein, *Philosophische Untersuchungen* (Frankfurt am Main: Suhrkamp, 1971), nos. 66-77.

tify the typical elements with respect to his own situation. However, on a very general level the question of the *common element* of different normative clusters surfaces anew. Is it a minimum, perhaps a rule, to treat equals as equals and unequals as unequals? Is it a certain moral evidence, experienced by most human beings, that there must be justice however it may be defined?

Since the understanding of justice is vague, each serious discussion of its meaning includes an on-going discussion which relates the different views of already proposed conceptions of justice.[1] Procedures of this kind attempt either to arrive at a consensus or at disagreement. To the extent that dissenters respect the lives of others, they seem to maintain at least some *minimum intuition of justice*, fragments of an idea which are very often not articulated at all.[2]

3. *Attempts to Define Justice*

Such suggested (and often hidden) processes of explication or definition of justice may transcend the intellectual sphere; they may very well accompany processes of *social struggle*.[3] Whatever the procedure adopted, dissidence frequently condenses as attempts at semantic precision. One pursues either an extensional mode or an intentional tendency. However, the strictly extensional path evokes the problem of defining and fixing the meaning of justice (see above). By way of contrast, the intentional procedure concentrates on specification and attempts to deepen our understanding of justice by offering a special case for consideration; for example, justice means to assist widows and orphans and to offer them possibilities for a decent life within or against the framework of a given social environment. This path is frequently followed in prophetic preaching in the Old Testament.[4] However, the prophetic attempt does not exhaust the possible cases in which justice is or could be relevant.

An *extensional procedure* would try to define justice with reference to some general norm such that all relevant cases would seem to be

---

1. See 'Gerechtigkeit' and, for further details, C.H. Perelman, *Justice et raison* (Brussels: Presses Universitaires de Bruxelles, 2nd edn, 1972).
2. See H.L.A. Hart, *The Concept of Law* (London: Oxford University Press, 1961).
3. See D. Miller, *Social Justice* (Oxford: Oxford University Press, 1976).
4. Compare the prophetic call for justice: Amos 5.10-15; Isa. 56.1; etc.

covered by it. The formula, 'equals should be treated as equals, unequals as unequals', could be regarded as an attempt at an extensional definition of justice.

The *intentional way* tends to rely on some particular case which sets our understanding of justice in relief. The extensional approach to justice is concerned to determine the limits of the concept of justice and the sorts of cases which may be subsumed under it. The intentional approach emphasizes rather more subjective, the extensional one rather more objective, evidence.

4. *The Variety of Biblical Understandings of Justice*

Although a biblical example was used to illustrate the more intentional procedure and a formula close to Aristotle[1] was quoted to illuminate the extensional way, it is illegitimate to confront the so-called 'Hebrew' (and biblical) mode of thought on the one hand with the so-called 'Greek' type of thinking on the other. Demonstration by means of oversimplified alternatives often produces mere caricatures of the reality. This 'dogma' of the exegetical schools, that is, Hebrew versus Greek thought, distorts the problem of justice.

Ideas of justice are enclosed within the *elementary patterns of every civilization*. Wherever men have lived and in whatever epoch they have formed their lives, there have been norms of just distribution and just exchange. Therefore some notion of justice is comprehended by every form of everyday life, already prior to the transposition of the question of justice into the realm of scientific discourse. Today's committed Christians often point to the parable of the workers in the vineyard.[2] Although the lord of the vineyard disregards the number of hours worked by the people in his employ, the rebellious workers nevertheless claim that wages should be related to duration of effort, which seems to be the normal case. Can the astonishing and inexhaustible goodness of the lord of the vineyard, that is, of God, be transformed into a social programme? Is it possible to relate it to the question of social justice?

Proportional justice is well known in the Hebrew Bible. It contains exact prescriptions for buying and selling, and it emphasizes that

1. Cf. Aristotle, *Nicomachaean Ethics* 5.6 (1131a-b). Compare G. Stählin, 'ἴσος. . . ', in *TWNT*, III, pp. 343-56.
2. Cf. Mt. 20.1-16.

scales must be correct: a hint at elementary conditions of justice in connection with exchanges.[1] Fraud and overcharging should not be allowed to dominate. We may assume that there was (or is) no society without regulations comparable in their function to those which dominated social interaction in ancient Israel.

Elementary regulations of this kind have been expounded and theoretically elaborated by Aristotle, but not by the Bible. The Bible is evidently not very interested in generalizing elements and examples of justice so that they might figure as consistently defined notions. The Hebrew words which are most often assumed to be equivalents of 'justice', namely צדקה, צדק, and משפט (or even Greek δικαιοσύνη) are not, in a strictly semantic sense, compatible with definitions of justice; rather, their meanings tend in other directions.

5. *Some Remarks on the Western Tradition of Interpreting Justice*

The foregoing passages were intended to provoke some reflection on

a. an element which is typical of justice and governs its understanding,
b. the extension of the definition of justice which is founded on elementary ideas of justice, and
c. the possible enlargement of its understanding, including a continuous effort at precision.

These three aspects which characterize the *definiendum*. To these we should add a further aspect:

d. the question of a *definiens* which, due to its degree of abstraction, includes all the necessary elements of a definition of 'justice'.

The latter has been intensively discussed throughout the history of Western ethical thought. In the process, two definitions of justice have emerged: *distributive* and *poetic justice* (the latter including the question of jurisdiction) (*iustitia distributiva* and *iustitia commutativa*).[2] The most general but very abstract *definiens* of justice relies always on a certain relation between states of equality and inequality among men. Poetic justice investigates the parity to be maintained between

1. Cf. Lev. 19.35-36.
2. Cf. Aristotle, *Nichomachean Ethics* 5.6-8 (1131a-1133b).

dissimilar objects, such as houses and shoes, in connection with exchange procedures (on Aristotle's example, no one exchanges a house for a pair of shoes),[1] or the relationship to be maintained between crime and punishment. Distributive justice decrees equal rewards for equal merits or needs, but proportional rewards if the quantities involved be unequal. The *natural-law tradition*, which got its impulse from Stoicism, tried to concentrate these definitions in the *suum cuique* formula, which entails equal rights for all who can claim rights (in the best case all men), or equal care of all needs which are basic to human life, special care being granted to those with special needs, the legitimacy of which is acknowledged. The idea of equity conjoins with the last point.

This type of more or less abstract reasoning has been associated with consequences which are rather concrete. 'Give us this day our daily bread', the fourth request of the Lord's Prayer,[2] has spurred numerous interpretations across the centuries which distinguish between those goods which are necessary and hence to be distributed equally and those which exceed the necessary (and which therefore have been seen as luxuries). Today, the United Nations and other international institutions continue this line of thought by establishing catalogues of *basic goods*.

Section 5 above began by exhibiting certain distinctive marks of justice. The viewpoint 'c' may be understood as part of these reflections: when and by what means can the catalogue of basic goods be enlarged? Striking examples are the rights of access to medical care and to education. Intuitively, people who have been influenced by the notion of human rights recognize the common right of all men, in whatever culture, to medical care and education. However, this is not a matter of the distribution of such basic goods as may be acquired by hunting, collecting or primitive agriculture, activities which include the members of larger families. It concerns goods whose production presupposes special efforts of individuals and societies.

An example may serve to demonstrate the difficulties typical of attempts to define justice today: should the licenses to produce some 300 medicines which, according to the WHO, are basic for human beings and their welfare, be expropriated and their production be permitted to peoples who, living in very different cultures, are not

1. Aristotle, *Nicomachean Ethics* 5.8 (1133a).
2. Mt. 6.11.

able to invent such medicines? These inventions do not represent natural goods which are simply present in God's creation or in nature; they are products of intensive research and complicated work. Do the education and work of inventors demand a fair countervalue?

6. *Normative Images of Man*

The example just expounded above demands a conclusion: if justice is discussed or invoked, the discussion includes *differing images of man* and visions of his existence. These are very often taken for granted and play their role in the background of the debate. The basic assumptions underlying the example just posed are: (1) that each person has a legitimate claim on the fulfilment of his basic needs, and (2) that each inventor (e.g. of a medicine) and each worker has a legitimate claim on the rights and benefits accruing to the products of his labour.

Philosophy today is aware of the various and often countless difficulties posed by different claims which are presented as legitimate. It seeks to bypass them by concentrating on (d), that is, by formalizing the idea of justice. Justice so understood presents the rule of rules of social life. Thus the notion of justice tends to become an aspect of *metaethics*. The most prominent and intensively discussed theory of justice was developed by the American philosopher J. Rawls.[1] Rawls did not succeed in developing a unified theory of the notion of justice; instead, he combined two rules in a lexical order:

1. a rule of equal access to basic goods necessary for surviving and attaining the changes granted by society, and
2. a rule of unequal treatment within a given society according to which advantages and privileges are only justified if they produce the greatest advantage of the least privileged.[2]

Even extremely formalized philosophical definitions of justice prove that certain views on human life are necessary to form a normative perspective from which justice may be defined. According to Rawls's first rule, what kind of basic goods necessarily belong to truly human life under certain social conditions (i.e. what kind of medical care should never be refused to any person)? A normative view of

1. J. Rawls, *A Theory of Justice* (Oxford: Oxford University Press, 1972).
2. Rawls, *Theory*, pp. 14-15, 60-83.

human life is even more prominent when the idea of justice is derived from a so-called 'original position'. Rawls studies the vision of an *original situation* in which the people reflect their future social status before they enter into an existing society. They have sufficient knowledge of the structures of possible societies, but they are prevented by a 'veil of ignorance' from seeing their own social position in the future. If contingent events could place them into every type of position, the highest as well as the lowest, they would favour a type of society which would offer them the best chances even in the lowest position.[1] Reason, represented by the vision of an original position, would tend towards social equalization. This view includes within it a *basic anthropology*, as is partly revealed by asking the critical question: why should man not be a gambler who risks all his chances by risking even the worst? Rawls omits this possibility. In choosing to do so, Rawls proves that even such highly formalized definitions of justice as those proposed by modern philosophy cannot avoid respecting a normative view of good or integrated human life. This view does not present us with an *a priori* understanding; rather, it is transported by historically developed designs of human life which seek a consensus from among as many people as possible. For this reason, the questions (b) and (c) are important. They affect Christian ethics in particular, and may be stimulated by (a).

7. *Types of Justice*

The above-mentioned questions arise frequently in connection with the analysis of certain *social conditions*. Typologically, societies can be distinguished as

1. early societies with a *family-related* or clan *ethos*, e.g., the more segmentary associations of tribes, as in ancient Israel, in which membership was the ground of the claim for just treatment, and in which the 'stranger' presented an extraordinary problem;

2. *vertically structured societies* of the *feudal period*, in which the legal status of the person was the warrant of justice, and in which legal claims varied according to the position of the

---

1. Rawls, *Theory*, pp. 118ff.

people involved, but in which the special position of the poor was regularly acknowledged;

3. *market societies* which respect merit as well as deserts and special legal claims as the basis of just treatment, and in which the value of one's contribution to society forms the main concern of the ideology of justice.[1]

These three types, which are only roughly sketched out above, tend historically to overlap and to produce social tensions which reproduce themselves in a variety of concepts of justice. Some examples:

1. The Israelite society of the monarchical period was challenged by prophetic criticisms which appealed to the standards of ordinary life in the order: family- or clan-type-society, in which, at least ideally, all human needs and demands are integrated.

2. Today a certain type of Christian criticism of market economies and societies frequently appeals to the standards of the late Roman patriarchal ethos; thus documents of the Ecumenical movement favour the economy of the household, where God is regarded as the house father.[2]

3. How could it affect the Third World? Mannoni[3] demonstrates that Madegassian societies know the hierarchical subjection to the greater power, especially the European one, a position between the stages 1 and 2 which collides with ideas of autarchy and autonomy on the third level. Apparently, the ecumenical pathos of justice tries to transpose motifs from the first or second level to the third one:

a. a familial solidarity or even equality to the *familia Dei* as humanity,

b. the later Roman ethos of the house and the *oiko-nomia* to the 'one world', and

c. the biblical—and it might be, in some cases feudal—obligations to care for the poor in a welfare state which should be extended over the entire world.

Is it illegitimate to exalt older ideas of justice in a new situation? Any

1. See Miller, *Justice*, pp. 265-335.
2. Cf. K. Raiser, *Ökumene im Übergang* (Munich: Christian Kaiser, 1989), pp. 162-70.
3. D.O. Mannoni, *Prospero and Caliban—The Psychology of Colonization* (London: Methuen, 1956). Compare K. Nürnberger, *Ethik des Nord-Süd-Konflikts* (Gütersloh: Gütersloher Verlagshaus Gerd Mohn, 1987).

criticism of given situations can only grow by comparison. But any call for justice which links up with older models can only be effective when it discloses the need-structure and the vulnerability of each human life anew and posits the basic right to live, in a determinative way, shaped by social conditions, above the criteria based on deserts or merits.

8. *Guidelines for Justice*

Are there any visions or guidelines for a justice which transcends the socially organized and historically conditioned ideas and foundations of justice? The teachings of the *natural law* depended on the conviction that there is a secure basis of justice not affected by changes of time and epoch. This theory presupposes a *substantialist view of man* which cannot be analysed and criticized here. A modern *minimalist theory* does not rely on general and substantialist views of human nature; it favours criteria which regulate the access of men to rights (e) and acknowledges the legitimacy of deserts and needs (f).[1] A very important question is the continuous expansion of the number of candidates for treatment according to these criteria (g). The propositions implied by these criteria tend towards a *universal consensus.* Luther, for example, explained that the sum as well as the true content of the Decalogue is the exhortation to place oneself in one's fellow man's position.[2] Love and human justice approximate to one another. This is the key to the decisive views of man which guide human perspectives on justice (see above). Moreover, to return to the prophetic criticisms of Israelite society, it is apparent that the *regress* to prefeudal forms of justice was actually a *progressive* step. But in order to become progressive, the ancient conceptions had first to be translated into the language and the structural knowledge of another period. Similarly, the idea of a natural law (combined with the vision of man's original nature) has sometimes stimulated a progressive movement (especially among small and very often persecuted groups).[3]

1. See Hart, *Concept.*
2. M. Luther, *Unterrichtung, wie sich die Christen in Mosen sollen schicken*, in *Weimarer Ausgabe*, XVI, pp. 371-74, 378-80, 384.
3. See E. Bloch, *Naturrecht und menschliche Würde* (Frankfurt am Main: Suhrkamp, 1961).

The criteria of justice presented here are indicators of a steady and permanent redefinition of justice in new circumstances. They must be accompanied by certain basic assumptions concerning the essence of human life in order to become concrete and effective. According to the central content of the Bible, they must be interpreted within the horizon of that reality which God chooses and creates for man.

This integrated understanding of the Bible demonstrates a *permanent universalization*. The Old Testament tradition of law and custom relies mainly on a centralist perspective: of primary relevance is the neighbour belonging to one's own people; then comes the stranger, tolerated as a guest; and finally the member of some other nation.[1] However, prophetical preaching and instruction depicts God as calling all nations to Jerusalem;[2] foreign peoples are no longer seen from an unbridgeable distance, but socially and locally.

When foreign peoples start to adore the true God in Jerusalem the boundary between the two concentric circles of human commitment, the first containing the members of one's own nation, the second the foreigners, begins to weaken. If there is only one true God, and if pagan gods are nothing, then all nations and powers are under the same God, and perhaps one is as near to God as the other. The ambiguous passage in Rom. 13.1ff. is to be interpreted in this sense: none other than the true God has the power truly to legitimate political authority.

In a parable ascribed to Jesus this process of concrete universalization reaches its climax: a Samaritan, that is, a social and religious outcast, performs what love commands.[3] Thus the tradition inaugurated by Jesus is a type of universalization which moves away from the centristic point of view.

Law and justice include the limitation of power. Therefore the most *powerless* is the minimal criterion of just law. The *biblical view* of the poor, however, does not indicate precisely what we should do or aspire to do today. The poor of the Old Testament (in the prophetic tradition) are either innocent victims who shall therefore profit from just actions,[4] or else they are lethargic, and hence require to be activated to participate in actions consonant with the order of divinely

1. Lev. 19.18b, 33, 34.
2. Isa. 55.4-5.
3. Lk. 10.25-37.
4. Zech. 7.10.

founded justice (the Wisdom tradition).[1] Insensitive readers of the Bible might conclude from this that the poor should receive alms rather than be encouraged to prove their own responsibility. Feudal societies tried to implement the biblical call to justice for the poor by the institutionalized *charity of alms*. The modern conception of human rights calls for participation in all the essential and life-sustaining possibilities of a given society. The institution of alms, widespread especially among religiously grounded societies, marks a static social pattern with an imbalanced assymetric power hierarchy. A naive reading of the Bible may be the first step towards liberation taken by oppressed peoples in some Third World society, but it cannot replace *sophisticated social ethics* in industrialized societies where the patterns are different and where societies are learning to defend themselves against the state. Although practical norms of justice (in actions and structures) must be identified within given societies, they must be chosen in the light of more general perspectives; then Christians rely on an inspiring interpretation of more general biblical–theological lines of thought.

Such practical norms may assist in forming a *lexical order of basic values* within a given social context, and with a view to the establishment of a future world society. The following scheme is an attempt of this kind:[2]

---

1. Prov. 10.4; 20.13.
2. Cf. C. Frey, 'Grundwerte und ihre politische Verwirklichung', *Die Mitarbeit* 30 (1981), pp. 47-59.

Basic welfare includes the maintenance of the elementary conditions of human life (cf. the idea of goods essential to life in the Aristotelian tradition and the exegesis of the Lord's Prayer, esp. the 'daily bread').

Basic welfare should lead to *participation* in the *economic* and *political affairs* of societies, but even more to a kind of responsibility which should activate the destination of the image of God.

The participation of most men should be realized by *creative labour*, by productive contribution to the common life of present and even of possible future generations (a social transposition of some aspects of the love of one's fellow man).

Participation includes *freedom* realized in a community and directed by social relations (which may be interpreted as an implication of man's creaturehood, that is, his creation in the image of God).

Both aspects conjoin in a socially organized *communal life* which respects individuality and autonomy in communication, cooperation, education and culture.

All basic values presuppose a *life-sustaining environment* (the ecological foundation of social and individual life): nature is to be treated as a life-sustaining context, rather than as a conglomerate of resources; creation is to be discovered in nature.[1]

The basic values indicated in the scheme above are criteria of justice in given societies. They have no meaning without a very exact analysis of the actual circumstances. Many prophetic attempts to call for justice refrain from such analysis and may themselves be prey to self-deception or projection; they may be expressions of the extremely personal views of those who act as prophets. Models of an ethos of the extended family (or clan) (for example, those which represent God as

---

1. Cf. D. Bonhoeffer, *Ethik* (Munich: Kaiser, 6th edn, 1963), pp. 152-59.

an 'economist' and which advocate the economy of a house!)[1] are without analytical force: they cannot really influence and shape institutions. They result from a misinterpretation of social ethics and their substitution by a pseudo-spontaneous and highly moralistic appeal to justice. Although the Bible sometimes addresses us immediately and existentially, it directs that the choice of our preferences of basic values (or goods) take place solely by deliberation, analysis and reflection.

9. *Conclusion*

Biblical images or ideas of justice do not aim to establish a semantic equivalent, but a pragmatic analogy in historical and social contexts very different from those of the biblical authors. Therefore, if they seek to anchor their perspectives, readers of the Bible today have perforce to rely on some *comprehensive biblical–theological view* which reveals a very general aim of human life towards which the process of establishing social justice should move.

The main options implied in these perspectives are:

1. *universalizability* (there is only one God for all men; all are possibly important for our moral convictions);[2]
2. the emphasis on *needs* (because the life of creatures is a gift, all men are essentially poor and vulnerable);[3]
3. *participation* or the appeal to it (justice does not produce clients);[4]
4. the analogy between *justice* and *love*: each pattern of proportional treatment is to be transcended if life demands it (because love transcends the *do-ut-des* of *philia*, i.e. friendship);[5] and
5. the relation between *justice* and *law*: justice seeks to establish life-sustaining and participatory patterns of communal life because God loves the law.[6]

1. Cf. *Christian Faith and Economic Life. A Study Paper. . . of the United Church of Christ* (New York, 1987), esp. passages 18-47.
2. See C. Frey, *Theologische Ethik* (Neukirchen–Vluyn: Neukirchener Verlag, 1990), pp. 142-49, 197-209.
3. Frey, *Ethik*, pp. 207-209.
4. Frey, *Ethik*, p. 238.
5. Frey, *Ethik*, pp. 140-49.
6. Frey, *Ethik*, pp. 28-41.

OBSERVATIONS ON SOME RECENT HYPOTHESES PERTAINING TO EARLY ISRAELITE HISTORY[1]

Siegfried Herrmann

I

Now you might think that the theme of my presentation has nothing to do with the subject to be treated by this symposium, namely 'Justice and Righteousness in the Bible'. I have nevertheless chosen to offer the historical theme for consideration, because I am convinced that every topic studied by Old Testament scholars gains in sharpness and definition only when its historical presuppositions have been thoroughly observed.

Let me pose my question in the following simple manner: is the Mosaic law really a law deriving from ancient times? If the answer to this question is 'yes', then this has decisive consequences for our understanding of Israel. If, however, the law of Israel was not the law of Moses, that is, if it is not an ancient law, then we have to ask when it emerged, under which presuppositions, and on which conditions. When and how did the Torah become Israel's Torah?

These matters could perhaps be very simply answered with the remark that the Torah is the word of God, the God of Israel. But must we enquire as to its historical origin? This would be the answer of tradition; it is possible to defend it, and there are reasons for defending it. However, there are also reasons for posing historical questions as to the origin and developmental character of the law—not for the purposes of entering upon an intellectual adventure, but for the sake of the law. After all, every law is the product of historical and social conditions, just as knowledge of God comes into being in historical

1. I have retained the style of the original oral delivery of my lecture, which corresponds to the nature of the original symposium. I should like to thank my assistant, Dr Frederick H. Cryer, for the translation of my German text.

time, rather than in the course of theological and philosophical theorizing. Who has God, as the God of world history, ever taught better through his prophetic word and his law than Israel?

What I mean to say is quite clear. The correspondence between history and the spiritual development of a people is unquestionable. This is, to say the least, a legitimate object of scholarly investigation. What, then, are we to say to those scholars and so-called historians who claim that Moses never existed, that he was an invention?

This claim is not new. One might even have been able to pass over it in silence had it not been for the fact that it has recently popped up in the literature. Quite a number of young scholars no longer want to see Israel wander through the southern desert towards Canaan. According to them, Israel was from the beginning the product of social processes which took place within Canaan. Thus Israel is supposed to have 'detached itself' from the Canaanite populace towards the close of the Bronze Age, around 1200 BC, either through revolution or through evolution, that is, through a gradual process of separation from the Canaanite social system of the city-states.

For such theories, the Moses tradition, which is connected with the south, is inconvenient. It is for this reason that it is usually disqualified as 'ahistorical'. This is particularly clear in the statements of one of the more radical scholars, the learned professor from Copenhagen, Neils Peter Lemche. In his book, *Ancient Israel. A New History of Israelite Society*, which appeared in 1988, Lemche says (p. 256):

> In other words, we do not know just who and what this Moses was before the late sources elevated him to the status of founder of the religion. We only know what the tradition made him into. It is important to acknowledge this, because the figure of Moses is frequently cited as the last bastion of the Old Testament account of the history of Israel and her religion. One sometimes even hears the remark that 'if Moses didn't exist, one would have had to invent him'. To which we may reply, with Mario Liverani, that they did in fact invent him!

If we take Lemche and Liverani seriously for a moment, then the questions remain as to why the Israelites invented Moses or had to invent him, and as to why they made him into the great authority-figure behind the law.

This is not the place to discuss the historicity of Moses. After all, the understanding of justice and the law in Israel is not directly dependent on this matter. The second question, however, which recent research has provoked, is important. If Israel did not really come from outside, from out of the desert and the steppes, how then are we to understand the emergence of Israel? Is it possible to conceive of Israel as the product of a special internal Canaanite evolution? Moreover, what could have brought this to pass?

The answer to such questions is crucial not only for the evaluation of the specific character and nature of Israel, but also for that of its law. The shibboleth of contemporary historians of Israel has become, 'What is your opinion of the protohistory/early history? The desert and a nomadic existence, or not?' The consequences for the history of Israel which follow our answers to these questions are quite extensive. They have not only to do with the organization of Israel in the so-called 'Period of the Judges', but also with the character of the two Israelite monarchies in Israel and Samaria.

Finally, however, can the specific nature of Israelite religion, its henotheism, which opened the path to monotheism, be explained against the Canaanite background? And, above all, how did the understanding of Israelite law and its views on justice and righteousness come about? How are we to account for the dominant role of the Torah? Is it not on precisely these points that Israel differs significantly from its neighbours? Is it really possible to explain all this as the result of movements in the late monarchic or, especially, the postexilic periods? Is this not to claim more for Wellhausen than he himself did?

Of course, my brief presentation here cannot solve these problems. I can do no more than to call to your attention just how important our evaluation of Israel's history is for the history of Israel as a whole, and to indicate how I seek to solve these problems myself.

II

The recent re-evaluation of the early history of Israel to which I have alluded above did not suddenly appear from nowhere; it has a variety of presuppositions and components which cohere in a particular way. Here I can only sketch them out briefly.

1. *The Literary Criticism of the Old Testament Sources*
Until the middle of this century, the dominant conviction was that the Old Testament writings, including the historical books, are of

considerable worth, even though they may derive from various times and be of uneven historical quality. The view was thus that even though the Pentateuch was first concluded in the postexilic period, old and reliable materials are contained in the patriarchal and Exodus traditions and (neither least nor to be under-estimated) in the laws of the Pentateuch.

Accordingly, the goal of scholarship based on such premises was to search behind every text to determine the nature of its historical background and its source value. Such efforts revealed that, as is the case with the traditions of every people, the reconstruction of ancient events is more difficult than the reconstruction of more recent times. It is understandable that less can be known with certainty concerning the historical background of the patriarchs and of the Mosaic period than is possible in the case of the monarchic period. Nor is it coincidental that, for example, the traditions of the books of Kings may be directly synchronized with Assyrian and Babylonian texts, or indeed, that these materials correct each other reciprocally.

As far as the close of the second millennium is concerned, when the tribes of Israel appear on the horizon, matters are more complicated. Contemporary external sources contain only a little which may be read so as to confirm the Old Testament texts. Thus archaeological finds must be taken into consideration, and in this connection they receive more weight than their nature entitles them to.

2. *What Does the Archaeology of Canaan Tell us about the Close of the Second Millennium?*

If we date the exodus from Egypt to the reigns of Rameses II or his successor, Merenptah, that is, to the thirteenth century, we are dealing with the end of the Late Bronze Age and the beginning of the Iron Age. At this time, Canaan experienced a decline in Canaanite culture and the city-states which is difficult to explain. The Ephraimite and Judaean hill country was only thinly inhabited. Moreover, the centuries-old hegemony of the Egyptians over the coastal plains collapsed during the Rameside period. In other words, in the Late Bronze Age, Canaan was a political and cultural vacuum. Incidentally, in 1984 I spoke with the late Yigael Yadin, the excavator of Hazor and Masada, concerning this problem of the decline of the Canaan city-state system in the Late Bronze period. He regarded it as an open question as to whether external influences were responsible for this phenomenon, or whether the cause was to be sought in internal cultural and civilizational difficulties arising after the centuries of Egyptian dominance, coupled with economic collapse.

Now, it was at precisely this time that the Israelites began the first consolidation of their hold on the country. This apparent or correctly diagnosed vacuum at the end of the Late Bronze Age has provided both temptation and a *point d'appui* for those desirous to compose hypotheses as to the origins of Israel.

Although there are signs of several population movements towards the close of the Bronze Age and the beginning of the Iron Age, as, for example, the arrival of the Philistines in the coastal regions, the American George Mendenhall presented the hypothesis that Israel did not come from the desert or the steppe, that *Israel had no nomadic past*, but rather that Israel was the result of a revolutionary movement on the part of those already settled in the country against the decadent Canaanite cities. In a now-famous sentence, Mendenhall declared,

> In summary, there was no real conquest of Palestine (i.e. by the Israelites) at all. What happened instead may be termed, from the point of view of the secular historian interested only in socio-political processes, a peasant's revolt against the network of interlocking Canaanite city states.[1]

Mendenhall's view signalled the entry of a third approach among the arguments pertaining to the emergence of Israel.

3. *The Sociological Approach*

By the sociological approach I mean the attempt to explain a political event, or in a seemingly reliable fashion to illuminate its background, on the basis of a more or less assured knowledge of sociological facts. Mendenhall regards himself as a historian who is solely concerned with the sociopolitical process, and he seems to have little respect for other factors contributing to an evaluation. He prides himself on being a *secular* historian. The fact that the biblical texts never speak of any sort of 'peasants' revolt' does not daunt him. The witness of archaeology is also of only secondary importance to him.

Originally, Mendenhall found little support, at least in Germany.[2]

---

1. G.E. Mendenhall, 'The Hebrew Conquest of Palestine', *BA* 25 (1962), p. 73.

2. As a rule, Mendenhall was ignored in Germany. The first extensive, if critical, appreciation of his approach was presented by Manfred Weippert in his *Die Landnahme der israelitischen Stämme in der neueren wissenschaftlichen Diskussion*

However, in the 1970s, as sociological interest in history not only grew, but also become—in places—perceived as decisive for all historical research, Mendenhall's theory received renewed life, if only in modified form.

Norman K. Gottwald built further on the foundation of Mendenhall's work in a mammoth study which, however, received only partial support from Mendenhall himself.[1] At the beginning of the 1980s, the previously-mentioned Danish scholar, Lemche, departed from the peasant-revolt hypothesis by employing the collapse of the Canaanite city-states in a different way. According to Lemche, individuals who served these organizations separated themselves from them, moved to the more thinly populated mountainous regions and established themselves there. In the course of a gradual process the later quantity known as Israel evolved in conscious opposition to Canaanite life, which, being autocthonous, had ancient traditions at its disposal. Thus, in contradistinction to Mendehall's model, Lemche advocated an evolutionary model.[2]

Of course, this contradicts everything that we know from the Old Testament. The Old Testament says that Israel came from the east and gradually settled the territory west of the Jordan, in the beginning, at least, not including the coastal regions. Lemche stands all this on its head: it was precisely from these coastal regions that a west-to-east population movement occurred which eventually produced Israel.

I have here drawn out the main lines of recent theoretical work, unavoidably in a very concentrated and simplified manner. The question is: what are we to make of such theories? My first observation is that they are one-sided. It is unacceptable to parenthesize the biblical texts in this manner, as far as their historical source-value is concerned. Not only I, but also many other scholars note with regularity

---

(FRLANT, 92; Göttingen: Vandenhoeck & Ruprecht, 1967), pp. 59-66.

1. N.K. Gottwald, *The Tribes of Yahweh* (Maryknoll: Orbis/London: SCM Press, 1979); G.E. Mendenhall, 'Ancient Israel's Hyphenated History', in D.N. Freedman and D.F. Graf (eds.), *Palestine in Transition* (Sheffield: Almond Press/ Winona Lake: Eisenbrauns, 1983), pp. 95-103.

2. N.P. Lemche, *Ancient Israel. A New History of Israelite Society* (Sheffield: JSOT Press, 1988); more extensively and with attention to the history of research *idem, Early Israel. Anthropological and Historical Studies on the Israelite Society before the Monarchy* (VTSup, 37; Leiden: Brill, 1985).

how frequently the Bible communicates and reworks with astonishing precision details which cannot have resulted from invention, but which instead contain detailed knowledge and facts which could only have arisen in particular periods. I am thinking in this connection of linguistic phenomena, of culture–historical materials and, above all, of certain stages of the evolution of ideas and of theology.

Increasingly, adherents of the sociological approach, but also some exegetes and source critics, are advancing the opinion that the biblical texts are tendentious and useless as source materials. The 'uselessness' of the biblical texts is also held to be proved by a number of general ethnological investigations which derive, for the most part, from quite remote cultural areas. Thus, for example, it seems to be modern to compare African tribal organization patterns with those of earliest Israel. One might say that these scholars make a picture which conforms to the theory.[1]

In his doctoral dissertation, Frederick H. Cryer[2] comments on Lemche's position with the remark that,

> After having laboriously and with great learning striven to show how poorly informed and tendentious is the Old Testament account of the formation of the Israelite people, he proffers instead a model based on modern sociological studies of nomadism, ethnicity, and the like. In so doing, Lemche is in reality composing a new 'source'. . . that is, he proposes for our consideration a narrative of his own devising.

Lemche feels that, with reference to the biblical text, the only thing of decisive importance is what archaeology can tell us, that is, the material witness which time has allowed to survive for our use. And since we possess no archaeologically unambiguous evidence as to the early history of Israel, it follows that it is not possible to say anything with assurance about any immigration of the Israelite tribes into Canaan. Recently, however, this picture has apparently changed.

Because of recent archaeological excavations and surveys it may

---

1. As is well known, most of the studies of African societies were done in the heyday and under the auspices of the structural–functionalist approach to anthropology. An explicit criticism of the attempts of the 'Africanists' to expand the scope of the claims made on the basis of their studies also to non-African societies has been made by no less a scholar than I.M. Lewis, *Religion in Context. Cults and Charisma* (Cambridge: Cambridge University Press, 2nd edn, 1987), pp. 10-11.

2. F.H. Cryer, 'Divination in Ancient Israel and her Near Eastern Environment. A Socio-Historical Investigation' (Dissertation, Aarhus, Denmark, 1989), pp. 15-16.

now be held that it was precisely during the transition from the Late Bronze to the Iron Age that a striking population growth took place in the mountainous regions. In this connection the most important single publication is that of the Israeli archaeologist Israel Finkelstein, *The Archaeology of the Israelite Settlement*.[1]

To mention merely the main points: Finkelstein reports that the distribution of Iron I sites (i.e. sites dating from the actual period of Israelite settlement, around 1200 BC) reveals no more than 10 in Judah and circa 12 in Benjamin, whereas approximately 120 have been found in Ephraim and about 100 in Manasse.[2] This points not only to a very differentiated process of settlement, but also to a population growth in this period whose cause cannot have been an entirely natural one; rather, we must assume an additional influx of settlers from outside.

Finkelstein further says that approximately 90 per cent of the sites between Ramallah and the plain of Jizreel are Iron I sites; they comprise 70 per cent of the total of Iron I sites in the whole of the territory west of the Jordan. Naturally, it is possible to ask the question: can we be sure that all these sites were really founded and settled by the *Israelites*? What assurance do we have that this population increase could not have been the result of settlement by non-Israelite groups? This bring us to my own appreciation of the situation.

I personally believe that an important part of the Israelite population came from without, mainly from the south and southeast. Beyond this, the total settlement pattern of Israel in all the various regions of the country must have been of extraordinary complexity. In consequence, it seems to me that *no single theory or hypothesis* is able to explain the entire process. It will only be possible to determine the probable course of the settlement of what was later to become Israelite territory through careful testing of the various *regional* presuppositions.[3]

Of course, there are enduring limits as to what can and cannot be demonstrated by archaeology. For example, potsherds do not allow us

1. Jerusalem: Israel Exploration Society, 1988.

2. Finkelstein, *Archaeology*, p. 353.

3. I have advocated this thesis already in my study, 'Basic Factors of Israelite Settlement in Canaan', in *Biblical Archaeology Today. Proceedings of the International Congress on Biblical Archaeology (Jerusalem, April 1984)* (Jerusalem: Israel Exploration Society, 1985), pp. 47-53.

to determine with certainty just who may have used the implements in question, particularly when we consider that the Israelites adopted the material culture of the autocthonous Canaanites. Finkelstein has correctly said in this connection,[1] 'No total cultural break should be expected. Even when new groups of people enter a given area, their material culture is soon influenced by the material culture prevailing in that area, and thus a seeming link to the previous period is forged.' In other words, the adoption of pre-existent indigenous artefacts prevents us from drawing conclusions as to the previous developmental stages of the immigrants.

In my opinion, the immigration of populations from outside the cultivated territory should not be drawn into question. Such immigrations are, after all, well known throughout the history of the entire ancient Near East, and they have sometimes produced centres of material and spiritual culture. This applies as much to Syria and Canaan as to the vastness of Mesopotamia. But we cannot pursue this topic further here. In any case, it will certainly be necessary to attempt to understand the Israelite immigration in conjunction with the Aramaic population movement. However, the population which was later to become Israel underwent its own independent development and had its own past, as its very language shows. Aramaic did not assert itself from the very beginning in the regions south of Lebanon on both sides of the Jordan, as it did in Syria. Rather, in and with the emergence of Israel, Hebrew became an independent dialect which lasted for a very long time. In this fact we see that Israel had started on a different course from its neighbours already at an early date.

This brings me to the last issue, which is of particular importance to me: how did the distinctive spiritual and religious nature of Israel come about? Can it really be claimed that the Canaanite religious inheritance simply evolved, that Canaan was, in a manner of speaking, the substratum of Israel? Are we not instead dealing with a number of characteristically Israelite presuppositions which were modified in the course of the encounter with Canaan, in many cases in defence against Canaanite conceptions and practices?

In the field of Israelite law, it was long ago noted that Israel adopted impulses stemming from both Canaanite and Mesopotamian law, but

1. Finkelstein, *Archaeology*, p. 338.

also that Israel often refashioned such influences in its own spirit. Israel's own concepts of justice cleared a path for themselves. The sovereignty of the God of Israel had also to find expression in the law. In the evaluation of Israelite law, it is essential to distinguish between a mainly casuistically formulated common law which emerged under Canaanite influence and a normative law whose most eloquent expression is to be seen in the Decalogue. It was primarily this normative law which established standards and enabled the development of sophisticated legal thought, features which were only partially achieved in Israel's environment.[1]

It was also on this basis that the specific nature of the formal concepts of משפט and צדקה, the internal correspondence of which circumscribed the formulated 'applicable law' and the 'right behaviour' of the individual, emerged. Normative adherence to the rights which were anchored in the משפטים made צדקה possible, which is to say, made it possible for 'justice' to be established among men. Whoever lived up to the norm became a צדיק. This is transferable to the religious sphere, as occurs prototypically in Gen. 15.6, in the famous sentence in which God acknowledges the faith of Abram:

והאמין ביהוה ויחשבה לו צדקה
Then he believed God and he reckoned it to him as righteousness.

These are statement-forms of the religion of Israel in which the relationship of the individual to the one God expresses itself in a special way. צדקה is more than *uistitia*. צדקה is based on the relationship of correspondence to the reality of God. This seems to me to be a feature specific to Israel, the presuppositions of which are to be sought in the acknowledgment of its one God.

Man sees his behaviour from the viewpoint of the eye of God, of

---

1. The distinction raised by A. Alt (in his fundamental study, 'Die Ursprünge des israelitischen Rechts' [1934], reprinted in *Kleine Schriften*, I [Munich: Beck, 1953], pp. 278-332) between 'apodictic' and 'casuistic' law retains its applicability, even though attempts have been made to characterize the so-called 'apodictic' law as merely a special variety of casuistic law. Apodictic law is above all distinguished by its use of similarly formulated legal sentences, and its statements are not concerned with individual cases, but are rather of normative significance for the entire legal sphere. Thus apodictic law is by the same token also normative law. Cf. S. Herrmann, 'Das "apodiktische Recht". Erwägungen zur Klärung dieses Begriffs', in *Gesammelte Studien zur Geschichte und Theologie des Alten Testaments* (TBü, 75; Munich: Kaiser, 1986), pp. 89-100.

the God who is neither a mere fertility god like the gods of Canaan, nor a pure concentration of unpredictable power. The God of Israel is the God who determines the life of man existentially and individually and who intends that justice be done to him.

Where did the spark occur which kindled such an understanding of God? Did it really first appear at some time in the seventh century, in the time of Deuteronomy, as some scholars believe, or does it not have much more ancient roots which are connected with the God of Sinai?

Thus the question of Israel's relationship to its earliest history, to the roots of its independent thought and activity, poses itself anew. What was it that led Israel to localize both the proclamation and sanction of its law at the Mount of God? Israel knew that also its existence in 'justice and righteousness' was founded at the place of origin of her religion.

III

The crisis in which the study of the early history of Israel now finds itself has largely been brought about by rather one-sided theories. Characteristic of these theories is that they underrate the biblical tradition and overrate the archaeological evidence. The significance of sociological theories is also exaggerated; not all of them are suitable to contribute to our understanding of Israel's early history. The hypotheses of Mendenhall, Gottwald, Lemche and others develop their own picture of the early history of Israel, but this picture is by no means better and more reliable than the biblical tradition.

In point of fact, recent archaeological results tend rather to confirm than to contradict the biblical tradition. The population growth in the Ephraimite territory, which has recently been demonstrated by Israel Finkelstein, at the beginning of the Iron Age, opens the possibility to connect the beginnings of Israelite settlement with Ephraim. It does not permit wider conclusions, however.

I personally believe that no single hypothesis is sufficient to explain and illustrate the settlement of the country by the Israelites. We must assume that the settlement process was widely differentiated according to the geographical situation in the various regions.

The independent evolution of Israel's religion and law can by no means be derived from Canaanite presuppositions alone. It was the result of the encounter between an independent population group and the native culture. In the context of Israelite law we note points of contact with Canaanite law, and in particular with casuistic laws. However, they were modified by the influence of the specifically Israelite concepts of law. Israel was able both to define legal norms and to abstract on their basis, as we see in the Decalogue. It was therefore possible to regard משפט and צדקה as concrete and also normative concepts which circumscribed Israel's relationship to its God, and which it was possible to summarize in the Torah.

THE CREATIVITY OF THEODICY

Yair Hoffman

There are some criteria by which the scientific character of a theory might be measured, the most common and popular being the coherence, accuracy, or 'correctness' of the theory. Karl Popper, the philosopher, denied this criterion. He pointed to the historical fact that most of the theories which had been regarded as 'scientific', that is, 'correct' at their time were later proved to be wrong; he also realized that most of the present theories are probably doomed to the same fate. However, he claimed, this should not deprive any theory from its scientism. He therefore suggested the replacement of the criterion of 'correctness' with a more modest one—the principle of refutability:

> But I shall certainly admit a system as empirical or scientific only if it is capable of being tested by experience. These considerations suggest that not the *verifiability* but the *falsifiability* of a system is to be taken as a criterion of demarcation. In other words: I shall not require of a scientific system that it shall be capable of being singled out, once and for all, in a positive sense, but I shall require that its logical form shall be such that it can be singled out, by means of empirical tests, in a negative sense: *it must be possible for an empirical scientific system to be refuted by experience.*[1]

Another important criterion by which a scientific theory may be judged is its *fertility*. If a theory stimulates new ideas which direct the scientists towards new relevant questions; if it opens new horizons; if it evokes novel theories—contradictory as they might be—it would be highly regarded. I am suggesting the possibility of considering theodicy, or the biblical concept of retribution—reward and punishment—as a sort of scientific theory, and a very comprehensive one.[2] It pro-

1. K. Popper, *The Logic of Scientific Discovery* (New York: Harper & Row, 1961), pp. 40-41.
2. A vice versa comparison between religious dogma and scientific theory is men-

vides systematic explanations of various phenomena, and to a certain extent it might stand the demand of refutability. It is my intention in this paper to demonstrate the stimulating, fertile character of the concept of retribution, or, to use a term taken from our previous symposium, its intellectual creativity in the Bible.[1]

1. *Is There a Doctrine of Retribution in the Old Testament?*

In the above preface the concept of retribution is treated as a matter of fact. Yet there is no common agreement among scholars as to the existence of such a concept in the Hebrew Bible. The title of this section of my paper is taken from an article by Klaus Koch based upon his dissertation *SDK im Alten Testament*.[2] To the question 'Is there a doctrine of retribution in the Old Testament', Koch gives a categorically negative answer. He claims that the Bible considers the connections between people's acts and their consequences as automatic, naturally inevitable. They key phrases which are repeated in his article time and again, are *human actions have built-in-consequences* or *action–consequence construct*. These phrases, which eliminate heavenly intervention between man's acts and their consequences, represent Koch's claim that there is no concept of retribution in the Hebrew Bible, that is, there is no concept that 'Yahweh actively administers punishment' (or blessing; p. 62). Indeed, he agrees, in some cases Yahweh is regarded as the one who sets in motion, brings to completion or even speeds up the sin–disaster connection or the

tioned by Z. Bechler, *Philosophy of Science* (Tel-Aviv: Synthese Library, 1979), p. 70, while reviewing T. Kuhn's philosophy: 'For a time, and this might be a very long period, it is very important for the scientist to treat the scientific theory as a religious dogma, as a religious creed, which should not be attacked and should not be put into a decisive test. Dogma is an untested principle, it is rather a tool by which other things are being tested. And a scientific theory should serve in the long run as a dogma in order to prove its capability of organizing the phenomena.'

1. See B. Uffenheimer and H.G. Reventlow, *Creative Biblical Exegesis* (JSOTSup, 59; Sheffield: JSOT Press, 1988).

2. K. Koch, 'Is There a Doctrine of Retribution in the O.T.', in J. Crenshaw (ed.), *Theodicy in the O.T.* (Philadelphia: Fortress Press/London: SPCK, 1983), pp. 57-87. This is an English version of the German original published in *ZTK* 52 (1955) (reprinted in *idem, Spuren des Hebräischen Denkens* [Neukirchen–Vluyn: Neukirchener Verlag, 1991], pp. 65-103).

good action–blessing connection, but he cannot determine the unavoidable process.[1]

It is not my intention here to examine Koch's arguments one by one. However, I would like to point out what seem to me to be two methodological fallacies in his argument. (1) We are correctly advised (pp. 59, 79) not to impose on the biblical writings our modern, Western way of thinking, but in fact he falls into this methodological pit, by examining the Bible with the analytical sharpness of Western philosophy. Thus I wonder if his intricate, sophisticated distinctions are valid to the understanding of the Israelite way of thinking. (2) Most of the verses that have been chosen to make his point are of the same kind: they deal with the connections between acts and their consequences *per se*, using metaphorical language and therefore they cannot escape a hermeneutical vicious circle.

Allow me to demonstrate both my arguments by a single but representative example. Ps. 58.12 reads,

אך־פרי לצדריק אך יש־אלהים שׁפטים בארץ

Surely there is a fruit[2] for the righteous, surely He is God who judges the earth.

On this Koch comments as follows:

> Fruit will be provided for those who are faithful members of the community, thus [Yahweh sets] in motion the *built-in* consequences of their actions which already have a *pre-determined result*. . . Thus when the psalmists speak of Yahweh's judgment they are not thinking about how Yahweh applies some 'objective' norms in order to assess human action so that an equivalent punishment is administered (p. 74).

This example demonstrates what a sophisticated, abstract, non-Israelite way of thinking is applied here; one can also see the hermeneutical vicious circle: should the very common metaphor of the fruit be taken literally as if to say 'there is an automatic, built-in

---

1. For example, speaking about the apparent doctrine of divine retribution in the book of Proverbs, Koch claims that 'they all stress that blessing follows an action which is faithful to the community but that an action which is judged ethically to be wicked will result in disaster for the one who did it. Yet they do not say that Yahweh is the one who sets this disaster in motion. . . These verses initially give one the impression that a *wicked action*—just like the laws of nature. . . *inevitably results in disastrous consequences*. . . ' (p. 58).

2. KJV; NKJV translates פרי (= LXX καρπος) as 'reward', which is a decipherment of a metaphor rather than a literal translation. Luther translates literally 'Frucht'.

connection between man's acts and their consequences', or rather be interpreted as saying the Lord is so pedantic, so persistent in keeping his doctrine of reward, that a metaphor taken from the world of nature may well describe it? I am *not* claiming that Koch's evidence has been refuted by this argument, but that methodologically his proof is invalid, because it yields to two contradictory interpretations. And since most of Koch's examples bear the same character, they are not good enough to test his thesis.

Hence, my methodological suggestion is that the question of whether or not a concept of retribution existed in ancient Israel could be better answered by examining writings that *indirectly* touch the subject. My methodological assertion is that only a deep-rooted *theological* concept—*not a mere law of nature*—could have been influential on a variety of subjects of Israelite thinking. Therefore I will try to demonstrate how biblical historiography, eschatology and abstract thinking (I avoid the term 'philosophy' which should be reserved for the Greek genre of abstract thinking) were shaped by a certain concept of moral connections between acts and consequences, which can only be a theological concept, therefore a *doctrine of retribution*.

2. *Retribution and Historiography*

It is unnecessary to elaborate here on the widely accepted view that the whole Deuteronomistic and Chronistic historiography is based upon the idea that the nation's acts determine its history. The very essence of the book of Kings is to prove that the exile and the destruction of the state came as a heavenly punishment for Israel's iniquities. In fact, the book of Kings as a whole is an answer to the question, why did such harsh calamities befall Israel? Is it reasonable to assume that such a book would have been composed simply in order to prove a law of nature, with which the Lord has nothing to do? The spontaneous negative answer to this question, based upon logical speculation, is supported by some writings expressing unequivocally the idea that the national calamity was the Lord's punishment, and hence by no means can it be interpreted as an automatic connection between men's acts and their consequences. Let me point only at one of them: 2 Kgs 17.7-23. Apparently this is the explanation, or rather justification, for the destruction of the Northern Kingdom, but in fact it also anticipates the destruction of Jerusalem, which is not justified later on in the book by any special speech.[1] Thus it might be regarded in a way as the theological summary of the whole book of Kings.

The most significant verses for our purpose are 13-14 and 18-23:

> Yet the Lord testified against Israel and against Judah by all His prophets, namely every seer, saying: Turn from your evil ways, and keep My commandments and My statutes. . . Nevertheless they would not hear, but stiffened their necks like the necks of their fathers who did not believe in the Lord their God. . . Therefore the Lord was very angry with Israel. . . And the Lord rejected all the descendants of Israel, afflicted them and delivered them into the hand of the plunderers. . . So Israel was carried away (ויגל ישראל) from their own land to Assyria. . .

Surely there is no pre-determined, built-in action–consequences construct here.

A proper indication of the validity and influence of a certain concept in any society is the degree of its entanglement with other concepts: to what extent does it shape other concepts? What happens when it contradicts other concepts? Can it survive while facing a reality which does not approve it? Does it collapse, knocked out, and give place to an alternative concept, or is it so deeply rooted that its vitality is kept, either by ignoring reality or by supplying new answers, that is, being flexible?

Here are two examples which demonstrate the vitality of the action–consequence concept (not construct!), and prove it to be a theological concept rather than one related to the laws of nature.

a. *The Delayed Consequence*

The Deuteronomistic historiographer, coming to unveil the rules which determine history, using the key of action–consequence con-

---

1. One can appreciate it as an example of the literary sensitivity of the author. He gave up the expected 'grand finale' sermon at the end of the book of Kings, allowing the devastating information about the total destruction to speak for itself. Instead, he has planted enough hints of the (still-to-come) destruction of Jerusalem in the sermon which concludes the account of the destruction of Samaria. A different opinion is expressed by M. Brettler, 'Ideology, History and Theology in 2 Kings xvii.7-23', *VT* 39 (1989), pp. 268-82. He advocates the view that vv. 7-12 is 'a unit condemning Judah for specific sins. This unit was probably originally written as part of 2 Kings xxv but it became misplaced. . . ' (p. 281). Brettler admits that 18b-21 is an 'exilic unit bringing the chapter up to date by referring to the exile of Judah' (p. 282), and since I regard the whole sermon in 7-32 as exilic I see no reason to regard 18b-21 as an editorial addition.

nections, had to face a serious problem: in too many cases the events did not 'obey' the rules of sin and punishment: King Solomon, who worshipped Ashtoret, Milkom, Kemosh (1 Kgs 11.1-10) was not punished; Menashe, the most vicious king of all, who

> built altars in the house of the Lord. . . and built altars for all the host of heaven in the two courts of the house of the Lord and made his son pass through the fire [2 Kgs 21.4-6]. . . shed innocent blood very much till he had filled Jerusalem from one end to another [16]

ruled as a king for no less than 55 years (probably 698–642 BCE) and passed away in peace at the age of 67. On the other hand his most righteous grandson Josiah, who abolished Menashe's and Solomon's abominations, was killed by a foreign king at the age of 39. The solution to these difficulties is that retribution is not always executed immediately, history should be judged in perspective, the roots of some crucial events should sometimes by sought in the far past. I wonder if one can exaggerate in evaluating the theoretical importance of such a solution for any future historiographical methodology. However, it is a very intricate solution, too complicated to be invented just for the sake of having a theory about a law of nature, which was surely not the concern of the Deuteronomist.

b. *The Conflict with Future Expectations*
How can a sinful nation be saved if the concept of retribution is valid? Of course, there is the solution of repentance; there is also the solution of Second Isaiah, 'for her warfare is accomplished, her iniquity is pardoned' (40.2). However, these solutions have nothing to do with historiography. In our context I would like to mention the solution given by Ezekiel. Living in the exile, the national salvation for him was more than a theological concept; it was an existential need. But being realistic (some would say pessimistic) he reckoned that Israel would not repent; he also understood that any stipulation between repentance and salvation would only discourage the exiles. He was therefore driven to bridge the gap between the concept of retribution, the conviction of salvation and the awareness of the stubbornness of the people in a new way. And since salvation for him was an event which should and would take place within the course of history, not beyond it, he had to deduct the certainty of salvation from the laws of history, which he was trying to expose through a review of the history

of Israel. This attempt is attested in ch. 20.[1] In this survey Ezekiel reaches the conclusion that the dominant law which governs and determines history is not the causality between the people's acts and their consequences, but rather quite a different factor: the contribution of the historical event to the establishment of the glory of God among the nations. To use Ezekiel's own terminology, which is the key phrase in this chapter:

ואעש למען שמי לבלתי החל לעיני הגוים

But I acted for My name's sake that it should not be profaned before the Gentiles (vv. 9, 14, 22, 39);

and the conclusion of this prophecy—

וידעתם כי אני הי בעשותי אתכם למען שמי לא כדרכיכם הרעים
וכעלילותיכם הנשחתות בית ישראל נאם הי אדהים

Then you shall know that I am the Lord, when I have dealt with you for My name's sake, *not according to your wicked ways nor according to your corrupt doings*, O house of Israel, says the Lord God (v. 44).

Only such a rule can explain, says Ezekiel, why the Lord did not annihilate Israel neither in Egypt, nor in the desert, nor later on in the Land of Israel, and not even in the exile. And since 'the name of God' is the dominant factor in history, and the salvation of Israel is the best way now to glorify this name, this salvation is inevitable in the nearest future.

Apparently the concept of retribution has been totally given up here, but then comes the idea of the מדבר העמים—*desert of nations* to save the concept of retribution:

And I will bring you out from the peoples and gather you out of the countries where you are scattered. . . And I will bring you into the wilderness of the nations and there I will plead My case with you face to face. . . I will make you pass under the rod. . . I will purge the rebels from among you and those who transgress against Me: I will bring them out of the country where they sojourn but they shall not enter the land of Israel (34-38).

A sophisticated adaptation of the idea of the 'delayed response' can be found here: a punishment which should have been activated immediately during the exodus, was changed (from annihilation to exile) and postponed until the exile; but Ezekiel also raises here a new idea

---

1. See Y. Hoffman, 'The Structure and Significance of Ez. 20', *Beth-Miqra* 63 (1972), pp. 473-89 (Hebrew).

which is the negative (using a metaphor taken from photography) of
the delayed response: *the premature response*. It says, sometimes the
Lord rewards the nation *before* the merits for this reward have been
gained. To use another metaphor: being the master of history, God
can allow himself 'to be in the red', since he can always collect his
debts—Israel's repentance, in our case.

This example proves that a moral concept of retribution was
believed to have been an active factor in history, and was not regarded
as a mere built-in automatic connection between acts and their
consequences.

The Chronicler is not very keen on accepting the sophisticated rule
of the delayed response, although he does not totally reject it.
Accordingly, to come back to the previous examples, the Chronicler
does not tell us about the idolatrous practices of King Solomon, since
he was not punished, and the division of the state did not occur in his
time, while Rehoboam is denounced as a sinner who therefore paid
for his own sins. Menashe is said to have been punished and then
repented (2 Chron. 22.10-16), while Josiah's death is said to have been
a punishment for his refusal to obey 'the words of Necho from the
mouth of the Lord' (35.22). Hence, facing the need to reconcile the
contradiction between acts and the expected moral consequences the
Chronicler preferred to ignore the known facts of the past or even to
change them, rather than compromise by accepting the idea of the
delayed response, which seemed too sophisticated for a dogmatist like
him. Is it reasonable, I wonder, that he has been pushed into reshaping
the past just in order to save a built-in concept, in which there is no
room for God? He surely did it as a doctrinaire, trying to protect
God's justice by an oversimplistic, easy-to-grasp representation of his
acts in history.[1]

3. *Retribution and Biblical Eschatology*

The problem of 'biblical eschatology' is too vast and complicated to be
discussed here in even the briefest way. Nor is it the occasion to
present my own overall view on this matter. But in order to clarify

1. On the Chronicler's concept of retribution in history, see S. Japhet, *The
Ideology of the Book of Chronicles and its Place in Biblical Thought* (Jerusalem:
Môsād Bialik, 1977), pp. 132-72 (Hebrew) (ET: Frankfurt am Main: Lang, 1989,
pp. 125-98).

the argument a delineation of my basic concept is unavoidable. I have learned a lot about eschatology from Professor Uffenheimer, and one of his virtues as a teacher was encouraging the students' self-thinking, rather than imposing on them his own ideas. I must confess that I have taken advantage of this privilege, though I do not fully share some of his ideas about the antiquity of biblical eschatology.[1]

I assume that not until the exile had the major motifs, which later on turned to be eschatological, been integrated to form a coherent concept. Motifs such as immense catastrophe, ideal king, peace and wealth and fertility of the land existed, I believe, prior to the emergence of the idea of the end of history followed by a new era, which is the core of eschatology. This abstract idea was developed gradually[2] by the absorption and adaptation of different concepts such as the covenant, history being conducted according to some detectable rules, etc., and only then did the previously mentioned motifs gain their eschatological character. To this relatively late stage I would like to refer here.

I claim that one of the concepts that contributed to the shaping of biblical eschatology, if the gradual model is accepted, is the concept of retribution. Let us examine some passages—eschatological or on the verge of eschatology.

Isa. 2.1-4 (= Mic. 4.1-4): Nothing is said here about events that would anticipate this final situation of a universal peace. It is certainly not stipulated in any way. The phrase באחרית הימים which is here an eschatological term, isolates the prophecy from any previous specific situation. The same holds true of some other prophecies such as Isa. 11.1-9; Amos 9.13-15; Mic. 5.1-8.

This very feature, namely detachment from any previous events of developments, and a total absence of conditionality, also characterizes prophecies dealing with the catastrophic aspects of the eschatological period, for example, Jer. 25.15-38. There is no hint here either to the context of the catastrophe or to its reasons: why and when should all

---

1. See B. Uffenheimer, 'From Prophetic Eschatology towards Apocalyptic', in Z. Brass (ed.), *Messianism and Eschatology* (Jerusalem, 1984), pp. 27-72 (Hebrew). An ardent advocate of the antiquity of Israelite eschatology is Y. Kaufman, *Toldot Haemuna Hyisraelit*, III (Jerusalem, 1960), pp. 626-56.

2. See Y. Hoffman, 'אחרית הימים and ביום ההוא as Eschatological Terms', *Beth-Miqra* 71 (1978), pp. 435-44 (Hebrew); *idem*, 'The Day of the Lord as a Concept and a Term', *ZAW* 93 (1981), pp. 37-50.

the nations including Jerusalem 'drink from the cup'? What would happen after they got drunk and unable to rise 'because of the sword which I will send among you' (v. 27)? What would anticipate and what would follow the universal catastrophe described in vv. 32-33? These questions remain unanswered. The same enigmatic characteristics are found in other prophecies such as Ezekiel 37–38; Zeph. 1.14-18; Zechariah 14.

On the other hand in some late passages there is a clear sequence between the two opposite eschatological motifs, and the catastrophe is represented as the introduction to the salvation. One example is Isaiah 24–27, which is commonly regarded a late complex, known as 'The Apocalypse of Isaiah'.[1] Here the catastrophe is described as the wicked world's punishment which would be followed by the salvation of the righteous people (24.5-6, 16-17, 20-23; 25.1-5, 9-12; 26.1-5, 20-21). In this way the concept of retribution is intertwined into eschatology to create one integral concept. Another example is the editorial complex Isa. 1.1-22. Three independent prophecies were edited here to create a coherent unit bearing a clear message: human wickedness (vv. 6-10) would be annihilated in the 'day to Yahweh Zebaot' (vv. 12-22) and consequently the eternal peace of באחרית הימים would come (vv. 1-4).[2] This sequence of events, dictated by the concept of retribution, is best represented in prophecies which are governed by the motif of the Judgment, for example, Joel 4.

The concept of retribution could have penetrated eschatology through non-eschatological prophecies of salvation, which were always attached to the concept of retribution. This could have

---

1. For example, G.B. Gray (*The Book of Isaiah I–XXXIX* [ICC; Edinburgh: T. & T. Clark, 1912], pp. 397-404) dates the complex to the Maccabaean period; O. Ploeger (*Theocracy and Eschatology* [Oxford: Basil Blackwell, 1968], p. 77) suggests the second half of the third century; O. Kaiser (*Isaiah 13–39* [OTL; London: SCM Press, 1974], pp. 173-79) dates it to the first third of the second century BCE.

2. I regard vv. 5 and 11 as editorial connections between the 'original' units, whose sequences have been determined by a rhetorically minded editor. Starting with the latest future the complex stresses the huge gap between the expected eschatological period and the gloomy present. Thus a strong doubt is created as to the possibility of bridging this huge gap, which is answered by the last section: the Day of the Lord is the bridge, at the end of which human pride will vanish, and the new era will come. For a recent study dealing with the editorial aspects of the book of Isaiah see M. Sweeney, *Isaiah 1–4 and the Post-Exilic Understanding of the Isaianic Tradition* (BZAW, 171; Berlin: de Gruyter, 1987).

happened prior to the fixing of generic and conceptual boundaries between these prophecies and the eschatological prophecies. It could have also infiltrated through prophecies against foreign nations, some of which developed to be semi-eschatological (e.g. Isa. 13; 63.1-6; Zech. 9). Indeed, the intermingling of the concept of retribution and eschatology was surely too complicated and dialectical a process to be meticulously traced and put into a rigid chronological scheme. Moreover, I believe that the integration of eschatology with any concept—historiographical, nationalistic or whatever—was disputable in Israel, which is only natural in a process of systematization of such an important theological concept.

However, at the end of this intricate process the concept of retribution became one of the most important factors in postbiblical Jewish eschatology, and a catalyst to the development of new motifs, such as personal eschatology.

4. *The Concept of Retribution and Abstract Thinking in Israel*

By abstract thinking I mean enduring attempts to reflect on any concept in a semi-philosophical manner, the model for the 'philosophical' being Greek–Western philosophy. In other words, to reflect about our reflections on a certain concept. 'Semi-philosophical' since it is obvious that no genre identical to 'Greek philosophy' exists in the Bible. My claim is that the concept of retribution is the only subject in biblical thinking which evoked such a quasi-philosophy. Here are three examples to make my point.

1. The book of Job: one of the most important indications of abstract thinking is the attempt to organize ideas systematically around one common axle. I suggest that the book of Job can be considered such a work. It is the only book in the Bible which lacks any historical context, a fact which was recognized by the Sages who admitted that איוב לא היה ולא נברא אלא משל היה ('Job never existed nor was ever created, it was just a parable', *B. Bat.* 14.2). Although built as a story, the plot is minimized and functions only as a tactical literary tool which enables a meaningful organization of the speeches. These tactics helped the author to create the only book in the Bible which is devoted to a single theoretical subject—the concept of retribution. My description of the book of Job is, therefore, *a systematic anthology of reflections, problems and possible (or impossible) solutions regarding*

the concept of retribution.[1] This approach to the book of Job makes
the conventional question, 'what is the book's solution to the problem
of theodicy' irrelevant. The solution is not found because the book
does not intend to suggest any single one. Being a quasi-philosophical
anthology it only aimed at the systematic organization of reflections
about the concept of retribution, which thus became the only concept
to be dealt with in the Bible in such a manner.

2. Solutions to the problem of theodicy have been suggested in the
Psalter, but not all of them fit my definition of abstract thinking as
'reflections about our reflections' on the concept of retribution. One
solution which does fit this definition is איש בער לא ידע וכסיל
לא יבין את־זאת ('a senseless man does not know nor does a fool
understand this', Ps. 92.6) or ואני־בער ולא אדע בהמות הייתי עמך ('and I
was senseless and did not understand, I was like a beast before you',
Ps. 73.22). This is indeed a reflection about our reflections; it does not
address the classical question, why are there wicked people who
succeed or righteous ones who suffer? Instead it answers a quite
different question: why do we human beings, in spite of all the
evidence that the world is conducted according to just principles, still
tend to disbelieve this fundamental fact? Both the question and the
answer belong to the field of our reflections about our reflections, that
is, they are associated with abstract thinking.

3. My last example is Psalm 1. Here, I suggest, the abstract thinking
is represented in a very sophisticated manner of solving problems by
using the most reflective tool we have—the language. Wittgenstein
claimed that the essence of philosophy is the criticism of language.
'Philosophy is concerned with tracing the limits of language and
therefore of thought from within' (*Tractatus* 4.114). That means that
an ordinary language disguises thoughts, and it is the task of the
philosopher to clarify them by clarifying the language. I am arguing
that in Psalm 1 the author expresses the idea that the phenomenon of a
suffering righteous man or a successful wicked one is non-existent in
our world, and the apparent 'problem' is created by an improper use
of language.

Many answers have been suggested to the question of what is the

---

1. This apparent underestimating definition by no means intends to demote the
book from being one of the greatest literary works of all time. On the contrary, the
possibility of shaping a dramatic plot out of anthological materials is one aspect of
this artistic greatness.

main idea in Psalm 1, and I am venturing to contribute another one. I propose the following: the psalm is a sort of an exercise in logic, or in the criticism of language. It says that one of the most tantalizing theological problems, the problem of heavenly justice, is caused by a false and corrupted use of the language. To be more specific: a mistaken use of the terms רשע and צדיק (righteous and wicked). What is the definition of צדיק according to this psalm? It is one who

> walks not in the counsel of the ungodly,
> nor stands in the path of sinners
> nor sits in the seat of the scornful. . .
> is like a tree planted by the rivers of water
> that brings forth his fruit in its season (vv. 1-3).

And who is the wicked? The one whose *conduct and fate* is—not *are*, since it is one entity—the utmost opposition to that of the righteous. Hence, *by definition* there can be no such logical expression as 'a suffering righteous' or a 'successful wicked', and therefore no such phenomena exist.[1]

Thus, indirectly the psalm relates to theodicy in the same way as the previous examples; there is no real problem; what seems to be a problem is a consequence of human stupidity or inaccurate use of language.

---

1. Hence והיה in v. 3 (והיה כעץ שתול על פלגי מים) should *not* be interpreted as a future verb anticipated by verbs (either in perfect or in imperfect forms) expressing repeated actions in the past (הלך . . . עמד . . . ישב . . . יהגה). I am suggesting that all these verbs are expressing a permanent (hypothetical) situation. The variety of forms (*qtl*; *yqtl*; *wqtl*) is either for the sake of literary variety or in order to express some nuances of modality. In any case the biblical verbal system is still a riddle. 'The central difficulty in the Hebrew verbal system has been, and still is, the correct understanding of the two principal verb forms, the Prefix- and Suffix forms (i.e. *yqtl* and *qtl*) and their respective *waw* consecutive constructions (i.e. *wayyqtl* and *wqtl*)' (L. McFall, *The Enigma of the Hebrew Verbal System* [Sheffield: Almond Press, 1982], p. xii). These introductory words of McFall are actually the conclusion of his study, in which he reviews and criticizes the major theories up to 1954 regarding the above-mentioned problem. Recently A. Rainey suggested a new theory of the Hebrew verbal system, yet he deals with the *yiqtol* rather than with the *wqtl* (והיה) forms. See 'The Ancient Hebrew Prefix Conjugation in the Light of Armarnah Canaanite', *Hebrew Studies* 27 (1986), pp. 4-19. A collection of articles discussing Rainey's theory was published in *Hebrew Studies* 29 (1988).

5. *Conclusion*

The few writings that have been dealt with in this short paper do not reveal, of course, the whole picture of the concept of retribution in the Bible. Thus, for example, discussion of the biblical concept of retribution which ignores the book of Qohelet cannot represent the wide range of biblical views in this subject. I have also avoided any comparison with extrabiblical ancient Near Eastern sources, such as some historical documents, the Egyptian literature dealing with the concept of Maat, the Mesopotamian Wisdom literature, etc., which can illuminate the question of the uniqueness of the Israelite concept of retribution. Yet I hope the centrality of the concept of retribution in the Bible has been demonstrated and perhaps even proved.

Do my conclusions refute Koch's interpretation of some biblical passages? Not necessarily. Since no systematic philosophy is attested in the Bible, the two contradictory concepts, the concept of retribution and the action–consequences construct, could have coexisted. However, I claim that no concept was as creative and influential as the concept of retribution.

The paper commenced with a comparison between the concept of retribution and a scientific theory. At the conclusion I must raise serious doubts as to this premature impression. Fertile, yes; but what about refutability? What we have seen is that the biblical concept of retribution is in fact indestructible; it is so flexible, yields to so many adaptations and excuses, that it is practically irrefutable. Should the conclusion be, then, that the concept of retribution has nothing to do with a scientific theory, being a *religious axiom*, or perhaps that its indestructibility is a decisive proof of its correctness as a 'scientific' theory? The inverted commas within which the word 'scientific' is put express my personal answer to this question.

RIGHTEOUSNESS IN PAUL[1]

Gottfried Nebe

1. *Introduction*

The New Testament contribution to the complex of problems associated with justice and justification, in the context of the Jewish–Christian Symposium's theme 'Justice and Righteousness in the Bible and the History of its Influence' ['Recht und Gerechtigkeit in der Bibel und ihrer Wirkungsgeschichte'] is provided by several writings and their authors. The concentration on Paul in the following study is due both to the limited scope of the essay and the importance of the apostle Paul's statements on the subject, within the framework of the New Testament writings and authors. On the other hand, we must recognize at the outset that, while Paul's voice in the New Testament must be heard, historically and exegetically it is still only one among several.

Within the larger question 'Justice and Righteousness' this study will focus on 'justification/righteousness'. The limitation has been made with consideration. For the very inquiry into justification/righteousness itself belongs to the 'first principles' of Paul's theology, and it is along these lines, in my opinion, that Paul's special contribution to the topic 'Justice and Righteousness', can be examined.

To be sure, the aspect of justice also makes itself felt in Paul. This is true, for example—to mention only a few texts—in Romans 1–2, where the argumentation is from a kind of natural theology tinged with natural law, probably with a Stoic background, or, in Romans 13, in the statements concerning state government. It can be observed

---

1.   This is a revised, annotated and somewhat expanded version of my symposium paper, 'Gerechtigkeit bei Paulus', read on 20 June 1990. The English translation from the German has been provided by Paul Cathey of the Institutum Judaicum Delitzschianum, Münster (Westfalia).

further from the structures of congregational life in certain offices and functions, as well as in connection with the relationships between Law and Spirit, Office and Charisma,[1] hotly debated since the famous controversy between Rudolf Sohm and Adolf von Harnack.[2] One is reminded in this connection of the so-called 'Sätze heiligen Rechtes', enunciated with such effect by the Protestant exegete Ernst Käsemann in the post-war period.[3]

Nonetheless, the reader of Paul's letters sees that righteousness carries incomparably more impressive and fundamental weight than justice or juridical rulings. This is already clear in the usage and conceptual choice of the special and prominent δικαιο-formulations, such as δικαιοσύνη, δίκαιος, δικαιόω.

Although in the following I particularly investigate righteousness in Paul, this should be considered as no more than an attempt to open some important roads and blaze some 'trails' in this problematic field.

Before proceeding further it is necessary to make clear which books we are examining. The letters I consider authentically Pauline are Romans, 1 Corinthians, 2 Corinthians (with the problems of the composition deriving from several individual letters), Galatians, Philippians, 1 Thessalonians, and Philemon.[4] The following remarks are based on these letters or parts of them. I date them, along with numerous other scholars, c. 50–56 AD. This means that these letters

1. For this discussion see, e.g., H. Conzelmann, *Grundriß der Theologie des Neuen Testaments* (Munich: Kaiser, 1967), pp. 58ff.; (adapted by A. Lindemann; Uni-Taschenbücher, 1446; Tübingen: Mohr [Paul Siebeck], 4th edn, 1987), pp. 121ff.

2. Cf. R. Sohm, *Kirchenrecht*, I (1892); A. von Harnack, *Entstehung und Entwicklung der Kirchenverfassung und des Kirchenrechts* (1910 [= 1980]).

3. See E. Käsemann, 'Sätze heiligen Rechtes im Neuen Testament' (1954/55), in *Exegetische Versuche und Besinnungen*, II (Göttingen: Vandenhoeck & Ruprecht, 1964), pp. 69-82, and elsewhere. Cf. also, e.g., R. Bultmann, *Die Geschichte der synoptischen Tradition. Ergänzungsheft* (adapted by G. Theissen and P. Vielhauer; Göttingen: Vandenhoeck & Ruprecht, 4th edn, 1971), pp. 51-52; M. Sato, *Q und Prophetie. Studien zur Gattungs- und Traditiongeschichte der Quelle Q* (WUNT, 2.29; Tübingen: Mohr [Paul Siebeck], 1988), pp. 264ff.

4. See the New Testament 'Introductions' for the problems of the classification— disputed, in part, by scholarship—of authentic and inauthentic letters of Paul, and the composite nature of 2 Corinthians and other Pauline letters.

originate in 'the period of the height of Paul's missionary activity and its end'.[1]

2. *Roads and 'Trails' into the Field of Problems Surrounding 'Righteousness in Paul'*

I would like to approach the problem by, above all, examining the characteristically Pauline statements on righteousness/justification. The reader of the Pauline Epistles quickly notices particular key passages where the accent is laid on righteousness, such as Rom. 1.16-17 and 3.23-24:[2]

> For I am not ashamed of the gospel: it is the power of God for salvation to every one who has faith, to the Jew first and also to the Greek. For in it the righteousness of God is revealed through faith for faith; as it is written, 'He who through faith is righteous shall live' (Rom. 1.16-17)

> since all have sinned and fall short of the glory of God, they are justified by his grace as a gift, through the redemption which is in Christ Jesus. . . (Rom. 3.23-24).

Such passages lead already to important contexts, connotations and interpretations, but also to special exegetical tendencies of the justification statements in Paul

But how are we, exegetically and theologically, to understand and interpret more precisely Paul's characteristic statements on justification particularly in the context of its aspect 'righteousness'? In what follows I will attempt to delineate in *five points* the Pauline understanding of righteousness in the context of the teaching on justification.

a. *Righteousness and the Problem-complex: Judgment, Law, Jesus Christ*

I begin with this point because I consider it to be the most basic and the most explosive, not only for my topic here, but also for a Jewish–Christian symposium. It will therefore be dealt with more compre-

---

1. Cf. W.G. Kümmel, *Einleitung in das Neue Testament* (Heidelberg: Quelle & Meier, 21st edn, 1983), pp. 216, 219 (ET based on the 17th edn, *Introduction to the New Testament* [trans. H.C. Kee; Nashville: Abingdon Press, 1975], pp. 251, 254-55).

2. The following translations are taken from *The New Oxford Annotated Bible with the Apocrypha* (Revised Standard Version), 1973.

hensively than the other points. First of all, the horizon of an eschatological judgment must be presupposed for Paul's teaching on justification and his understanding of righteousness no matter that this jars
with some tendencies in modern exegesis.[1] To be sure, we must differentiate here.[2] On the one hand we picture a final judgment that
judges deeds which, so to speak, have been recorded, and is thus far a
forensic judgment such as would occur in a court of law (cf., e.g.,
Rom. 2.1ff.). From this perspective it is understandable when scholarship understands Paul's teaching on justification to be referring to a
quality of relationship (as opposed to an ethical quality) in a forensic–
eschatological sense.[3] I presume, as do other exegetes,[4] that this conception of judgment according to deeds (works) stems particularly
from Paul's Pharisaic past, whatever influence one might ascribe here
to apocalyptic.

It seems that for Paul the concept of righteousness cannot represent
simply a salvation concept in the sense of the ancient Old Testament
tradition of mutual relationship and covenant faithfulness.[5] In my
opinion, something like a *iustitia distributiva*, which we know above
all from the ancient Aristotelian tradition, comes into play here—
certainly a type of righteousness which judges impartially and justly

---

1. See in any case studies such as that by E. Synofzik, *Die Gerichts- und
Vergeltungsaussagen bei Paulus* (GTA, 8; Göttingen: Vandenhoeck & Ruprecht,
1977).

2. For such a differentiation see, e.g., already J. Becker, *Das Heil Gottes. Heils-
und Sündenbegriffe in den Qumrantexten und im Neuen Testament* (SUNT, 3;
Göttingen: Vandenhoeck & Ruprecht, 1964), particularly pp. 199ff., 251ff. Cf. also
P. Volz, *Die Eschatologie der jüdischen Gemeinde im neutestamentlichen Zeitlalter.
Nach den Quellen der rabbinischen, apokalyptischen und apokryphen Literatur* (1966
[1934]), pp. 93ff. In my dissertation, *'Hoffnung' bei Paulus. Elpis und ihre
Synonyme im Zusammenhang der Eschatologie* (SUNT, 16; Göttingen:
Vandenhoeck & Ruprecht, 1983), I also attempted something of this sort (cf.
pp. 55ff.).

3. So Bultmann, *Theologie des Neuen Testaments* (Tübingen: Mohr [Paul
Siebeck], 9th edn, 1984 [1948]), §§28-29, especially §28.2 (ET, *The Theology of
the New Testament* [trans. K. Grobel; 1951–52]).

4. Cf., e.g., Becker, *Heil*, pp. 251-52.

5. For such an Old Testament understanding of righteousness cf., e.g., G. von
Rad, *Theologie des Alten Testaments*, I (Munich: Kaiser, 4th edn, 1962),
pp. 382ff., and K. Koch (ed.), *Um das Prinzip der Vergeltung in Religion und
Recht des Alten Testaments* (WdF, 125; Darmstadt: Wiss. Buchgesellschaft, 1972),
esp. pp. 87-180 (Fahlgren, K. Koch).

according to law, and therefore can even condemn and punish.[1] Is this the background for the later rabbinic tradition's attempt to differentiate God's righteousness, grace, justice and mercy and to bring them into relationship with one another, an attempt in itself to demonstrate the primacy of mercy and grace? The key words מדת הדין and מדת הרחמים must be mentioned here.[2]

Paul also speaks of an eschatological judgment in language that contains no notion of an express judgment of individual deeds.[3] Above all Paul's 'eschatological-present' statements indicate such a judgment. I refer here, for example, to the remarks concerning the ὀργῆ θεοῦ (Rom. 1.18ff.), which reveals itself in the present, as compared with the δικαιοσύνη θεοῦ (Rom. 1.16-17), which reveals itself in the gospel. Here God's righteousness and wrath appear clearly together as power. This leads rather to a powerful judgment of destruction and salvation that, although an eschatological judgment, does not proceed by computing the balance of deeds, but simply separates good and evil, light and darkness.

Impressive testimony to such a conception of judgment at about the beginning of the Christian era is found in the Qumran texts, which, to my knowledge, according to the currently accessible texts, know only this type of judgment. Apparently, they can also bring this process of separation and judgment into the present. The 'Thanksgiving Hymn' in 1QH 3.19-36, with its so-called apocalypse, especially in 3.26ff., can be instructive here.[4] In this connection, other presuppositions may be given for the righteousness of God as well. Thus, just here, the ancient Old Testament tradition of God's צדקה as salvation concept in the context of community and covenantal relationship and faithfulness to

---

1. Cf. Aristotle, *Ethica Nicomachea*, V; Ulpianus, *Digesta Iustiniani*, X. We also find a *suum cuique* already in Plato, *Politicus*, Iff. (esp. 331eff.; 433aff.).

2. See K.E. Grözinger, 'Middat ha-din und Middat ha-rahamim. Die sogenannten Gottesattribute "Gerechtigkeit" und "Barmherzigkeit" in der rabbinischen Literatur', in *Frankfurter Judaistische Beiträge* 8 (1980), pp. 95-114. See also already W. Bousset and H. Gressmann, *Die Religion des Judentums im späthellenistischen Zeitalter* (HNT, 21; Göttingen: Vandenhoeck & Ruprecht, 4th edn, 1966), pp. 350-51, 378ff.

3. E.g., 1 Cor. 3.12ff. already indicates differentiated types of judgment.

4. Cf. to the Qumran texts here H.-W. Kuhn, *Enderwartung und gegenwärtiges Heil. Untersuchungen zu den Gemeindeliedern von Qumran mit einem Anhang über Eschatologie und Gegenwart in der Verkündigung Jesu* (SUNT, 4; Göttingen: Vandenhoeck & Ruprecht, 1966), and further, G. Nebe, *Hoffnung*, esp. pp. 152ff.

the covenant could have established itself more easily. It is thus certainly not by chance that, under such rubrics, we find conspicuous words in the Community Rule, e.g., 1 QS 10.10-12; 11.11-14. In the second of these passages (11.12) we read:

> As for me, if I stumble, the mercies of God shall be my eternal salvation. If I stagger because of the sin of flesh, my justification shall be by the righteousness of God which endures forever.[1]

Indeed, it is the very baseness and sinfulness themselves, which the pious covenanter expresses in such extreme terms before God (cf., e.g., 1QS 11.9-10; 1QH 3.23-25), plus the Qumran community's manifest constitution of itself under the rubric of increasing the demands of the Torah, that make this all the more striking (cf. 1QS, etc.).

We see then, from contemporary or even older early Jewish texts—and this has already been thoroughly investigated—that important analogies or presuppositions for the concept of righteousness as a salvation concept are available to inform Paul's understanding of the righteousness of God and justification. This clearly shows the tenacity of the typically Old Testament structures of the concept of righteousness.

To be sure, it must be kept in mind that Paul does not understand the righteousness of God simply as continued and renewed covenant faithfulness, for he sets out decidedly with God's new eschatological act of salvation, effected through a new revelation and a break with the past. From this point also we are led again to aspects of the Pauline teaching on justification described by scholars as relational and eschatological. What is new in Paul is that the intensification of the Torah's demands, extreme consciousness of sin, and righteousness of God as a salvation concept are no longer held together or side by side as in Qumran—in Paul, alternatives have arisen. In the place of Qumran's 'and' is Paul's 'either–or', between Torah and the salvation concept 'righteousness of God', an alternative that is further intensified by Paul in the formulation 'Torah or Christ'.

How has Paul arrived at this, and how are we to understand him properly here? First of all we must examine Paul's understanding of

---

1. English translation by G. Vermes, *The Dead Sea Scrolls in English* (Harmondsworth: Penguin Books, 1962–70), p. 93.

the law—a difficult undertaking.[1] The conspicuous words in Paul for law and commandment are νόμος and ἐντολή. To begin with it is clear that Paul basically follows the usage of the LXX when he uses νόμος to include the (entire) Torah (cf. the Hebrew use of תורה), and ἐντολή, in conspicuous contrast, to refer to the individual commandments of the Torah (cf. especially the Hebrew מצוה).[2]

To find what such indicators reveal about the meaning, it is necessary to ask whether the Old Testament usage of תורה as instruction, teaching, precept, direction and, above all, as guidance [Weisung] plays a role in Paul.[3] Can the Greek word νόμος be so understood? Indeed, it seems to me that in the progression νέμω (dispense) to νόμος a strong sense of commandment-law comes into play. The word ἐντολή yields the sense of commandment/law even more clearly. Perhaps the LXX's translation of תורה with νόμος is not purely by chance. It may be that the LXX reveals here a shift of Torah understanding that can be observed in the postexilic period,[4] upon which Paul bases his own understanding.

This usage, which so emphasizes the 'law' character of the Torah, is further sharpened by Paul in that, as a rule, his own emphasis is on the inclusive expression 'the law', and that he consciously envisages (soteriologically) the fulfilment of the whole law. In certain respects the groundwork for this too could already have been laid through postexilic shifts and tendencies (cf., e.g., Ps. 1). To what extent Paul himself is a product of that particular form of Judaism that characterizes his life must be asked. At all events, Paul can speak of Judaism and himself as a Pharisee as having a 'zeal (ζῆλος, etc.) for the law'.[5]

---

1. For the literature see the references for the New Testament as a whole in *EWNT*, I, pp. 1121-22; II, pp. 1158-61. For Paul in particular see H. Hübner, *Das Gesetz bei Paulus. Ein Beitrag zum Werden der paulinischen Theologie* (FRLANT, 119; Göttingen: Vandenhoeck & Ruprecht, 3rd edn, 1982), pp. 9ff, 130ff. and the bibliography of earlier research on Paul; G. Strecker in *Neues Testament—Antikes Judentum* (ed. G. Strecker and J. Maier; Urban-Taschenbücher, 422; Stuttgart: Kohlhammer, 1989), pp. 75-76, 83-86.

2. See also M. Limbeck, *EWNT*, I, pp. 1122-23, 1124; H. Hübner, *EWNT*, II, pp. 1162-63, 1167ff.

3. Cf. the verbal root ירה (Hiph.) in the Old Testament as 'point out, direct, instruct, teach'.

4. Cf., e.g., Bousset and Gressmann, *Religion*, pp. 119ff. and elsewhere; see also H. Hübner, *EWNT*, II, pp. 1162-63.

5. This is also seen in the accounts of Paul in Acts.

Such a 'zeal for the law' may indicate an increased severity in the rule as well as an increased severity in the Torah's demands. Clearly, this would also effect an understanding of Torah which was more firmly rooted in the direction of commandment and law.

At the same time, when Paul speaks of the law as power, which, in his understanding, leads further into sin or the knowledge of sin (individually, i.e., in Paul's anthropology, through the relationship σῶμα–σάρξ, and collectively-cosmically, etc., by means of forces such as sin, called forth and empowered by the law (cf., e.g., Rom. 7–9; Gal. 3.19ff.; 5.16ff.), this too could lead to making the rule more stringent or even intensifying the demands of the Torah and the law as a standard.

This clearly indicates—despite, in my judgment, recent exegetical attempts to work out a development from Galatians' completely negative evaluation of the law to the somewhat more positive evaluation of Romans[1]—that for Paul, as is seen from his soteriological statements, the law is no longer the way to salvation, and thus neither is it the way to righteousness. And this is what Paul places over against the conceptions of Judaism.[2]

In this connection it is now necessary to investigate the alternative relationship of law and Christ in the context of seeking righteousness. In Paul's statements concerning righteousness and justification the decided soteriological stance of Christ/Jesus Christ over against the law is striking. This is seen for example in his autobiographical rehearsals and similar remarks in Galatians 1–2; Philippians 3; 1 Cor. 15.1ff.; 2 Cor. 11.18ff.; Rom. 1.1-6,[3] and, more generally, in the important texts treating righteousness and justification. From this arises the question concerning the nature of the relationship between law and Christology, and how that is ordered in connection with the problem of righteousness. Has the so-called Damascus experience already thrown the basic switches or does that not occur until later?

It seems to me that, *in nuce*, Paul from the very beginning understood his meeting with the resurrected, crucified Lord, whose disciples and adherents he persecuted as a Jew—according to his own

1. See now esp. H. Hübner, *Gesetz bei Paulus*.

2. Cf. Rom. 3.21 'apart from the law', and 3.28 'apart from the works of the law'.

3. Cf. here as well as the Lukan depiction in Acts 7.58–8.3; 9.1ff.; 22.1ff.; 26.1ff.

statement he did this as a zealous follower of the Pharisees, faithful to the law—as a crisis for the religion of Torah, which he practised as a Jew, and as a crisis for his self-awareness as a Jew seeking righteousness, whose piety was rooted in the Torah. Since this leads at once to the beginnings of the righteousness problem, I must express my criticism of remarks that characterize Paul's teaching on justification as a later 'polemical teaching' (W. Wrede) or 'minor crater' (A. Schweitzer), or that date its development in the later stages of Pauline theology, indeed, in favour of a christological early phase (G. Strecker).[1]

But how does the sharp soteriological alternative arise, as formulated in Rom. 10.4: 'For the end [this probably does not mean 'goal'] of the law is Christ, the righteousness of every one who believes'?[2] Or is this an alternative after all? Can it be that an inner-Jewish halachic clarification of the alternative Torah–Christ is considered here, such as we find already addressed by H.-J. Schoeps?[3]

Let us begin with the last named. The Jewish interpreter of Paul, H.-J. Schoeps, has maintained that the addition formula 'the law *and* the messiah' could have been sharpened in Paul's thinking to 'the law *or* the messiah' as the result of halachic reflection. According to Schoeps, then, in Jewish thinking Rom. 10.4 is a very precise judgment based on a conception that sees the era of the law and the era of the messiah in succession.[4] But, Schoeps maintains, the rabbis did not

---

1. Cf. G. Strecker in G. Strecker and J. Maier, *Neues Testament*, pp. 83f(f), or already his earlier 'Befreiung und Rechtfertigung. Zur Stellung der Rechtfertigungslehre in der Theologie des Paulus' (Festschrift Ernst Käsemann, 1976), in G. Strecker, *Eschaton und Historie. Aufsätze* (Göttingen: Vandenhoeck & Ruprecht, 1979), pp. 229ff.

2. In my judgment, the interpretation 'end of the law' for τέλος νόμου is in any case primarily set over against 'goal of the law'. This is valid despite the positive formulation 'law of Christ' in Gal. 6.2. For the latter refers, I believe, chiefly to the Christian life and not, soteriologically, to the basic principles of the doctrine of justification.

3. Cf. H.-J. Schoeps, *Paulus. Die Theologie des Apostels im Lichte der jüdischen Religionsgeschichte* (1959), esp. pp. 174ff.

4. Schoeps lists above all the following rabbinic and similar statements, texts, and proofs (cf. pp. 177ff. 'Christus des Gesetzes Ende'): (1) the tripartite 6000-year reckoning (2000 years each for Tohuwabohu, the aeon of the Jewish law, the age of the messiah)—cf. e.g., *4 Ezra* 5.55; *Barn.* 15.4; *b. Sanh.* 97a; *b. Abot Zar.* 9a; *y. Meg.* 70d; and Rom. 10.4; (2) the validity of the law/commandments only for the

share the Pauline premises that the age of the messiah as preparation for the future world had already begun with the death of Jesus and his resurrection.[1]

But the problem remains—and Schoeps himself has already addressed it[2]—whether this perspective clarifies Paul's statements regarding the law as a 'law unto death' (cf. Rom. 8.2). Therefore I must still question whether the alternative 'Torah or Christ', in its Pauline form, in fact originated in the contemporary Jewish framework, that is, contemporary halachic reflection. It seems that something new has appeared here.

Thus it may be that the Pauline alternative 'Torah or Christ' is not to be understood as a purely inner-Jewish problem, but should be reckoned as an alternative between Judaism *per se* and a 'Christianity' which is freed from the law, or at least Torah-critical. And this alternative, 'Torah or Christ', in the pointedness of its formulation and its sharpened theological gravity, appears to originate with Paul. Neither the Gospel of Matthew nor, it should be noted, the Epistle of James nor even the Paul of Acts make such a sharp distinction.

Since Paul has formulated the concept thus, the question arises as to how this is to be understood and whether it has already grown out of the so-called Damascus experience. I believe that it has, that is, that just here we find the roots of the 'something new' mentioned above.

To be sure I do not wish to proceed as does U. Wilckens in an essay from 1959.[3] According to Wilckens, for Paul the Christ-event formally acquires (since the Damascus experience) exactly the position and function which the law had in Jewish apocalyptic. Wilckens, however, was working from the perspective of a problematic relationship between a Pharisaical-rabbinical understanding of the law (the law as a bundle of divine individual precepts), and an apocalyptic under-

---

life of a man (and thus the Christian-Pauline understanding that they ended at the resurrection of Jesus)—cf. e.g., Ps. 88.6; *b. Sab.* 30a; 151b (cf. already R. Shimon ben Gamaliel); *Nid.* 61b (cf. R. Joseph bar Chiyya, a fourth-generation Amoraite); *Pes. R.* 50b; *y. Kil.* 9.13; and *Vit. Mos.* 3.22; the apocalyptic writings, also Mt. 5.17-20 and Rom. 7.1, 6 (cf. also Gal. 6.2; Rom. 3.27).

1. Cf. Schoeps, *Paulus*, pp. 177ff., esp. 179-80.

2. Schoeps, *Paulus*, pp. 181-82.

3. U. Wilckens, 'Die Bekehrung des Paulus als religionsgeschichtliches Problem', *ZTK* 56 (1959), pp. 273-93; also in Wilckens, *Rechtfertigung als Freiheit. Paulussteudein* (Neukirchen–Vluyn: Neukirchener Verlag, 1974), pp. 11-32.

standing of the law (the law as a fundamentally unified magnitude).[1]

I would rather think further along the lines of more recent attempts such as those offered in a 1985 study by C. Dietzfelbinger.[2] This study attempts to anchor the principles and lineaments of Paul's theology in the Damascus experience and thereby in the context of Hellenistic–Jewish Christianity (the group around Stephen).[3] Paul's meeting with Christ on the road to Damascus, according to Dietzfelbinger, plunged him into a dangerous and saving self-confrontation. The Torah and the Christian message of the cross were the two bases for Paul's persecution of Christians. Thus these two also determined the character of the turnaround after the appearance of Jesus. Therefore the Damascus experience was at bottom the event in which Paul recognized Jesus, rejected by and cursed by the law, as the Christ and the Son of God.[4] Dietzfelbinger refers deliberately here to Gal. 3.13 where Paul, citing Deut. 21.23, calls the crucified one 'cursed by the law'.[5] The Temple Scroll has once again generated current interest in Deut. 21.22-23.[6] Dietzfelbinger reminds us as well,

> that Jewish polemic used Deut. 21.22f. against Christian preaching already very early on and independently of Paul. . . that Paul for his part, already in his pre-Christian life, knew Deut. 21.22f. as an anti-

1. Wilckens saw the Jewish understanding of the law in a way also shared by D. Rössler (*Gesetz und Geschichte. Untersuchungen zur Theologie der jüdischen Apokalyptik und der pharisäischen Orthodoxie* [WMANT, 3; Neukirchen–Vluyn: Neukirchener Verlag, 1960]). To be sure, Wilckens later changed his view. He now understands righteousness in Paul as a polemical doctrine developed in Galatians (cf. U. Wilckens, 'Christologie und Anthropologie im Zusammenhang der paulinischen Rechtfertigungslehre', *ZNW* 67 [1976], pp. 64-82, esp. 68-69.).

2. C. Dietzfelbinger, *Die Berufung des Paulus als Ursprung seiner Theologie* (WMANT, 58; Neukirchen–Vluyn: Neukirchener Verlag, 1985).

3. Cf. also, e.g., the recent article by M. Hengel, 'Der vorchristliche Paulus', *Theologische Beiträge* 21 (1990), pp. 174-95.

4. Dietzfelbinger, *Berufung*, p. 126.

5. Dietzfelbinger, *Berufung*, pp. 33ff. See also Schoeps, *Paulus*, pp. 186ff., for such questions.

6. Cf. 11QT (Temple Scroll), col. 64.6ff. For the German translation and commentary on this text see also J. Maier, *Die Tempelrolle vom Toten Meer* (Uni-Taschenbücher, 829; Basel: Reinhardt, 1978). Dietzfelbinger also expressly treats this Temple Scroll text (pp. 33ff.); it was of course not available to Schoeps. Cf. also Hengel, 'Paulus', p. 195.

Christian argument from the synagogue, and may have used it himself in
his conflict with Christians.[1]

When I attempt to pursue this line of thinking further, I am confronted with the question whether one can set aside the problem of the
law for a Pharisee, who persecuted Christians with 'zeal', after this
Pharisee has become a 'Christian', that is, whether Paul can isolate
Christology from his understanding of the law.

Moreover, I must consider whether Paul the Pharisee, and then
Christian convert, can by any means judge the problematic crucifixion
of Jesus as messiah (pretender)[2] apart from the Torah, particularly
since this Jesus had himself exercised a Torah critique in word and
deed. Thus Paul's accounts of himself reveal that he saw his conversion and call as critically aligned over against his hitherto Jewish
soteriological understanding, in which the striving for righteousness
had played a fundamental role. Thereby, it was also necessary for
Paul to take the position—as is apparent from Gal. 3.10ff.[3]—that the
death of Jesus, his failure and crucifixion, had from a Jewish
perspective led to a Torah reflection which portrayed the crucified
one as accursed and unrighteous. Indeed Pharisaic circles, with their
orientation towards Torah and messiah, were the very milieu where
this problem could become acute. Here it was possible, as I have
already said, to comprehend the crucifixion of Jesus as punishment
and as curse. This may point to a subsequent reflection and evaluation
of Jesus' crucifixion fate after his death.[4] It may also go back to a
subsequent reflection and evaluation in direct conflict with the
disciples of Jesus as they maintained and proclaimed that Jesus was
raised and had appeared to some of them, so that they were not
operating in the authority of this Jesus who had died on the cross but
had been resurrected and exalted by God.

1. Dietzfelbinger, *Berufung*, p. 38.
2. By formulating thus we keep the historical circumstances of Jesus' crucifixion
in view. The early Christian tradition as well took this as its point of departure, that
Jesus (of Nazareth) was crucified as 'messiah' (1 Cor. 15.1ff., among others).
3. Cf. already, e.g., Bultmann's perspective (*Theology*, §7.3, pp. 45-46) particularly in connection with the early church's understanding of the cross.
4. However, it may point to a judgment in the Sanhedrin before his delivery to the
Romans and crucifixion. I will not address this here. In any case it seems to me that a
subsequent evaluation of Jesus' crucifixion fate after his death should at least be
considered, particularly in view of Paul's history.

Within this horizon Paul the Pharisee was able, with 'zeal' and striving for righteousness, with 'traditional' Jewish Phariseeism, to participate in the conflict with the disciples of Jesus—indeed, clearly Hellenistic–Jewish disciples—and especially in their persecution. When Paul met this resurrected Jesus on the road to Damascus, it not only forced the issue of Jesus as messiah, but also that of the truth of the Torah. The alternative 'Torah or Christ' could have arisen here, perhaps expressly, but at least *in nuce*, no matter that the later definition and development in conflict with Jewish-Christian and Jewish opposition takes place within the doctrine of justification as finally expressed in Galatians and Romans.[1]

Whether Paul already recognized and represented the full Gentile mission, the consequences and extent of which are not seen until later, may (somewhat in contrast to his autobiographical accounts) be questioned.[2] But that Paul had already in Damascus become aware of the opening to the Diaspora and to the Gentiles, and of his own commission, can certainly, in essence, already be seen in his autobiographical accounts.

b. *The Righteousness of God: A Salvation Concept*

The recent discussion on the understanding of righteousness, or particularly the righteousness of God, in Paul has above all been

1. In all such attempts, I want first of all to begin more generally by examining Paul's horizon and the front he established over against the Judaism of his time. For me, therefore, Palestinian Judaism also continues to be important, structurally and theologically. Thus the Qumran texts, of Palestinian provenance, offer an important background or contrasting horizon. They are for this reason dealt with above. One distorts a proper understanding of such backgrounds by focusing too narrowly on Paul as a Diaspora Jew, in particular as a Greek-speaking Hellenistic Diaspora Jew. And this is what I see in many cases as a dubious tendency in contemporary research on Paul. Hellenistic Greek-speaking (Diaspora) Judaism, Greek-speaking Jewish-Hellenistic Christianity and, finally, Hellenistic-Gentile Christianity were certainly extremely important for Paul and the development of his theology. However, one must guard against a 'Hellenistic stretto', a danger of the many-faceted so-called Hellenistic interpretation of Paul. For this can result in the fundamental beginnings and contrasts of Paul's doctrine of justification and their genesis being ignored, or at least reduced in significance.

2. The Christian community in Syrian Antioch may, just here, already have been very important, both early and later. It is once again commanding attention in recent research. Cf., e.g., already Bultmann, *Theology*, §16, and now J. Becker, *Paulus. Der Apostel der Völker* (Tübingen: Mohr [Paul Siebeck], 1989), esp. pp. 87ff.

determined by the question of whether this is a gift or an aspect of power, or whether both form a focal point of understanding.[1] It seems to me important to re-emphasize what research has already determined, that is, that the righteousness of God in Paul is, above all, a salvation concept. I would like to develop this thematically.

It should first of all be emphasized that in this framework we see the aspects of gift, power (i.e. the power that generates salvation), covenant faithfulness, God's new eschatological act of salvation, etc., which have become so important in recent research. Within this purview also fall such questions as how the genitive relationship δικαιοσύνη θεοῦ is to be interpreted. Is this a *genitivus subjectivus*, a *genitivus objectivus* or a *genitivus auctoris*? At all events the content and linguistic–grammatical categories are somewhat confused here. It is well known that H. Lietzmann posited 'an iridescent double-meaning' for the concept 'righteousness of God' in Paul, which he appropriately describes and the 'divine characteristic', but also 'God's gift of δικαιοσύνη to man' .[2] Thus the terminus δικαιοσύνη θεοῦ may express aspects of what God does as well as a characteristic of God himself. The well-known text, Rom. 3.26, expresses, with the verb and the adjective, both an act and a characteristic of God: 'that he himself is righteous and that he justifies him who has faith in Jesus'.[3]

Along with many other exegetes, I am of the opinion that Paul's main emphases are on the aspect of God's righteousness as (1) a gift of salvation and (2) the power that generates salvation (*genitivus auctoris*), and this within the larger framework of God's righteousness as a decided salvation concept. This is already connected to the righteousness of God in Paul (in the framework of the concept of 'righteousness' *per se*) representing a relational and a forensic–eschatological concept. Moreover, this idea of salvation stems from the background of the Old Testament in so far as righteousness there

1. See here particularly Bultmann, *Theology*, §28ff.; *idem*, 'δικαιοσύνη θεοῦ', *JBL* 83 (1964), pp. 12-16; E. Käsemann, 'Gottesgerechtigkeit bei Paulus', in *Exegetische Versuche und Besinnungen* (Göttingen: Vandenhoeck & Ruprecht, 1961), II, pp. 181-93. Cf. also Hübner, *Gesetz bei Paulus*, esp. pp. 104ff.

2. Cf. H. Lietzmann, *An die Römer* (HNT; Tübingen: Mohr, 4th edn, 1933), p. 30, and also E. Jüngel, *Paulus und Jesus. Eine Untersuchung zur Präzisierung der Frage nach dem Ursprung der Christologie* (HUT, 2; Tübingen: Mohr [Paul Siebeck], 2nd edn, 1964), p. 33.

3. English translation from *The New Oxford Annotated Bible*.

describes a mutual relationship, where the righteousness of God is a salvation concept in the sense of God's covenant faithfulness.

At the same time I want to consider the possibility that at a certain point in Paul the character of God's righteousness as a salvation concept is broken through, or at least viewed differently, so that righteousness becomes a kind of characteristic of God. This affects the conceptions of Jesus' vicarious death, atonement and reconciliation.

Recent research has been apt to put such an idea back into the context of a critical attitude to the so-called 'satisfaction theory' and cultic–juristic thinking in the interpretation of Paul.[1] On the other hand, it should be noted how important the theme 'reconciliation' has recently become. This is true for the area of Pauline theology itself.[2] Furthermore, it has become a leading motif in the context of seeking a 'biblical theology'.[3] Moreover, this topic can be important for Jewish–Christian dialogue itself, as I was able to observe at a Jewish–Christian symposium in July, 1989 in Augsburg on the theme 'Reconciliation in the Liturgy'. Here the New Testament and particularly Paul were addressed.[4]

It us just such questions as these that bring statements of Paul such as Rom. 3.24-26 into view:

> They are justified by his grace as a gift, through the redemption which is in Christ Jesus, whom God put forward as an expiation by his blood, to be received by faith. This was to show God's righteousness, because in his divine forbearance he has passed over former sins; it was to prove at the present time that he himself is righteous and that he justified him who has faith in Jesus.[5]

Nevertheless recent research shows that it is necessary to differentiate strictly (in the tradition history) between the individual conceptions

---

1. Cf. here Bultmann, *Theology*, §§31, 33.3, or more generally, Becker, *Heil*, p. 121.

2. See now C. Breytenbach, *Versöhnung. Eine Studie zur paulinischen Soteriologie* (WMANT, 60; Neukirchen–Vluyn: Neukirchener Verlag, 1989).

3. Cf. here, e.g., P. Stuhlmacher and H. Class, *Das Evangelium von der Versöhnung in Christus* (Tübingen: Mohr [Paul Siebeck], 1979), and also Breytenbach, *Versöhnung*, pp. 1-2, and elsewhere.

4. See the published papers of the symposium, *Versöhnung in der jüdischen und christlichen Liturgie* (ed. H. Heinz, K. Kienzler and J.J. Petuchowski; 1990), esp. H. Merklein, 'Der Sühnetod Jesu nach dem Zeugnis des Neuens Testaments', pp. 155-83 (for Paul in particular, pp. 166ff [163ff.]).

5. English according to *The New Oxford Annotated Bible*.

and motifs, thus also, between the conception of reconciliation in καταλλάσσειν, κτλ, and the conception of atonement in ἱλάσκεσθαι, κτλ.[1] To be sure other exegetes assume a closer connection in their interpretation here.[2]

If one views such conceptions and motifs as the vicarious death of Jesus, atonement, and reconciliation in connection with the conception of the righteousness of God, it may be asked (in my judgment) whether Paul is not thinking on various levels in Rom. 3.24-26, rather than simply defining himself by means of corrections and additions over against a given tradition.[3] Is it not possible that, under such tokens as these, the aspect of atonement through the death and blood of Christ shows itself at the level of Pauline thinking in such a way that the death and blood of Christ work vicariously here, and that thereby—and this seems to me to be very important—it becomes manifest in the world how an *avenging* 'righteousness of God' is absorbed and at once integrated into the *salvation concept* 'righteousness of God'?[4]

Is it also possible in this connection that Paul—in the very same way, grounding it christologically—attempts to gather up the forensic ideas of the Last Judgment and the relational qualifiers of grace and justice, righteousness and mercy (as already provided for him in Jewish reflection),[5] into the concept of the righteousness of God as a salvation concept?

Having offered these questions for consideration, I will not pursue them here. At all events, I believe that it has once again been

---

1. Breytenbach (*Versöhnung*) has recently attempted such a differentiation which is at the same moment a critique of the traditio-historical connections postulated by a 'biblical theology'.

2. For the history of research see now Breytenbach, *Versöhnung*, pp. 5ff.

3. For the relation between tradition and redaction cf. here esp. E. Käsemann, 'Zum Verständnis von Röm. 3,24-26' (1950–51), in *Exegetische Versuche und Besinnungen*, I (Göttingen: Vandenhoeck & Ruprecht, 1960), pp. 96-100; P. Stuhlmacher, 'Zur neueren Exegese von Röm 3,24, 26 (Festschrift W.G. Kümmel, 1975)', in *idem, Versöhnung, Gesetz und Gerechtigkeit. Aufsätze zur biblischen Theologie* (Göttingen: Vandenhoeck & Ruprecht, 1981), pp. 117-35. See also Breytenbach, *Versöhnung*, pp. 166ff., and Merklein, 'Sühnetod', pp. 163ff.

4. Cf. in this direction already G. Schrenk, 'δικαιοσύνη', *TWNT*, II, p. 205 l. 33ff.; p. 206 2.35ff.

5. Cf. the relationships already mentioned between מדת הדין and מדת הרחמים in the rabbinic tradition.

very clearly seen from this that in Paul the righteousness of God—as an overriding framework—is a salvation concept. It binds together at once giver, gift and the power that generates salvation.

c. *Man's Righteousness: Righteousness by Faith*
In describing the human predicament Paul denies that man, whether Jew or Gentile (i.e. the Jew, with the law, or the Gentile, without it, but by analogy having 'what the law requires is written on their hearts', Rom. 2.15), is 'righteous' or 'justified'. This can occur from the human perspective only through righteousness by faith.[1] Righteousness by faith then is so far connected with to the righteousness of God. The 'free gift' and 'by grace' bind them together, as is shown by such texts as Rom. 1.17 and 3.21ff.

Christians must be careful here not to accuse 'sight unseen' the Judaism of that time of being a religion of 'performance'. We find in the Tannaitic-rabbinic tradition of *Pirqe 'Aboth* the remarkable pre-Christian maxim of Antigonus of Sokho, one of the so-called 'pairs' of scribes: 'Do not be like slaves who serve their master expecting a reward, but be like slaves who serve their master expecting no reward...' (*Ab.* 1.3). Doubtless this stands in the face of many a traditional Christian judgment of Judaism as a religion of Torah-performance. And despite this, Paul sets justification by grace and righteousness by faith over against Jewish striving after righteousness.

An interesting aspect of such statements by Paul is that, in the righteousness by faith, the structure of a forensic judgment is retained; in this respect, faith replaces works in this judgment, or is appealed to for the judgment. Since faith here has reference to the grace of God, which is contained within faith in Christ, a change of categories comes into play now for Paul. He sets this over against his own righteousness (from the law; cf. Rom. 10.3; Phil. 3.9). From the righteousness by faith, then, righteousness becomes decidedly a salvation concept, a gift of salvation. And just here, as well, it is clearly seen that this is the point of departure for the gift.[2]

---

1. Cf. for terminological perspective Abraham's 'righteousness of faith' at Rom. 4.11.

2. In connection with 'righteousness by faith' I mention the interesting situation that the epithet 'the Just' referring to Christians—particularly, a given, individual Christian—is absent in Paul. That Christians are 'just' remains for Paul strictly within the structural and functional framework of the doctrine of righteousness. This

The question which now presents itself naturally is how Paul's concept of faith is to be understood historically and in the context of tradition and motif history. According to Paul's accounts of himself, its roots are already in his early Christian period and in his apostolic commission (cf. Rom. 1.5; Gal. 1.23; Phil. 3.9). Individually, the very inception is at the beginning of the Christian existence (cf. Rom. 1.17, etc.), and collectively, historically and eschatologically, it is the coming of Christ or the Christ-event (cf. Gal. 3.25). Paul clearly refers to an Old Testament concept of faith (cf. the faith of Abraham according to Rom. 4.1ff. and Gal. 3.6ff.). However, the motif-tradition history of the concept is not limited to the range of the Old Testament (cf. also the LXX) but also that of the contemporary Jewish, Hellenistic and syncretistic environment, as well as that of the early Jesus traditions, and of pre-Pauline and contemporary non-Pauline Christianity.[1]

d. *The Message of Righteousness and Justification: The Gospel*

The very orientation on the word of God, brought about by the Reformation–Protestant adoption of Paul, gives prominence to this problem field.[2] Indeed it is supported by Paul's statements in connection with justification. Exegetically these statements must be more precisely examined, particularly since law and gospel do not appear to be terminologically comparable in Paul.

That justification, and also especially the righteousness of God and righteousness by faith, are part of the content of Paul's gospel is clear in Rom. 1.16-17. It is also clear that the gospel points to the proclamation, to the verbal process (cf. also 1 Thess. 2.2, 9; Gal. 2.2), that the gospel is a power or that the gospel proclamation is made in

---

is in contrast to Judaism where we find the צדיק or, e.g., a name like 'Simon the Just', or the 'Teacher of Righteousness'. However, this can also occur elsewhere or later in Christianity, since there (albeit with a characteristically Jewish background) the epithet 'the Just' does play a role, as, for example, in the name 'James the Just' (cf. K. Niederwimmer, *EWNT*, II, pp. 411-12, 413; also Eusebius, *Hist. eccl.* 2.23, 4, 7, and elsewhere). The Jewish background for the usage in Mt. 13.17 and Lk. 2.25 should also be mentioned.

    1. For these backgrounds see, e.g., G. Barth, *EWNT*, III, pp. 217-18, 220ff.

    2. Cf. already *Confessio Augustana*, articles IV-V, and further, e.g., 'Gesetz', V-VI in E. Wolf and W. Joest, 'Gesetz und Evangelium', *RGG* (3rd edn), II, pp. 1519ff.; C. Andresen and W. Loew, 'Wort Gottes' III-IV, *ibid.*, VI, pp. 1812ff.; H.-M. Barth, 'Gesetz und Evangelium' I, in *TRE*, 13, pp. 126ff..

power (cf. already the composite εὐ-αγγέλιον). Here the gospel, according to Rom. 1.16-17, empowers man with righteousness, and especially does the righteousness of God empower man with righteousness by faith. Here it is seen that the gospel at once means a revelation process and the realization of the righteousness of God, that it creates this and mediates it.

Much can still be said in this direction about the 'gospel' in connection with righteousness and justification. But we will only briefly ask, as above, how the concept of gospel is to be understood historically and in the context of tradition and motif history. I begin historically with the life of Paul himself. According to Paul's autobiographical account in Galatians 1–2 (cf. also 1 Cor. 15.1ff.; Rom. 1.1ff.), he saw the gospel in play already in his so-called Damascus experience, that is, at his conversion and call. To be sure, the topic of righteousness and justification is not always addressed, as such texts from 1 Thessalonians in relation to those of Galatians and Romans show (cf. 1 Thess. 1.5, etc.—Gal. 1.11, 16; 2.14; Rom. 1.16-17, etc.). This again brings into play at this point the problem of Paul's development or even the connections of his thought within the transmission-historical development. But the connection of the gospel concept with the beginnings of Paul's Christian existence remains striking.

The possibilities are various for investigating the backgrounds to the tradition and motif history both before and contemporary with Paul. The following are almost all the main types which are currently being discussed on the (non-literary) gospel concept, as possible root and origin:[1] (1) Old Testament prophetic tradition (cf. Deutero-Isaiah, etc.); (2) contemporary Judaism's adoption of this and its own early Jewish conceptions (cf. the Qumran texts, Apocalyptic); (3) pagan usage, particularly in the ruler-emperor cult; (4) special early Christian origins, regardless of how these are traced back to the historical Jesus.

e. *The Context of Creation, History, Eschatology*
I begin by pointing out that since the discovery of the Qumran texts it can no longer simply be said (as did, e.g., Bultmann) that the difference between Paul and Judaism is that for Paul what has become real

---

1. Cf., e.g., G. Strecker, *EWNT*, II, pp. 173ff.

is for Judaism still hope, whereby Paul, to be sure, still retains an unrealized future.[1] At the same time it is necessary to investigate the presuppositions and connections which determine that the present already plays a role.

Christology is here certainly the central point for Paul, that is, that the messiah has come; the crucifixion, resurrection and exaltation are central. Over against this the messiah for Judaism, the two messiahs of the Qumran community have not yet come. It follows then, according to Paul, that Christ Jesus has become our (i.e. Christians') righteousness, not only in a future-eschatological perspective, but now and universally (1 Cor. 1.30), and that the righteousness of God, which has been revealed, is the righteousness of God through faith in Jesus Christ (Rom. 3.21-22). Accordingly, there are many Pauline statements which express becoming righteous by faith, for the sake of Jesus Christ in a present or universal sense (cf. Rom. 3.24, 26, 28; 5.1; 8.30; 1 Cor. 6.11; Gal. 2.16; 3.24).

To be sure Paul retains a future perspective since the coming judgment continues to play a role for him in this respect (cf. Rom. 2.13, 16; 3.30; etc.). In Gal. 5.5 Paul also speaks clearly of 'righteousness' as a coming element of hope and salvation which we, that is, the Christians, await through the Spirit on the basis of faith. This leads to Paul's well-known 'now but not yet'.

Now in this connection scholarship has assumed that Paul makes a double declaration of justification, once in the 'justification of the sinner by faith alone', effected through baptism, and once in the 'justification by faith at the last judgment', which is effected through love.[2] But in my opinion this is hardly to be seen as *the* solution of Paul's 'now but not yet'. There is still room here for further discussion in exegesis.

In the framework of creation, history and eschatology a good many aspects and problems indeed appear. There is, for example, a type of thinking in salvation and doomsaying spheres like that which occurs—analogous, in certain respects, to Qumran statements—in 2 Cor. 6.14ff.[3] E. Käsemann's thesis should also be remembered which sees

---

1. Cf. Bultmann, *Theology*, §§28-29, and the critique by Käsemann, 'Gottesgerechtigkeit', pp. 181-82 (footnote).

2. Thus, e.g., J. Jeremias, *Die Gleichnisse Jesu* (Göttingen: Vandenhoeck & Ruprecht, 8th edn, 1970 [1947]), p. 207 n. 4. Cf. Becker, *Heil*, pp. 267ff.

3. However there is a lively scholarly discussion on this text concerning genuine-

the righteousness of God in Paul in the context of God, on the apocalyptic horizon, asserting his right as creator by going beyond anthropology and a present eschatology:

> God's power reaches out to the world and is the salvation of the world, so
> that the world is brought back under the rule of God. Even for this reason
> it is God's gift and the salvation of the individual that we are obedient to
> the righteousness of God.[1]

Then what sort of a concept of justice do we have here?

I will close this section, in which still more could be said, and
thereby the main portion of my remarks on the Pauline statements on
righteousness, with a glance at Israel in Romans 9–11. There we
find—and this seems clear to me in all problems of understanding
which this section of Romans continues to present[2]—on the one hand
that salvation is withheld from Israel because of justification by faith,
and on the other, that because of God's faithfulness a future hope still
remains for Israel, which helps Israel in such a way that the Gentiles
also attain to salvation. Thus Paul expresses in Rom. 11.25 as a
'Geheimnis/mystery': 'Verhärtung (Verstockung) ist Israel zum Teil
widerfahren, bis daß die Fülle der Heiden eigegangen ist' / 'hardening
has come upon part of Israel, until the full number of the Gentiles
come in. . . ' and in Rom. 11.28, then: 'Nach den Evangelium sind sie
zwar Feinde um euretwillen, aber gemäß Gottes Erwählung sind sie

---

ness and literary-redactional questions. Cf. Kümmel, *Einleitung*, pp. 239-40, 249ff.

   1.   Käsemann, 'Gottesgerechtigkeit', p 193.

   2.   For the interpretation of Rom. 9–11 and the voluminous literature see the following exemplary studies: *Die Israelfrage nach Röm 9–11* (ed. L. De Lorenzi, with
contributions from W.G. Kümmel *et al.*; Monographische Reihe von 'Benedictina',
3; Rome: Abtei von St Paul vor den Mauern, 1977), there particularly on the history
of research, W.G. Kümmel, 'Die Probleme von Römer 9–11 in der gegenwärtigen
Forschungslage', pp. 13-33 (discussion pp. 34-56); H. Hübner, *Gottes Ich und
Israel. Zum Schriftgebrauch des Paulus in Röm 9–11* (FRLANT, 136; Göttingen:
Vandenhoeck & Ruprecht, 1984); N. Walther, 'Zur Interpretation von Röm 9–11',
ZTK (1984), pp. 172-95; E. Brandenburger, 'Paulinische Schriftauslegung in der
Kontroverse um das Verheißungswort Gottes (Röm 9)', *ZTK* 82 (1985), pp. 1-47;
H.-M. Lübking, *Paulus und Israel im Römerbrief. Eine Untersuchung zu Römer 9–
11* (Europäische Hochschulschriften, 23.260; Frankfurt am Main: Lang, 1986);
W. Schmithals, *Der Römerbrief. Ein Kommentar* (1988), esp. 320ff.;
E.E. Johnson, *The Function of Apocalyptic and Wisdom Traditions in Romans 9–
11* (Society of Biblical Literature Dissertation Series, 109; Chico, CA: Scholars
Press, 1989).

Geliebte wegen der Väter.' / 'As regards the gospel they are enemies of God, for your sake; but as regards election they are beloved for the sake of their forefathers.'[1] Paul brings here on the one hand an eschatological break in the sense of 'old-new' into play, to which the gospel refers, and on the other a salvation–historical continuity based on God's faithfulness to the forefathers, which, in the form of a future hope, also includes Israel.[2]

3. Conclusion

I come now to the conclusion of my remarks. It will have become clear that in reality it has only been possible to attempt to lay some roads and 'trails' into the problem area of righteousness in Paul. Thus, for example, one could also say much in the direction of effects and consequences of justification, or concerning righteousness in connection with the Christian realization of salvation and Christian lifestyle in the world, or also on the relationship of 'now but not yet', of indicative and imperative, of 'to declare righteous' and 'to make righteous' (cf. the so-called relationship of imputed to effected righteousness), or to a *theologia crucis*, or to the work of the Holy Spirit and much more. The possibility should also be investigated that the further development of the justification and righteousness statements in Paul are in the direction of syncretism. Reviewing my remarks, I would like our colloquium to give special attention to two focal points.

---

1. English translation from *The New Oxford Annotated Bible*.
2. This is perhaps in certain respects related to, or analogous to, the statements of Paul in Rom. 3.24-26, if it is true there that Paul on the one hand presents the righteousness of God as an eschatologically new salvation event in Christ and as a gift of salvation mediated through faith in Jesus (cf. Rom. 3.21-23, 26 or 26b and the Pauline *theologoumena* 'faith', etc. in 3.24-25), and, on the other, takes up the righteousness of God in the sense of God's faithfulness in connection with atonement and forgiveness through the blood of Christ, based on Israel's ancient cultic salvation traditions (cf. Rom. 3.24-25 or 3.24-26a without the specific Pauline *theologoumena* 'faith', etc.). To be sure the relationship between tradition and redaction must be expressly considered in this text (cf. Käsemann, 'Verständnis': to the tradition 3.24-25, the Jewish-Christian motif of the renewed covenant, 3.26 is a corrective addition from Paul; cf. also Stuhlmacher, *Exegese*, who sees 3.25-26a as a pre-Pauline tradition, with a typological reference to Lev. 16, going back to the Stephan circle). But in any case Paul considered the tradition important and took it up, indeed, perhaps 'exalted' it (in Hegel's sense: 'aufgehoben').

1. The first point concentrates especially on the soteriological aspects and there on the relationship of Torah/law to Christ. This seems to me in Paul—despite all possibilities of a development of his thinking as a Christian—soteriologically to be sharpened finally and fundamentally to a contrast, an alternative between Christ and Torah/law. Can Paul still be understood within the framework of ancient Judaism with this alternative, or has he thereby forsaken the fundamentals of Judaism?

At the same time Paul distinguishes himself through the sharp antithesis from other early Christian solution models for the concept of righteousness and justification, such as occur in Matthew (there based on, or in connection with, the Jesus tradition)[1] and in James.[2]

2. The second point, as I see it, concentrates on the reality and realization of justification and righteousness in the world. What is the outlook—from the Christian standpoint—for a smooth derivation of church law from the Pauline concept of righteousness, particularly in the connection of 'law' and 'spirit'? In the relationship between Judaism and Christianity, where is the eschatological dawn of salvation to be located?

How can justification and righteousness, especially today, be understood in a wider and more comprehensive horizon? How can a bridge be built to such great themes as moral law, categorical imperative, ethics of discourse, etc.? How do we find the way from a concept of righteousness rooted in the Old Testament to the Greek–Western tradition of thinking, on which basis does—in the sense of *suum cuique* and perhaps also of idealism—above all, the understanding of universal human rights rest? From there one may then attempt to go further in what we at present discuss in the ecumenical movement under the keywords 'righteousness, peace and preservation of creation'.

1. Cf., e.g., Mt. 5.20; 6.33.
2. Cf. Jas 2.20ff.

REFLECTIONS ABOUT SOCIAL JUSTICE WITHIN THE ECUMENICAL MOVEMENT

Konrad Raiser

I

The quest for social justice on the level of a nation or internationally has been a central concern of the ecumenical movement between the Christian churches since its beginnings. 'Justice' and 'peace' were the two key concepts on which ecumenical reflection about the social responsibility of the churches concentrated. One would therefore think that this ecumenical discussion which has been carried on passionately for almost 70 years would have led to something like a basic consensus regarding the understanding of social justice. However, the last major ecumenical conference which dealt with these issues, that is, the 'World Convocation for Justice, Peace and the Integrity of Creation', which took place at Seoul in March 1990, indicated that 'justice' continues to be an issue which is highly charged with conflict. I will return to this point later.

Does this mean that the intensive ecumenical reflections on social justice have not led to any results? If this were the case I would hardly have chosen this topic for my contribution. The nature of the difficulty rather arises from the fact that these results cannot be formulated within the framework of a consistent theory which integrates convincingly the biblical understanding of justice and is critically related to the contemporary debate among social philosophers, political scientists and lawyers. The ecumenical reflections do not make scientific claims; following the method of action and reflection they are always related to concrete areas of social conflict. Thus it is characteristic of the ecumenical discussion that rarely is an attempt being made to define 'justice' or clearly to differentiate the respective understanding of justice from other philosophical, political or legal uses of the concept. The ecumenical discussion arises out of everyday experience in contexts where justice is at stake, where injustice is unquestionably evident. The reflection is oriented towards searching for ways to overcome apparent injustice and not so much guided by an ideal concept of social justice which could then serve as a basis to formulate clear criteria for the building of social order.

The emphases of the ecumenical discussion on justice have therefore changed several times depending on the specific character of the social conflict. Ecumenical social thought does not have the systematic coherence of the social teaching of the Catholic church based, as it is, on the central concepts of personhood, subsidiarity and solidarity with their roots in the tradition of natural law. This framework has most recently been restated and expanded in an impressive way in the papal encyclical *Solicitudo rei socialis*. Nevertheless I believe that a number of basic insights have been gained in the course of ecumenical discussion which are of significance for any reflection about social justice in the framework of the biblical tradition.

II

Ecumenical thinking about social justice began to crystallize for the first time at the ecumenical world conference on 'Church, Community, and State' in Oxford (1937). Against the background of the unresolved conflict regarding the foundation of Christian ethics either in biblical tradition or in natural law the conference affirmed the fundamental significance of the biblical commandment of love for any Christian understanding of social order. Following J.H. Oldham, the conference endeavoured to formulate 'middle axioms' which could provide a bridge between the biblical tradition, in particular the teachings of the Sermon on the Mount, and the challenges of contemporary social life, between general norms of Christian ethics and prescriptions for concrete action. Thus, the Oxford conference spoke of the 'principle of justice' as the adequate translation and mediation of the Christian commandment of love into the institutional requirements of contemporary social life. Justice here was understood in the sense of the goal of a harmonious relationship between all members of society which tries to define what each member of a given community can equitably claim within the harmony of the whole. Obviously this understanding of justice, which follows Reinhold Niebuhr, is strongly inspired by the tradition of natural law with its roots in the Greek notion of justice as 'equity', that is, the equitable distribution of social goods.

This relatively traditional approach to the problem of justice proved to be too narrow as the confrontation between the Western liberal and the communist concepts of social order deepened in subsequent years. Continuing the search for 'middle axioms' the first Assembly of the World Council of Churches in Amsterdam (1948) adopted the concept of the 'responsible society' as developed by J.H. Oldham. This concept was to respond to and take seriously the competing claims of freedom and justice in building an order of society. It was J.H. Oldham in particular who emphasized the priority of freedom over all other elements of social order. He was convinced that only the free society 'can in the long run ensure progressive approximations to social justice. It alone provides the opportunities by which men can discover by common discussion and by experiment what social justice means and thereby progressively achieve it.'[1]

Our experience today in the context of the reordering of societies in the countries of Eastern Europe is that this is anything but a dated discussion. Here we encounter again the tension between freedom and justice, between equality and the liberal insistence on the primacy of freedom. In most of the constitutional democracies in industrialized countries this tension is mediated through the principle of legality, that is, by means of a legal order which guarantees civil as well as economic liberties and safeguards a minimum of social justice. This also was the interest behind the concept of the 'responsible society' which therefore has remained an important point of orientation.

III

Since the end of the 1950s this early phase of ecumenical discussion which had been characterized by basic liberal assumptions has been replaced by the new quest for international economic justice in the context of the emerging development conflict. The beginning of a new phase became publicly visible for the first time at the conference on 'Church and Society' held at Geneva in 1966. Since then, social justice has become the decisive criterion for all ecumenical initiatives

1. See J.H. Oldham, 'A Responsible Society', in *The Church and the Disorder of Society* (The Amsterdam Assembly Series, 3; New York, 1948), pp. 120ff. (p. 146).

regarding world development, taking issue with an understanding of development oriented primarily towards modernization and economic growth.

This new challenge progressively led to a change of emphasis in the understanding of justice. Instead of the attention given to distributive justice in the earlier discussion, the emphasis now was increasingly placed on the demand for equality, for rights and opportunities for all people and nations. Thus, the Fourth Assembly of the World Council of Churches in Uppsala (1968) stated programmatically:

> The application of social justice to all human relations demands a common understanding between nations for the recognition and protection of the inherent dignity of men, and of full human equality between men of all races and nations, and respect for the adherents of all religions and ideologies.[1]

According to the Indian economist, Samuel Parmar, who has strongly influenced the ecumenical discussion with his ideas rooted in the Gandhian tradition, social justice finds concrete expression in 'greater equality of opportunity, a more egalitarian social order, a diffusion of economic and political power from the few to the many. . . Thus social justice incorporates equality and human dignity'.[2] The explicit link which is established in these two quotations between human dignity and equality is not accidental in situations which are characterized by a complete lack of reliable legality and the absence of the rule of law. The defence of human dignity becomes more and more the elementary expression of the claim of freedom in society, while equality is regarded as the basic criterion of justice.

The statement by the Central Committee of the World Council of Churches concluding an ecumenical study on 'Violence, Non-Violence, and the Struggle for Social Justice' (1973) tries to describe in a succinct formula the goal of this search for social justice:

> The goal of social change is a society in which all people participate in the fruits and the decision-making process, in which the centres of power are limited and accountable, in which human rights are truly affirmed for all,

---

1. *The Uppsala Report 1968* (ed. N. Goodall; Geneva: CVB-Druck, Zürich, 1968), p. 63.
2. See S.L. Parmar, 'Goals and Process of Development and Objectives of Development Projects', in *Fetters of Injustice* (ed. P.H. Gruber; Geneva, 1970), pp. 41ff. (p. 42).

and which acts responsible towards the whole human community of mankind, and toward coming generations.[1]

Notable in this definition, which continues at least implicitly the earlier orientation towards a 'responsible society', is the broadened understanding of justice, emphasizing in particular the political dimension in the sense of opportunities for participation and democratic control of power. The explicit reference to responsibility over against coming generations introduces for the first time the ecological concern into the context of ecumenical discussion about justice. Both of these emphases have subsequently been integrated into the new concept of a 'just, participatory and sustainable society' which has served as a basic frame of reference since the Fifth Assembly of the World Council for Churches in Nairobi (1975).

IV

The challenge of structural injustice and oppression in many countries of the southern hemisphere had led to the conviction that basic human rights should be considered as minimal criteria for the establishment of a just order of society. In addition, the political dimension of a participatory order had received increasing attention. In many situations, the struggle for democracy and human rights had become a contemporary expression of the search for social justice.

Behind this strengthened ecumenical conviction a new conflict, however, became visible, that is, the tension between justice and peace as requirements for a durable international order. Certainly it had always been recognized that justice and peace are inseparably related according to biblical witness. However, the sharp confrontations regarding the question of security in an age of nuclear weapons, regarding the legitimacy of a liberation struggle against oppressive power structures, and the consequences of the sharpened conflict between North and South posed the dilemma that there are situations where the commitment to justice and the need for preserving peace cannot be easily reconciled.

This tension has overshadowed the ecumenical discussion since the

1. See ' "Violence, Non-Violence and the Struggle for Social Justice". A Statement Commended by the Central Committee of the World Council of Churches, August 1973', in *Ecumenical Review* 4 (1973), pp. 430-46 quoted from an offprint of the report p. 9.

beginning of the 1980s. More recently it has been replaced by the tension between social justice and the protection of the natural foundations of life. In both cases what is at stake is the opposition between fundamental interests: the rich and industrialized countries of the North are interested in preserving, strengthening and expanding the existing order; the poor and dependent countries in the South or at least the majority of their populations are vitally interested in changing this very same order which they experience as discriminating and oppressive, and therefore as unjust.

This conflict of interests which is at the root of the tension between justice and peace and which is basically a conflict about the distribution of power has objective causes and cannot be simply resolved. The Sixth Assembly of the World Council of Churches in Vancouver (1983), in formulating the programmatic thesis 'that without justice for all everywhere we shall never have peace anywhere'[1] has tried to link peace and justice as closely as possible. Further on, the same policy statement on peace and justice adds: 'True security for the people demands respect for human rights, including the right to self-determination, as well as social and economic justice for all within every nation, and a political framework that would ensure it'.[2] All this was understood as a contemporary interpretation of the word of the prophet that 'the effect of righteousness will be peace' (Isa. 32.17).

How little this profound inner connection between justice and peace is to be taken for granted became clear at the occasion of the ecumenical 'World Convocation on Justice, Peace, and the Integrity of Creation'. Here participants from the churches in the South, particularly, passionately claimed the primacy of justice not only over against the concern for peace but also over against the integrity of creation. However convincing the analysis of the profound inter-connection between the major world problems and its interpretation against the background of the biblical notion of *shalom* might be, the elementary experience of injustice had more immediate evidence for them as the starting point of reflection and action.

---

1. See *Gathered for Life. Official Report of the 6th Assembly of the World Council of Churches* (ed. D. Gill; Geneva: WCC Publications, 1983), p. 132.
2. *Gathered for Life*, p. 134.

V

Nevertheless, this world convocation has succeeded in summarizing much of the ecumenical discussion about social justice and in articulating this in its so-called 'affirmations'.[1] It is therefore appropriate to conclude this paper with a short glance at these statements coming from the world convocation.

1. The first point to be noted is that, even in this most recent ecumenical declaration on our subject, social justice is being understood primarily as a question of political order and thus as a matter of responsible and participatory, that is, democratic control of power. The tendency to narrow the concern for justice to the problems of distributive justice is thus overcome in a definitive way. The struggle for social justice embraces the defence of human dignity, the liberation from oppression, and the building up of a just and participatory system of government and of the economy.

2. Already at the time of the Vancouver Assembly the analysis of the problems of social justice had led to the conclusion that economic exploitation and discrimination on the basis of race and sex form an interconnected 'web of oppression'.[2] This insight is now being confirmed when, in the affirmations coming from the world convocation, the right of the poor to a life of human dignity, the equal rights of all peoples and races, as well as the fundamental equality of women are placed on the same level as fundamental dimensions of the goal of social justice.

3. This view of basic human rights as a criterion for the realization of social justice is present throughout the text of the affirmations. This presupposes, however, a broadening of the classical liberal notion of human rights in terms of civic and political rights with a view to including the collective social, economic and cultural rights of people. Thus, over and beyond the classical right of the freedom of opinion, the text explicitly mentions access to truth and education, information and the means of communication as a basic human right. 'All people have the right to be educated, to tell their own stories, to speak their

1. Cf. *Now is the Time. Final Document and other Texts from the World Convocation on Justice, Peace and the Integrity of Creation* (Geneva: WCC Publications, 1990), pp. 11ff.
2. Cf. *Gathered for Life*, p. 86.

own convictions and beliefs, to be heard by others and to have the power to distinguish truth from falsehood.'[1] It supports poor peasant populations, in particular indigenous people, in their struggle for their rights to land and sea. It finally underlines the rights and the dignity of children and of the younger generation and calls for respect of the human right to conscientious objection.

4. It is noteworthy therefore that these affirmations on justice, peace and the integrity of creation, which begin with a solemn statement about the exercise of power, culminate in a concluding summary affirmation about human rights which opens with the sentence: 'There is an inseparable relationship between justice and human rights'.[2] And the central passage of this affirmation can be read as a summary of the reflections presented in this paper: 'We *affirm* that human rights are God-given and that their promotion and protection are essential for freedom, justice and peace. . . '[3]

VI

It was the intention of this survey to show that ecumenical reflections about social justice have developed in response to changing patterns of basic social conflict. In the course of these reflections the conviction has taken shape more and more clearly that human rights are to be understood as minimal demands which are to be met by an order of society claiming to be just. By the same token they become the criterion for social and political responsibility of the churches. This position should provide important points of contact for the dialogue with the social teaching of the Catholic church and the way it had been developed further in recent years.

Where Christians and churches commit themselves to the defence of the rights of the poor and the oppressed they discover more clearly that the notion of human rights which is a fruit of the European enlightenment, nevertheless has its independent and specific roots in biblical tradition. The poor and the weak members of the community have a right before God to protection and to the basic sustenance of life. God in his justice watches over their right and, through the words of the prophets, defends this right before the rulers and the

1. See *Now is the Time*, Affirmation V, p. 16.
2. *Now is the Time*, p. 21.
3. *Now is the Time*, p. 21.

powerful. This biblical foundation of the basic social rights cannot be developed any further at this point. However, when the Fifth Assembly of the World Council of Churches in Nairobi (1975) began its listing of human rights concerns with the 'right to basic guarantees for life' including the protection of the weak members of society as well as the rights of future generations, this can be understood as a distant echo of the biblical understanding of justice and righteousness.

The re-affirmation of this fundamental commitment at the occasion of the world convocation should serve as a clear mandate for the churches' further reflections and actions regarding social justice.

RIGHTEOUSNESS AS ORDER OF THE WORLD:
SOME REMARKS TOWARDS A PROGRAMME

Henning Graf Reventlow

The idea of righteousness as a basic ethical demand for human living together belongs to the central content of the biblical heritage that is common to Jews and Christians. We hear together from the Bible that righteousness has to guide our acting, if other ethical aims such as peace, mercy and love are to be reached. Beyond the action of the individual we hear in the Bible also that the structures of a society have to be righteous if the individual is to get his rights. Even the intercourse between peoples is subject to this measure, which we encounter as the will of God. But if righteousness is known to us as a specific biblical demand, we cannot overlook that it had its impact in the Western world in manifold refraction with the ethical traditions of classical antiquity. The ethical principles of the Stoa especially have influenced via the humanists our Western thinking. The parallels which exist to a certain degree between both traditions have contributed to procuring for the standard of righteousness acknowledgment beyond the circle of Jews and Christians believing in the Bible. Secular institutions as the UNO and the KSZE in Europe are under obligation to the ideals of peace and human rights. However, important aspects of biblical righteousness-thinking have been lost in this development, above all its relation to God.

Righteousness in the Bible and the secular idea of righteousness are neighbours and can fertilize one another. This fact seems to find a correlation when we ask for the origins of righteousness-thinking, stepping back in the history of mankind. The opinion which was still very common in the seventeenth and early eighteenth century, seeing Moses as the first law-giver upon whom all heathen law-givers and even philosophers depend,[1] has nowadays lost its followers even in sectarian circles. Even the so-called Babel–Bible dispute,[2] in which the broad public in Germany for the first time was informed, though in a tendentious way, about the importance of the Babylonian–Assyrian texts for the question of the origins of the biblical traditions and was shocked to a large degree, is now about a century old. So the idea that biblical righteousness-thinking does not stand at the beginning of the old oriental conceptions of righteousness is not offensive any more today. Nevertheless there still exist many obscurities about the ways in which influences of this kind may have been effective. The opinions on this question are not free of ideology, either; on one side we meet emancipatory, on the other side apologetic interests.

In the following deliberations I want to discuss on approach to which, for a while, much attention was paid, but lately (and also because the author has nearly retired from research work) is rather seldom debated. I mean the book of H.H. Schmid, *Gerechtigkeit als Weltordnung*.[3] This work stands at the end of a series of enquiries beginning with K.H. Fahlgren's dissertation '*sᵉdaqa*, nahestehende und entgegengesetzte Begriffe im Alten Testament'[4] and furthered above all by K. Koch in several contributions.[5] In contrast to the modern Western understanding of righteousness, the peculiarity of the biblical 'righteousness'-thinking was detected here, which Fahlgren called a 'synthetic understanding of life'.[6] Fahlgren wanted to say that in the original Israelite thinking the different regions of life, such as religion

---

1. A famous example is the voluminous work of Theophilus Gale, *The Court of the Gentiles or a Discourse Touching the Original of Human Literature, both Philologie and Philosophie, from the Scriptures and Jewish Church* (4 vols.; 1669–76).

2. Cf. K. Johanning, *Der Bibel-Babel-Streit. Eine forschungsgeschichtliche Studie* (Europäische Hochschulschriften, 23.348; Bern: Lang, 1988).

3. Beiträge zur Historischen Theologie, 40: Tübingen: Mohr [Paul Siebeck], 1968.

4. Dissertation, Uppsala, 1932 (excerpts also in K. Koch [ed.], *Um das Prinzip der Vergeltung in Religion und Recht des Alten Testaments* [Wege der Forschung, 125; Darmstadt: Wiss. Buchgesellschaft, 1972], pp. 87-129).

5. Cf. his dissertation (manuscript), 'SDQ im Alten Testament. Eine traditions-geschichtliche Untersuchung' (dissertation, Heidelberg, 1953); *idem*, 'Wesen und Ursprung der "Gemeinschaftstreue" im Israel der Königszeit', *Zeitschrift für evangelische Ethik* 5 (1961), pp. 72-90; *idem*, '*sdq*', *TDOT*, II.

6. Cf. Koch, *Um das Prinzip der Vergeltung*, pp. 126-29.

and ethics, were not separated, but also that for the judgment on good and bad the relation to the community is decisive. The way Koch chooses his expressions, using the term 'faithfulness to the community' for 'righteousness', is intended to introduce a terminology better conformed to biblical thinking. Schmid went a step further beyond these first attempts. The starting point for his deliberations is the remarkable breadth of the term 'justice': it comprises, beyond the juridical scope[1] and wisdom, also nature/fertility, war/victory, cult/offering and kingdom.[2] Behind these special fields a comprehensive world-order becomes visible. which as a whole can be characterized by the term 'righteousness'.

The main part of the work[3] is dedicated to proving that the idea of such a comprehensive world-order as common to the ancient Near East forms the background also for the Israelite form of this thinking. Schmid tries to show this in several chains of argumentation: through the old oriental king ideology which describes the king as responsible for law, wisdom, nature, war and cult (offering); through the relation of the king to the respective highest god; above all through the Egyptian term *ma'at* which has the same breadth of meaning and corresponds most exactly to the biblical term 'righteousness'.[4]

Of special interest in our context, however, is the third part of Schmid's book, in which he discusses the question of how and in what manner the idea of righteousness as it was common to the ancient Near East was adopted by Israel.[5] The answer to the question how is remarkable only by offering thoughts on the content of Canaanite ideas which have been adopted,[6] but is silent about the circumstances and the places where such ideas could have been taken over. That seems to lie outside the interest of the author. On this first sub-chapter follows a second superscribed 'Specific Israelite Forms'.[7] It contains a

1. J. Scharbert ('Gerechtigkeit. I. Altes Testament', *TRE* 12 [1984], pp. 404-11) restricts origin and use of the term (in opposition to Fahlgren and Koch) explicitly on the forensic level.

2. Cf. l.c.14-23.

3. Part B, pp. 13-77; cf. also pp. 166-86.

4. In principle, however, Schmid takes the conceptual realm as common to the ancient Near East. Also the look upon the Sumerian term *me* belongs hereto (*Gerechtigkeit*, pp. 61-66).

5. *Gerechtigkeit*, pp. 78-165.

6. Superscription to part C, I, p. 78.

7. Superscription to part C, II, pp. 104-65.

detailed overview of the whole Old Testament from the Yahwist until Qohelet. As Schmid formulates it, he sees a decisive modification against Canaanite thinking in 'that for the Old Testament "order" is a basically historical entity'.[1] He means—and tries to show this in his overview of the Scriptures of the Old Testament—that the ideas of 'righteousness' in the biblical traditions are subject to a continual change. But he thinks also that certain parts of the 'righteousness'-thinking are historical—among them belong law and also wisdom in his opinion—while others are ahistorical—in his opinion nature and cult.[2] The latter were pushed back by Israelite thinking, the former adopted. 'Both one will have to see in the last resort as a consequence of the historical god- and world-understanding of Israel.'[3] Schmid developed these considerations still further in some essays. Related are especially the contributions 'Jahweglaube und altorientalisches Weltordnungsdenken' and 'Altorientalisch–alttestamentliche Weisheit und ihr Verhältnis zur Geschichte'.[4] In the second of these essays Schmid is interested in showing that the old oriental wisdom (especially the Egyptian) is also conditioned by the historical change of orders and answers upon them, and in refuting the common understanding of wisdom as 'ahistorical'. In the summary of the first essay Schmid expressly states that he is engaged in disproving the antiquated picture of Israelite religious history, as it had been stamped above all by von Rad, as marked by salvation history only and standing in opposition to the old oriental order-thinking. Instead this old oriental world-order-thinking is 'the self-speakingly presupposed horizon of intuition and thinking, in the frame of which Israel made all its experiences'.[5] The result, however, is not that now the identity of the Israelite faithful thinking with the old oriental thinking would be completed. On the contrary, Schmid is convinced of being able to observe the peculiarity of Israel in its environment, namely that Israel under the impression of its specific experiences in history—Schmid mentions exodus, pre-exilic prophets, threat to and destruction of city

---

1. *Gerechtigkeit*, p. 169; cf. p. 172.
2. *Gerechtigkeit*, pp. 172-73.
3. *Gerechtigkeit*, p. 173.
4. Both in the collection *Alttestamentliche Welt in der alttestamentlichen Theologie* (Zürich: Theologischer Verlag, 1974), pp. 31-63 and 64-90.
5. *Altorientalische Welt*, p. 59.

and nation—arrived at a continuous modification of this order.[1] In correspondence to that, in Israel 'nature and cult was put back by the (historical) order-thinking'.[2] However, 'in the postexilic period, in which faith was understood as ahistoric to a large degree', the order also became ahistoric: 'Law and wisdom are treated as inflexible entities, the word-group צדק is used for expressing a mechanistic teaching of retribution'.[3]

It would not be helpful to occupy oneself with the last cited utterance, in which still the approach of M. Noth, who spoke of the law as 'an absolute entity in the late period',[4] seems to be reflected. The question is more open, if the insight that the order is changeable and connected with history is to be regarded as specific for Israel in contrast to the order-thinking of its environment. Here Schmid seems partly to contradict his own theses in indicating so energetically the historical changeability of old oriental wisdom.[5] In addition to that, it has become more and more questionable whether the category 'historical thinking' is fitting at all for defining the peculiarity of the faith of Israel, above all after B. Albrektson[6] has proved that the historic acting of the gods is a common old oriental belief and not restricted to the faith of Israel. Also the other definitions of Schmid, for instance that nature and cult are 'ahistorical in their approach'—he identifies that with a cyclic understanding of time—could be debated.

Behind all, however, the question is hidden as to how the relation between the faith of Israel and the faith of the Canaanites is to be defined historically and systematically. To specify it in the frame of our symposium: what could one say on it in connection with the term 'righteousness'? This problem is becoming actual because of, among other things, the new model for the origins of Israel, which Niels Peter Lemche, in a voluminous book of theory, *Early Israel*,[7] has

1. *Altorientalische Welt*, pp. 61-63.

2. *Gerechtigkeit*, pp. 172-73.

3. *Gerechtigkeit*, p. 173.

4. See M. Noth, 'Die Gesetze im Pentateuch (ihre Voraussetzungen und ihr Sinn)', in *idem, Gesammelte Studien zum Alten Testament* (Munich, 1957), pp. 9-141, superscription p. 112.

5. 'Altorientalisch-alttestamentliche Weisheit'.

6. *History and the Gods. An Essay on the Idea of Historical Events as Divine Manifestations in the Ancient Near East and in Israel* (Lund: Gleerup, 1967).

7. *Early Israel. Anthropological and Historical Studies on the Israelite Society before the Monarchy* (VTSup, 37; Leiden: Brill, 1985). Cf. also S. Herrmann,

recently developed. In the following book, *Ancient Israel*,[1] he has added to the socio-historical description also a chapter on 'Israelite Religion'.[2] Lemche's theory is the most recent variety of the 'sociological' solution for the question of Israel's origins, as it was proposed by G.E. Mendenhall[3] for the first time and has been modified by N.K. Gottwald[4] in combination with a revolutionary model. In spite of their internal differences,[5] it is common to all advocates of this approach that they do not connect the origin of Israel with a group of nomadic immigrants, but with the Canaanite subject population of the country itself. They would have liberated themselves either by a revolution or—as Lemche thinks—by a gradual emancipation from the city-states, which ruled over them, and had risen to an independent political existence in the country. Such a picture of the earliest development must, of course, have important consequences for the origins of the religion of Israel. With special attention one opens therefore the relevant chapter in Lemche's *Ancient Israel*.[6] Here we meet many reflections, which are common with other recent works that have the same intention: to replace the traditional picture of the history of the religion of Israel, as it can be gained out of the present form of biblical tradition, by a reconstruction of the actual origins of this religion, as they can be proven critically. The presupposition for this method, which Lemche also shares, is that 'the oldest texts were revised when the Israelite legalistic religion was promulgated, so that these sources were more or less made to agree with "orthodox" Yahwism'.[7] Behind this revision, according to these scholars, one can detect, if with some trouble then also with a certain degree of certainty, an old Israelite form of religion which is, in important

above, pp. 110-11.

1. *Ancient Israel. A New History of Israelite Society* (The Biblical Seminar; Sheffield: JSOT Press, 1988).

2. *Ancient Israel*, pp. 197-257.

3. 'The Hebrew Conquest of Palestine', *BA* (1962), pp. 66-87.

4. *The Tribes of Yahweh. A Sociology of the Religion of Liberated Israel, 1250– 1050 B.C.* (Maryknoll, NY: Orbis/London: SCM Press, 1979). Cf. also the discussion in *JSOT* 7 (1978) and in D.N. Freedman and D.F. Graf (eds.), *Palestine in Transition* (Sheffield: JSOT Press, 1983).

5. On the historical questions I refer to the paper of S. Herrmann, cf. above, pp. 105-16.

6. Cf. *Ancient Israel*, pp. 197-257.

7. *Ancient Israel*, p. 224.

aspects at least, syncretistic, if not a species of Canaanite religion itself. For this more extreme opinion one can mention for example B. Lang, who in his essay 'The Yahweh-Alone-Movement' describes the pre-exilic Israelite religions as follows: 'During the four and a half centuries of Israelite monarchy. . . the dominant religion is polytheistic and undifferentiated from that of its neighbours'.[1] 'The Breakthrough to Monotheism'[2] according to Lang is but the result of the struggle of the 'Yahweh-alone-movement' which passed through several phases; not earlier than in the Babylonian exile it became victorious. In pre-exilic times Yahweh is only a national god like Kemos and the national gods of other small neighbouring peoples. For the rest every Israelite adores his personal protective god[3] and a multitude of special gods besides, who are in charge of special fields as, for example, fecundity, but above all El as creator god, who kept this role invariably.[4] Lemche differs from Lang in that he does not accept the polytheistic model even for the pre-exilic period. For him it is 'admissable to concentrate on the figure of Yahweh',[5] as he was doubtless the national god in Judah and presumably also in the northern kingdom, Israel. According to Lemche he, however, assumed important traits of El and even Baal.[6] As a *type* of god, Jerusalem's Yahweh was 'an El-type. . . '; as such he was the creator and maintainer of the cosmos and of Israel. As combater of chaos he also assumed traits of Baal.[7] But in his role as El, Yahweh in the earliest period is also the head of the pantheon, and Ashera is his consort. The study of certain psalms as sources for the pre-exilic religion of Jerusalem, which have remained the most unaffected by the later orthodox revisions of the tradition, shows this god as 'the main god in the royal sanctuary of Jerusalem' (in which according to 2 Kgs 23.1-

---

1. B. Lang, *Monotheism and the Prophetic Minority* (Sheffield: JSOT Press, 1983), p. 20.

2. *Monotheism*, superscription on p. 41.

3. Cf. especially H. Vorlaender, *Mein Gott. Die Vorstellungen vom persoenlichen Gott im Alten Orient und im Alten Testament* (AOAT, 23; Neukirchen–Vluyn: Neukirchener Verlag, 1975); R. Albertz, *Persoenliche Froemmigkeit und ofizielle Religion* (Stuttgart: Calwer Verlag, 1978).

4. Lang, *Monotheism*, pp. 20ff.

5. *Ancient Israel*, p. 238.

6. *Ancient Israel*, p. 238.

7. *Ancient Israel*, p. 238.

28 other gods were also worshipped).[1] As such he had special close
relations to the kingdom. In the course of the period of the kings the
relation between the Davidic king and his god had been formed in
such a way that the king was regarded as man and viceregent of god,
who was responsible for the maintenance of 'justice' and the order of
the cosmos. In the pre-exilic Israelite religion, which was of a
Canaanite type or 'a classical West Asiatic religion',[2] the later, postexilic form was already preformed in its system. The prophet, in
Lemche's opinion, had an important influence on the development, as
the cultic elements, which should secure fecundity, were pushed into
the background, and the stress instead was laid upon justice as an ethical demand. But in principle this was just a shift of accent, to which
later other points came such as the supersession of the relation
between god and king by the 'covenant' between god and people.

As we see, this approach ascribes to the Canaanite element a central
role for the fundamentals of Israelite religion. The origin of the
totally different historic traditions of Israel, which tell about the stay
in Egypt, exodus and wandering through the desert, and finally about
a conquest of the land from outward, remains an open question. In
Early Israel, Lemche moves on the line of scepsis, which is usual in
recent research, and denies the historical reliability of such traditions
because of their late origin in the period of the exile. In his opinion it
is impossible to reconstruct a history of Israel before the year 1000.[3]
In his more recent book the method has changed a little; here at least
passages such as Judg. 5.5 and Ps. 68.9 are quoted for Yahweh's
origin from Sinai. But all in all, the rather brief remarks on the whole
problem come to a rather negative result; the importance of Moses,
for example, is summarized in the way of Noth: just the tradition of
Moses' tomb is known.[4]

In my opinion this approach has methodologically grave weak-
nesses; above all it deals with the Pentateuch tradition without
sufficiently valuing the ways in which the traditions developed. But
that is not my topic and can be left aside at this point. However, the
rejection of one-sided theses should not seduce us into disregarding

1. *Ancient Israel*, p. 229.
2. *Ancient Israel*, p. 239.
3. *Early Israel*, pp. 377-85. Cf. the criticism of W. Thiel, 'Vom revolutionären
zum evolutionären Israel', *TLZ* 133 (1988), pp. 401-10.
4. *Ancient Israel*, pp. 252-57.

worthwhile observations which are contained in the model. One correct observation which was not made by Lemche, but is the result of manifold recent research, is the significant impact of the 'Canaanite' religion Israel met with in the country. This observation remains valid, even if one is prepared to allow the 'invasion-model' for the early history of Israel a much greater importance.

But then it is remarkable—and now I am coming back to Schmid with whom I began—that the pre-Israelite religion of the country has become important for the content of the later faith of Israel, especially in procuring central theological and ethical terms. One of Schmid's results was also that the term 'righteousness' (צדק/צדקה) appears in parallelism to other terms which likewise are related to the world-order; the most important is the term for 'peace, welfare', שלום.[1] Here the conclusions of Schmid meet with the results of others who stressed the role of Jerusalem for the transfer of Canaanite mythological and conceptual terms.[2] Even if singular contingent events such as the exodus were constitutive for the faith of Israel, and this people brought its god with it out of the southern desert, the inhabitants of the country made the cultural and terminological heritage available by which this faith and the method belonging to it articulated itself. The term 'righteousness' therewith played a central role.

From this it may be concluded that this faith, from its beginnings, was designed not to particularity but to universalism. There apparently existed a broad openness and readiness to adopt from the Canaanites world-understanding, ideas of god, ethos, presumably also the language, and to combine it with the Israelites' own, specifically salvation-historical traditions. What we can just presume because of the scarcity of sources is that this adoption was not restricted to Jerusalem. For the northern kingdom a similar development is likely; there the holy site of Bethel even kept its name containing the theophoric syllable, *el*.[3] If on the other side there existed also a determined delimitation—we just mention Hosea, Ezra/Nehemiah, the Maccabees—we are always dealing with critical junctions in Israel's

---

1. Cf. H.H. Schmid, *šalom. 'Frieden' im Alten Orient und im Alten Testament* (SBS, 51; Stuttgart: Katholisches Bibelwerk, 1971).

2. I mention F. Stolz, *Strukturen und Figuren im Kult von Jerusalem* (BZAW, 118; Berlin: de Gruyter, 1970); O.H. Steck, *Friedensvorstellungen im alten Jerusalem* (TSt, 111; Zürich: Theologischer Verlag, 1972).

3. On Bethel cf. K.D. Schunck, 'Bethel', *TRE* 5 (1980), pp. 757-59.

history where its very existence was at stake. The universal claim that the god on Zion is the Lord of the cosmos was never limited. As standard for this rule the idea of righteousness was erected. God's righteousness,[1] which includes mercy, forgiveness, love, has remained from thereon a central theme of Jewish and Christian theological thinking. Human righteousness as standard of ethical acts for both communities of faith is just then theologically qualified if it reflects divine righteousness.

1.　Cf. F. Crüsemann, 'Jahwes Gerechtigkeit (*s^edaqa/sädäq*) im Alten Testament', *EvT* 36 (1976), pp. 427-50.

Moshe Hayyim Luzzatto's Thought Against the Background of Theodicy Literature*

Rivka Schatz-Uffenheimer

R. Moses Hayyim Luzzatto of Padua (*Ramḥa''l*), who lived in the first half of the eighteenth century, is remembered among the Jewish people as one who bore the aura of an enlightened genius; as the father of modern Hebrew literature; as a Kabbalist whose writings were too profound to be understood by anyone, and as one who was persecuted for the sin of messianism; as an individual whose prolific writings were destined either to be burned of hidden away; and as one who was banned from the Jewish community, but whose glory increased together with the severity of the ban against him.

Bialik's essay, 'The Young Man from Padua', concludes with the words:

> If thus far the name of R. Hayyim Luzzatto has not been inscribed upon the gate of honor of the sanctuary of Hebrew creativity, to be touched reverently by everyone who enters or leaves. . . and if thus far we have not known how to make the radiance of his life and of his personality and the creation of his spirit reside in the soul of the generation, as an eternal light not to be extinguished—this is a sign of how greatly impoverished we ourselves are.[1]

I do not know if we are impoverished due to a lack of reverence, for already in the previous century, and even more so in our own time, many people turned their attention to his image, each one in his own fashion—beginning with Almansi and Gerondi, and continuing with

* Translated from a Hebrew article published in *Proceedings of the Israel Academy of Sciences and Humanities*, VII: 12 (1988), pp. 275-91, and based upon a lecture given at a conference commemorating the fifth anniversary of the death of Professor Gershom Scholem, Jerusalem, 24 February 1987.

1. 'The Lad from Padua', in *Kol Kitvei N.H. Bialik* (Tel Aviv, 1949), p. 229 (Hebrew).

Abraham Kahana, Joseph Kohen-Zedek, Rothstein, R. Samuel Luria, Simon Ginzburg, Isaiah Tishby, Meir Benayahu, and most recently Hayyim Friedlander, who has published a selection of Ramhal's writings amended on the basis of manuscripts. To this list one may add the dozens of studies concerning Luzzatto's literary output.

We are nevertheless impoverished in terms of our understanding of his thought and the focus of its concern, and its connections with his substantial creativity in the area of Kabbalah—both in *Zohar* and Lurianic Kabbalah. Luzzatto's writings carry, not only a message, but also a polemical thrust, whose concern has not been fully clarified to this very day. There are those who have already noted the inadequacy of the conventional explanation, that is, that his thought is essentially a defence of the Kabbalah against the attacks of R. Leone of Modena, who lived about one hundred years before him. Nor has there been any analysis of the sources of his theological–ethical thought, even though Luzzatto has been interpreted, more than anything else, as a Mussar author.

Luzzatto was familiar with the religious thought of his period, and read the works of contemporary Christian theologians in Latin and French. Girondi already noted that: 'he was learned in natural science, scholastic thought, Torah and divine science, and he studied Latin, Greek and French'[1]—divine science being none other than theology. Indeed, all of his writings bear the mark of the theological debates current in Europe at the end of the seventeenth and the beginning of the eighteenth century within what might be referred to as the 'theodicy' tendency—although it is clear that the remarks of Luzzatto and of the Christian theodiceans were only partly addressed to the same audience. The main representatives of this tendency were the philosopher Wilhelm Gottfried Leibniz and the archbishop of Dublin, William King.[2] From a certain point of view, the neo-Platonist

---

1. M.D. Girondi, *Kerem Hemed* 2 (1836), p. 55. In a letter dated 1735, the rabbis of Venice mention his involvement in Latin literature with contempt: 'How can one marry the Holy Tongue and the tongue of the holy *Zohar* one who has already married its sister Lotan, called the chosen by the Christians?' See S. Ginzburg (ed.), *R. Moshe Hayyim Luzzatto u-venei doro: 'Osef 'iggerot u-te'udot* (Jerusalem, 1934), p. 274. (Henceforth *Iggerot*)

2.   In an appendix to his book, *Essais de théodicée sur la bonté de Dieu, la liberté de l'homme et l'origine du mal* (1710). Leibniz brings a summary of W. King's book, *De Origine Mali* (London, 1702). The author's name is not mentioned, the work being described only as 'the book concerning the origins of evil published

movement in Cambridge, the most prominent member of which was Henry More, who was renowned for his knowledge of Kabbalah, also belongs to this stream.

Theodicy refers to the justification of God's guidance or rulership of the world through the free exercise of his will, thereby implying the freeing of God from responsibility for evil within the world and the strengthening of his exclusive status. It is directed against various forms of scepticism, such as that of the adherents of dualistic Manichaeism or of pantheism. In brief, theodicy takes a fundamentally theistic theological position; theodicy as a line of defence against scepticism is not new to human thought.

We shall discuss here those of its expression, which are relevant to the thought of Luzzatto—to wit, the theodicy of Leibniz and King, whose books were, in my opinion, influential upon the structure of his thought, its arguments and philosophical basis. Of relevance here are Leibniz's *Theodicy*, published in French in 1710, and King's Latin work, *Essay on the Origin of Evil*, published in 1702. An English edition of the latter was published in 1731 in London by the Anglican priest Edmond Law, with the addition of a commentary.[1]

recently in London'. At the beginning of this appendix, Leibniz relates that he encountered the book in its Latin version, that it is very learned and elegantly written, and that it was published in London and thereafter in Bremen. Leibniz made use of this book in his polemic with P. Bayle. Whether or not Luzzatto saw Leibniz's *Theodicy*—a point which seems certain to me—there can be no doubt that he knew King's book, particularly as King's arguments are literally implied by the structure of Luzzatto's book, *Da'at Tevunot*. My student, Ms Zvia Rubin, has pointed out to me that Rabbi David Cohen (the *Nazir*) already mentioned the possibility that Luzzatto was influenced by Leibniz's *Theodicy*: see his *Sefer Qol Nevu'ah* (Jerusalem, 1970), p. 307: 'R. Moshe Hayyim Luzzatto, 1707–1747, perhaps made some use of the views of the new philosopher (1647–1717), the author of the *Theodicy*—the justification of the Divine judgment—after which he was drawn by the way of reason and distinction'. It is a curious fact that another member of the Luzzatto family, the nineteenth-century thinker Samuel David Luzzatto of Padua, testifies to his great excitement at the ethical approach of the theodicy in his anti-Kabbalistic treatise, *Vikkuah 'al Hokhmat ha-Qabbalah ve'al Qadmut Sefer ha-Zohar* (Gorizia, 1851), specifically mentioning the approach of S. Clarke, King's partner. In my opinion, he refers to the very same book. He evidently found the book itself in the library in Padua. This fact strengthens further the conjecture that Ramhal had found this book there some one hundred years earlier. See below, for details of Shadal's description of the theory of theodicy.

   1. I will henceforth refer to the English edition: W. King, *An Essay on the Origin*

I would like to cite the following remarks of Scholem concerning our subject:

> These outspoken theists among the theosophists never ceased to reinter-pret the doctrine of the *Partsufim* in a sense designed to strip it of its obvi-ous mythical elements, a tendency particularly interesting in the case of Luzzatto whose doctrine on the world of divinity was the offspring not of pure theory but of mystical vision.[1]

Although I do not identify the essential problem of theosophy in this case the way Scholem does, it is incumbent upon me to mention the theistic note attributed by Scholem to the teaching of Luzzatto, against which I have complained for some time.

The ideational basis for the 'theodicy' literature returns us to the foundations of Platonic and neo-Platonic thought, its influence during the Middle Ages, and the crossroads which it created within Christian theology. In a few brief sentences, which are necessary for under-standing the logical structure and theological argumentation shared by the theodiceans and Luzzatto, this may be described as follows. Already in Plato we find the assumption that the absolute does not exist by itself, and that the world of ideas is translated into practical terms—that is, there is a realization of the ideas, requiring the exis-tence of the temporal, the material, and the limited, which are logi-cally connected to their source. Thus, the existence of all evil is derived from the idea of the good, because all ideal possibilities have a practical translation. It is the nature of the idea to be revealed in exis-tence, for were this not so the connection between the two worlds would be arbitrary[2] and unintelligible. On the basis of this assump-tion, namely, that there is no potential which cannot be realized, the concept of the good became identical with this realization; in other words, the world was deemed necessary for the perfection of God. There are those scholars who claim that this cosmic determinism is required by Plato's approach, which leaves no room for God's free-dom of choice—even though Plato himself was not interpreted in this manner in the Middle Ages. Plotinus as well, who saw evil as an inseparable part of being—the definition of the universe as 'the best of all possible ones' necessary including evil—arrived at the basis of

of Evil (trans. E. Law; Cambridge, 1731).

1. G. Scholem, *Major Trends in Jewish Mysticism* (New York, 1945), p. 272.
2. A.O. Lovejoy, *The Great Chain of Being* (Cambridge, MA, 1933), p. 52.

theodicy through his system concerning the metaphysical necessity of evil,[1] contending that one who removes evil from the world thereby removes providence itself.[2] In all of these systems, the concept of good was clearly identified with that of being, so that if being is good, it must be the best possible, and all possibilities must therein reach their fullest expression.

This theory was common in the seventeenth and eighteenth centuries under the name of optimism, which states that the goodness of 'the best of all possible worlds' is not defined by the absence of evil, but precisely through its presence.[3] Evil is defined as necessary within the rational structure of the cosmos, the appropriateness of whose order is so perfect that there can be nothing greater than it; the world is made more beautiful by the presence of evil. The possibility of determinism, which seems to be suggested by these fortuitous formulations, is mitigated by the introduction of the motif of divine will, which limits this determinism and introduces a new nuance—namely, that the universe is good, not only because of the marvellous order and grading within it, but because God chose it and determined its purpose, as expressed in the service done by graded evil on behalf of the good. Thanks to this motif, nature acquires an ethical meaning: the existence therein of destruction, annihilation and death serve the overall purposes of existence, so that that which seems lacking and evil is, in truth, nothing other than good. The adoption of this stance, in addition to its systematic and rational value *per se*, is also indicative of a change in the view of man's status in the cosmos: man is no longer seen as the reason for existence, nor is his happiness the be all and end all. The fact that there are some things which are not pleasant to human beings simply indicates the fact that the world was not created for him,[4] and that the reason for being must be sought in other centres of gravity. It is therefore clear that what is meant here by the concept of good is not identical with man's existential happiness; the cosmos, or the concept of unity and perfection, seem more likely as the *raison d'être* for the universe. This idea is very noticeable in the viewpoint

1. Lovejoy, *Chain*, p. 64.
2. See Plotinus, *Enneads* (London, 1980), 3.3, 'On Providence, ii', pp. 113ff.
3. Lovejoy, *Chains*, p. 72.
4. Luzzatto alludes, for example, to the idea that the world was not created for righteousness, but for the revelation of his unity; see *Da'at Tevunot* (ed. H. Friedlander; B'nai Berak, 1975), p. 32.

of Luzzatto, particularly in his books *Da'at Tevunot* and *Ql''h Pithei Hokhmah.*

Eighteenth-century thinkers do not attempt to belittle the fact of evil or to claim its unreality, but rather argue its necessity—not because God creates with his full potentiality, but precisely because he chose to create the best possible world.[1] Divine omnipotence—that is, God's ability to do everything within creation—became a point of contention among theologians, because it contradicted the idea of God's free-willed choice.[2] The view which allows God to choose one world from among the many possibilities allowed by his 'omnipotence' was considered an orthodox approach,[3] as opposed to the various heretical claims which stated that, if God is indeed omnipotent, he ought to have prevented evil, the downfall of man, or the original sin of Adam, which was anticipated from the beginning. Why does he not prevent the existential suffering of the human race in general?[4] And whence has he the right to punish and to reward, if from the outset he could have prevented man's difficult and problematic confrontation with evil and with the forbidden?

The optimistic theodiceans related to these questions through a thesis which justified God's way in a rational manner, drawing upon the debate conducted throughout the Middle Ages on the basis of

---

1.   The definition of omnipotence given in Luzzatto states: 'God, blessed be He, is certainly able to make. . . all of creation in the greatest perfection. Moreover, by His law it is fitting that this should be so. . . and it is as if He prevented the attributes of His perfection and his goodness from acting in accordance with the law of his greatness. . . but to act with that same quality that He wished according to the purpose intended by His sublime thought' (*Da'at Tevunot*, pp. 7-8). Again: 'Because, as it were, He withdrew His great and infinite ability' (pp. 7-8). Creation is defined: 'not according to the law of His perfection' (p. 20).

2.   It seems to me that in the Middle Ages one can see quite clearly the conflict between divine omniscience and the idea of free choice, and not necessarily between the idea of omnipotence and of free choice. See J. Guttman, 'The Problem of Free Choice in the Teachings of Hasdai Crescas and the Muslim Aristotelians', *Dat u-Mada'* (Jerusalem, 1955), pp. 149-68 (Hebrew). Concerning this matter, see Z. Harvey, 'The Authorship of the Reservations Concerning Determinism in Crescas' *Or ha-Shem*—The Testimony of MS. Firenze', *Qiryat Sefer* 55 (1980), pp. 794-801 (Hebrew). Luzzatto relates to the system of values located between an omnipotence of endless possibility and free choice, as strikingly expressed among the theodicists of the seventeenth and eighteenth centuries.

3.   This polemic is also to be seen in *Da'at Tevunot*, pp. 21-23, 29.

4.   See *Da'at Tevunot*, p. 26.

Platonic theories, as interpreted in the spirit of the churches. It was essential for them to prove that good is the result of the existence of evil, and that it cannot enter into the world save by means of the existence of evil. This is an acceptance of an unavoidable judgment which derives, not from the arbitrary will of the creator, but from the inevitable logic of the absolute.[1] Voltaire opposed this position with the empassioned cry: 'Vouz criez "tout est bien" d'une voix lamentable!'—'You say "everything is good" with a miserable voice!'

The above-mentioned works of Leibniz and of King, which were both reprinted in numerous editions over a short period of time, were directed against Pierre Bayle who, in his encyclopaedia *Dictionaire historique et critique* (1695–1697), argued against the dogmatic approach in philosophy and religion and attempted to expose the contradiction between religion and reason. Bayle, who for a brief period was close to Spinoza, cast doubt upon the intellectual credibility of theological proofs as rational arguments.

The Spinozists, of course, constituted an additional element opposed to the concept of 'divine freedom'. We no longer need to guess at Leibniz's attitude towards this phenomena; the nineteenth-century French scholar de Careil discovered a manuscript of Leibniz, which included the dispute of those days which revolved around what was then called 'modern Kabbalah'—that is, Lurianic Kabbalah—and its connection to Spinozist pantheism.[2] Various figures in the Christian

---

1. Lovejoy, *Chain*, p. 211.

2. In two works whose manuscripts were discovered by de Careil in the library at Hanover, we find extremely interesting expression of Leibniz's addressing himself to the question of theodicy within Maimonides and the importance of Maimonides to Spinoza. Through his reading of (the Latin translation of) Maimonides' *Guide*, Leibniz was interested to learn how theodicy appeared in the various schools influenced by Aristotelianism. It is clear that Leibniz thought that there were significant traces of Maimonidean thought in Spinoza. On this problem, which very much concerned his contemporaries, see S. Pines, *Bein Mahshevet Yisra'el le-Mahshevet ha-'Amim* (Jerusalem, 1977), pp. 306-14; A. Foucher de Careil, *Leibniz, la philosophie juive et la cabale* (Paris, 1861), Introduction. The second problem, concerning the relation of Kabbalah to Spinoza, is primarily discussed in A. de Careil, *Refutation inedite de Spinoza par Leibniz* (Paris, 1854). This latter book was directed against Spinoza's ethical theory, and was evidently written between 1706 and 1710. Johann Georg Wachter, in his *Elucidarius Cabbalisticus*, argues that there is a resemblance between Kabbalah and Spinozism, and an influence of the Kabbalah upon Spinoza. Leibniz was influenced by the approach of

world have pointed towards the responsibility of the Kabbalah for Spinoza's ideas regarding this question. In his book on Abraham Herrera, the Marrano Kabbalist who wrote in Spanish, Gershom Scholem has described in detail the history of this debate as it was conducted in Europe in the middle and end of the seventeenth century.[1]

When Luzzatto defended the Kabbalah in his book, *Hoqqer u-Mequbbal*, he spontaneously defended monistic theism[2] of the type of the theodiceans. The argument against the Spinozist approach arguing the unity of the creator and the created likewise appears in this book: 'For it is impossible under any circumstance to say that His light, may He be blessed, would be activated and emanate down so that the creator would become the created'. That is to say that Luzzatto attempted, among other things, to show that the Kabbalah is not heretical, and is neither pantheistic nor Manichaean—the anti-Manichaean argument being more greatly stressed.[3] There can be no doubt that this theological debate was also influential within the Jewish world, and that many people had begun to feel contempt for the Kabbalah as a result of the accusations addressed against Judaism because of it. Luzzatto's complaints against the negative attitude

Wachter, and in the above-mentioned book describes at length the identity between Kabbalah and Spinozism.

1. G. Scholem, *Avraham Kohen Herrera, Ba'al Sha'ar ha-Shamayim* (Jerusalem, 1978), esp. pp. 47ff. (in German: *Abraham Cohen Herrera. Das Buch Sha'ar Shamamyim, oder Pforte des Himmels*. Einl. G. Scholem. Aus dem Lateinischen übersetzt von Friedrich Häussermann [Frankfurt am Main, 1974], pp. 41-61). Scholem also discusses the incident of Wachter and Leibniz at some length.

2. This theodicy, including that of Luzzatto, is in fact monistic. See *Da'at Tevunot*, p. 89, where he summarizes as follows: 'we find that we cannot say that good and evil are two [separate] influences'.

3. I will only mention a few of the theses presented in defence of the Kabbalah in the book *Hoqqer u-Mequbbal* (i.e. *Ma'amar ha-Vikuah*), which are directly related to the approach of the theodicy literature: (1) the Kabbalah is rational; (2) the doctrine of *Sefirot* does not imply dualism; (3) God is not the primal matter from which the world is created; (4) there is no inquiry made into the essence of the Emanator; (5) *Ein Sof* is the omnipotent—that which was able to emanate—while the *Sefirot* are what he wished to emanate, the concept of will being related to rulership; (6) God's activity is purposeful and limited, and the world was not created by means of his omnipotence; (7) order and number are necessary according to the deliberate intention; (8) the Kabbalah documents the 'general intention' [of God], and infers the order of value of limit and law, meaning that it is 'the inclusion of all order'.

towards the Kabbalah are reflected between the lines of the above-mentioned book.[1] There were even Christians who appealed to Luzzatto to come to the defence of the Kabbalah. More than a hint of this appears in one of the letters[2] Luzzatto wrote to his teacher, R. Isaiah Bassan, in which he says:

> In passing I will tell his honor a new thing. Today I received a lengthy letter from the judge Aquila Picci, known to his honor from Vincenza, where he is a judge. He wrote to me pleading for me to write to him my opinion concerning a polemic which took place before the prince of that place with another person from that city concerning the matter of our Kabbalah; he asserted that it is a very holy and sublime wisdom, revealed from the secrets of the Torah in truth, while this city-dweller denied this, and said that it is vanity. The latter brought in support the words of R. Leone of Modena in his book, in which he demonstrates that it is without any basis and that it is all vanity of vanities.[3] Would the honor of his Torah see how far the bitter fruit of this person goes, that even among the Gentiles his poison has spread! Also a great noblewoman from Genoa, who is a very wise Frenchwoman, sent for me in Venice greatly beseeching to speak with me about this holy Kabbalah, to hear whether it is true or not. And she knows in truth all the words of the holy Ari, z''l, from beginning to end, as I was very astonished to hear.

R. Isaiah Bassan understood that Luzzatto wished to defend the truth and importance of the Kabbalah, but he explicitly weakened his hand when he stated that he did not have much chance of success, after Joseph Solomon Delmedigo (*Yashar*) of Candia and R. Aviad Sar-Shalom had been unsuccessful.[4] However, Luzzatto's teacher was not aware of the theological argument underlying his stand in support of the Kabbalah. Luzzatto repeatedly stated, not only that people did not

---

1. 'The entire world is amazed by the Kabbalah', and Luzzatto attempts to respond to this amazement and to define its significance; see, for example, *Hoqqer u-Mequbbal* (Jerusalem edn), p. 5.

2. *Iggerot*, pp. 255-56.

3. See his book, *Ari Nohem* (ed. N.S. Leibovitz, Jerusalem, 1929); as well as the testimonies of Isaiah Bassan and Aviad Sar-Shalom, that *Hoqqer u-Mequbbal* was a response to Moden's *Ari Nohem* (*Iggerot*, p. 347).

4. *Iggerot*, p. 245. Rabbi I. Bassan referred to the book, *Mazref la-Hokhmah* by Joseph Solomon Delmedigo, in which Delmedigo came to the defence of Kabbalah in its polemic with R. Elijah Del-Medigo concerning the latter's book, *Behinat ha-Dat*. See *Sefer Behinat ha-Dat* (ed. J.J. Ross; Tel-Aviv, 1984).

understand him, but that evidently not even the sages of the Kabbalah in his generation understood the Kabbalah.[1]

1. At the height of the polemic concerning the writings of R. Hayyim Moshe Luzzatto, R. Joseph Ergas—an important authority in his generation—claimed that there was nothing new in his writings; they are simply a condensation of R. Moshe Cordovero's *Pardes Rimmonim* and writings of other Kabbalists, for which one has no need of a *Maggid*. The claim of a maggidic revelation implies the presence of authoritative novellae—'and it is also proven that the Maggid will not say what is already written in books!' (*Iggerot*, p. 102). In another matter, namely, the question of the extent to which R. Isaac Luria interpreted the *Zohar* according to its true 'intention', there was a great debate between Luzzatto and his teacher, R. Isaiah Bassan. Bassan tried to guide his disciple to interpret only that which Luria had not already interpreted in the *Zohar*.

> 'On this they would have agreed with him', said Bassan. 'But indeed, Nathan of Gaza also said, that he followed in the footsteps of the *Ari*, and he also said that the souls of the righteous were revealed to him; but nevertheless, in the final analysis his words were for naught and were lost, apart from the fact that they caused what they caused. Let us ask from this, what is the difference between this and that? Only that with R. Nathan, the entire intention of his words were directed towards the point of the 'hart' [i.e. Sabbatai Zevi], which was not the case in your words. But in any event, whom does this calm? (*Iggerot*, p. 105).

Regarding the differences in meaning between his commentaries to the *Zohar* and those of Luria, Luzzatto states that Luria 'apprehended far more than me, and he also engaged more than me in asceticism'. The sense is that Luria corrected the external matters, while he himself corrected the inner ones, 'to gather light and strength within his exile' (*Iggerot*, p. 113). Luzzatto argues to his teacher that he sent his explanations to the rabbis of Leghorn 'concerning these passages', and that 'they did not understand them'. The true novellae of Luzzatto, in his own view, were those which he wrote concerning the book of Ecclesiastes, *Tiqqunim*, and Torah.

> But by way of truth I will say that the Rabbi J. Ergas did not fully understand them, and I know that this is because of their extreme brevity, and I did not record the questions and answers, but only presented the premises by means of which those questions would in any event fall. And the honor of his Torah [Bassan] already wrote to me once that you did not find new things revealed therein, and I wrote to you the meaning of their intention in one or two lines, and see what novellae are found in them. For it is all intended to remove the corporeality from the sayings of R. Simeon bar Yohai and R. Isaac Luria, of blessed memories, and to remove the crooked thoughts which were thought about them, to think that they found light rolling about in straight form or in circles, while even in the spiritual realm it is not known what these are. . . ' (*Iggerot*, p. 114).

Further on, he mentions other problems which troubled commentators on the Lurianic Kabbalah, which he sees himself (exclusively?) authorized to interpret. These problems are indeed discussed in his book *Ql''ḥ Pithei Hokhmah*, in which he engages in a principled exegesis with new tendencies (see on this R. Schatz, 'The

I would like to argue here that Luzzatto's theistic–Kabbalistic polemic did not take place in isolation from the general polemic among European Christian theologians concerning theological issues generally. On the contrary, the entire purpose of the book *Da'at Tevunot* cannot be understood, either in terms of its structure or its primary message, if we ignore the above-mentioned works by King or Leibniz. I do not wish to resolve definitely a certain question which is liable to arise here: namely, whether the theological–ethical question was more important to him than the defence of the Kabbalah, or vice versa. It seems to me that these matters are inextricably interrelated, as follows from the fact that Luzzatto presents theological statements even at the beginning of an explicitly Kabbalistic book such as *Ql''h Pithei Hokhmah*. Indeed, the very importance of Kabbalah for Luzzatto lay in the fact that it served theological concerns. The inter-

Metaphysics of Luzzatto in their Ethical Context' [Hebrew], in the forthcoming *Shlomo Pines Memorial Volume*).

> And it will be understood from how all the forms of holy wisdom, are forms of essence, without the quantity, according to the descent of light in the emanation of the actions; and we find that the overall intent of all these rules [*Kuntres Kellalim Rishonim*, 'The Tractate of First Rules'] is to explain the parable in the words of Luria, in his own way. And the "Second Rules". . . in which are answered many difficulties and doubts, concerning the words of the *Ari*, are all of this way, prefaces which remove the difficulties on the way [and in this matter there is of course no need for a *maggid*, for these are theoretical assumptions which come from the intellect] (*Iggerot*, pp. 114-15).

Luzzatto writes to his teacher concerning Ergas: 'Behold, the honor of your Torah has seen well that our teacher, R. Ergas, did not delve to the depth of the [first] Rules, but the Second Rules [i.e. *Ql''h Pithhei Hokhmah*] are difficult for me to send, for they are very long and they have not yet been completed [i.e. in April 1730]' (*Iggerot*, p. 148). See the remarks of R. Moses Hagiz, who persecuted Luzzatto for his own novellae:

> that his *maggid* made him err, to send him to us [i.e. in Venice] in order to reveal the mysteries in his heart, in this novellum made by this lad, as I showed the interpretation of the entire passage in the eyes of the whole household of Israel in all their journeys, that there is none who disagrees to suggest any other interpretation. . . And the main thing with us, *is that Israel in this orphaned generation does not need any new thing introduced from year to year*, as against the truth accepted by us and verified by the words of the early ones. For in my opinion, in this thing, all the communities of Israel, their sages and leaders, agree that innovation is naught but an evil thing, and nothing good comes out of it.

This may possibly be a dig at Luzzatto for his statements about the good which comes out of evil.

esting introduction to his *Hoqqer u-Mequbbal*,[1] which has now been published in full by Friedlander on the basis of a manuscript, attests strongly to the underlying theological background for his Kabbalah. Luzzatto says that the laws guiding this world are to be considered as a kind of esoteric teaching, which was given at Mt Sinai and then forgotten; today, we no longer know it, so we believe that, 'the world does not behave save according to this nature which is visible to our eyes'. In his opinion, such a relationship to the natural world leads to the mistaken world-view, held by many, who think that ethics is that which is revealed in nature; in fact, such an understanding is the temptation of the Other Side. The proper understanding of the world is found in the Kabbalah, which indeed sees 'according to nature', albeit not as is visible to the eyes:

> For the Holy One blessed be He showed them [on Mt Sinai] all of existence and what it is based upon, and they knew clearly that He alone rules, and there is no other rulership, either natural or accidental. . . but that rulership by which He, blessed be His Name, rules, through the profound counsel which He has revealed to them. And He commanded them to reflect in their hearts upon this truth, that they may dwell upon it without any doubt, as they have seen in complete clarity.[2]

Casual examination of this quasi-catechistic formulation reveals that the words, 'He alone rules', are directed against the Manichaean–dualistic approach, which both King and Leibniz also oppose—that is to say, the recognition of evil as an independent element. The sentence,

1.   The introduction is published from MS. Oxford 2593. On this introduction, see I. Tishby, 'A Collection of Kabbalistic Writings from the Archive of M.H. Luzzatto in MS Oxford 2593', *Kiryat Sefer* 53 (1978), pp. 193-94 (Hebrew). Tishby discovers in this introduction various matters which influenced the development of Hasidic teaching; see his 'Traces of Rabbi Moshe Hayyim Luzzatto in Hasidic Thought', *Zion* 43 (1978), pp. 224ff. (Hebrew). Interesting light is shed upon Luzzatto's influence on R. Shneur Zalman of Lyady's *Sefer ha-Tanya* by Yoram Jacobson, 'The Doctrine of Creation in R. Shneur Zalman of Lyady', *Eshel Be'er Sheva'* 1 (1976), pp. 307-68 (Hebrew).

2.   The central thesis of his book, *Da'at Tevunot*, is based upon the assumption that God does not reveal himself as he is in truth, in his omnipotence, but only with 'hiddenness of face'. This is the solution to the problem of the apparent success of evil. The strikingly polemical element in the book explicitly reminds one of the apologia found in theodicy literature concerning the contradiction between the teleological understanding of the world and the way it appears to the eye. See *Da'at Tevunot*, pp. 37-46, and also p. 145.

'there is no other rulership, either natural or accidental', is aimed against atheistic naturalism, as well as against the view that there is no divine providence, which the two above-mentioned theologians also advocated; that they should 'reflect in their hearts upon this truth' refers to the need for systematic and rational exposition of the world, with the aim of silencing scepticism.[1] Indeed, it was this at which Luzzatto aimed, and this is likewise the content of the rationalism of Leibniz and King. 'The profound counsel He has revealed to them' refers to the inclusive approach to understanding, a concept repeatedly used by Luzzatto as a technical term. He protests against the fact that the study of Kabbalah is on the decline due to external reasons pertaining to the accusations against Kabbalah.

> In our great sins, the distance grows day by day, and as the darkness and obscurity increase, it [the Other Side] has constructed fortresses against this thing, and thrust its ramparts in several cases which occurred in the world, with various shaky claims and argument, to send students away from learning this subject, in order to leave all of Israel in the slumber of their heavy Exile, heavier than stone and sand. . .

The controversy concerning the Kabbalah, both amongst the Christians and the Jews, would appear to have caused a decline in its prestige among Jews.

But before we relate to certain fragmentary hints, let us turn to the basic claims of the theodiceans, whose unique logic corresponds almost exactly to the ethical and Kabbalistic doctrine of Ramhal—with the obvious exception of their christological concerns, which under these theoretical circumstances are of no significance.

The dominant tendency of theodicy is to present the concept of divine perfection as one of ethical perfection.[2] Unlike Spinoza, Leibniz believes that the denial of God's freedom of will is a severe limitation of his nature. In his view, God's power of choice is unlimited, there being an infinite number of possibilities of kinds of existence. His wisdom teaches which is the best of them, while his

---

1. Luzzatto frequently stresses the need for rational understanding of the things that he 'wishes that one know with knowledge and understanding' (*Da'at Tevunot*, p. 12). This is true at the beginning of the book, where he distinguishes between verification based upon faith and verification based upon understanding. These were major points of principle in the teaching of Luzzatto, and in my opinion were very influential upon the Hasidisms of Iszbista-Radzin, a point to which I will relate elsewhere.

2. R.L. Saw, *Leibniz* (London, 1954), p. 86.

goodness moves him to bring them into the world. The actual cosmos must entail the maximal degree of perfection: had he not created matter, for example, the metaphysical world would be lacking in perfection, because there would then be several beings which would not exist.[1] In discussing the questions of evil—which is the point of departure of theodicy—Leibniz does not mean to deny that a particular situation is evil, nor does he intend to argue that it will become clear within a broader context that evil is an important component within a good situation of things. Rather, he says, it will become clear that evil is a necessary component in the best of all possible worlds, because the realization of the 'best' world means the existence of perfect beings or 'lacking' ones, whether in the ethical or the metaphysical sense. For the sake of the perfection of the totality, there must be components which, taken in isolation, seem incomplete.[2] Acts of choice do not flow from the nature of the actor by logical necessity, even though all given situations are, in retrospect, subject both to the law of contradiction and to the law of sufficient reason.[3] These assumptions of Leibniz are important in that they support the perception of a world which is both rational and volitional.[4] He likewise wished to avoid a mechanistic description of the world, which after its creation operates in a manner that is, so to speak, independent of the aims or will of its maker.[5] Leibniz remains loyal to the idea that there is a purpose to the world, albeit not necessarily one visible on the surface of things or 'in the sight of the eyes,' to use Luzzatto's words. In his introduction to the English edition of *Theodicy*, Farrer[6] says that, 'His discussions never lack ingenuity, and the system of creation and providence in which they result has much of that luminous serenity which colours

1. Saw, *Leibniz*, p. 87.
2. Saw, *Leibniz*, p. 89.
3. This concept likewise appears in Luzzatto; see *Da'at Tevunot*, pp. 67, 157-58.
4. The motif of will as an expression of a conservative theological approach follows from all of Luzzatto's writings. This motif is intended to explain that God does not perform things through his omnipotence, but with his will, which determines the dimensions of things. See, for example, *Da'at Tevunot*, p. 72. There is also a philosophical background to this stance, which states that one cannot know the things as they are in themselves, but only according to his will. See *Da'at Tevunot*, p. 72.
5. See Saw, *Leibniz*, p. 91.
6. See Leibniz, *Theodicy*, edited and with an introduction by A. Farrer (New Haven, 1952), p. 29.

the best works of the Age of Reason'. In his Introduction to the book, Leibniz declares that the understanding of existence as necessary undermines the freedom of will, which is essential to ethical action, as justice and injustice, praise and shame, reward and punishment, cannot be applied to necessary actions. It is important to realize that there are different levels of necessity, and thereby to recognize that there are those levels which do not cause damage, just as there are those which must inevitably lead to bad results. Leibniz explains further that permission is given for the existence of evil as a *conditio sine qua non* of the good—not out of necessity, but because of the degree of goodness of the things which caused them to be freely chosen by God. While there is in fact a certain predisposition, there is never a necessity for this, so that we may say that the physical necessity is built upon the moral force appropriate to his wisdom. This physical necessity is what brings about order in nature, and it is an axiom of the laws of motion (an interesting subject, utilized by Luzzatto in his description of Lurianic Kabbalah), as well as of several other general laws that God sought to leave in things when he gave them existence. He chose everything in accordance with the general good and order which brought him to this choice.

The three major elements connecting the physical world to the metaphysical world are purposiveness, rationality and ethicality; the framework of Luzzatto's teaching is constituted from these same elements. The common denominator between Leibniz and King is that, first of all, neither of them attribute evil to the perverse will of man or to the Devil, but seek to derive its necessity from divine nature itself: all evils are not only consistent with his infinite wisdom, the goodness and dominion of God, but derive therefrom.

King divides evil into three categories: (1) natural, metaphysical evil; (2) physical evil; (3) moral evil.[1] His main interest is in drawing a clear distinction between moral evil and metaphysical or natural evil. By means of this distinction, it is possible to deepen theodicy, and to remove it from the dualistic straits of Manichaeanism or of Epicureanism, which are also mentioned by Luzzatto in this context. King is opposed to the claim that ethical evil is responsible for the existence of natural evil. In his opinion, these are two different planes of the existence of evil: natural evil could have been prevented neither

---

1. The division of the chapters there represents the three criteria of evil. See *Da'at Tevunot*, pp. 90-91, 104-14, 126-32.

by the choice of good by old Adam or by the removal of choice from man; it is one of the elements of the structure of reality *per se*, whose purpose is the all-inclusive, absolute good. King thereby minimizes the centrality of Adam's sin, and weakens the note of Manichaean and Epicurean rebellion against the weakness of God, who did not wish, as it were, or was unable to prevent the anticipated choice of evil by Adam. King's argument, which emphasizes the necessary structural lack in natural existence, is also based upon Holy Scripture, which in his opinion nowhere states that evil would not have existed in any way had Adam not sinned. God does everything well in its proper time, meaning that he preserves everything in a situation and under conditions which are suitable to the entire system of being. Neither God's goodness nor the perfection which pertains to the nature of things require that all evil be removed: certain created beings tend by nature towards evil, which God must tolerate, for were this not so he would not have created these creatures at all. There are in fact several kinds of evil which would perhaps not exist were it not for sin, namely, those forms of ethical sin which are connected with the expulsion from the Garden of Eden: the cursing of the earth, the dominion of man over woman, the birth of children in pain, and, of course, the greatest of them all, the abolition of the grace of immortality. Everything that man has lost is grace; nothing demanded by nature has changed, as death is a necessity of matter and of the nature of man following the Fall. Refining his logic, King even adds that the barring of man from the Tree of Life following the Fall was for Adam's own good, once grace had been removed from his existence and he began to live according to nature. This punishment contributed to restrict the choice of evil, for which the fear of death is also a positive factor (pp. 195-200). In summary, King stresses that God's goodness goes beyond that justice which is visible to the eye, as did Luzzatto. Justice or divine recompense are connected with ethical evil, and stem from a mistaken choice. Good and evil are brought upon man by himself, in accordance with his own free decisions. King preserves both forms of free choice—that of God and that of man. He used the free choice of God to explain the non-contingent nature of the chosen object, which would otherwise, so to speak, restrict his choice; by the free choice of man, he explained the non-imposition of his choice from without—an imposition which exists among animals, who are dependent upon their physical instincts (p. 252). King thereby expressed his opinion against the determinism of human free will, as did also Luzzatto.

The three-way distinction drawn above is also made by Luzzatto; although the terms used are different, such as 'the way of hiddenness of the face' (*derekh hester panim*), 'the way of justice' (*derekh hamishpat*) and 'the righteous to whom evil befalls' (*zaddiq ve-ra' lo*), their meaning and message within a system of relations is the same. The understanding of evil as part of the structural–rational model is intended to explain the felicitous place of man in the scheme of being. Evil, as a structural concept, provides man with opportunity and does not bring upon him misfortune, but this depends upon his understanding the nature of this opportunity. It is clear that the tone of the traditional approach, stating that evil is connected with sin, is thereby lowered; on the contrary, according to this understanding even moral evil, which stems from sin, is a consequence of privilege, of man's free will, albeit in this case he was so unfortunate as to choose uncorrectly. Physical evil—that is, human suffering—is also seen by Luzzatto more as a consequence of structure than of ethical failure, and there is a subtle set of relations operating here. In any event, lack of 'non-existence' is a necessary part of natural evil, as well as the possibility or condition of moral evil. For King, the removal of evil is like the removal of the cosmos itself, for evil occupies a place within the nature of things similar to that of the radius within a circle, lack being necessary for the harmonious perfection of the mechanical act. The great emphasis upon natural sciences during the period under discussion relates the two systems—the mechanical and the ethical—to one another even more strongly, a point which is particularly striking in Luzzatto's interpretations of the foundations of Lurianic Kabbalah.[1]

The important thing is the relation to the creation and the nature of what is thereby intended—namely its purpose within the harmony of existence—which serves as an argument against all those who rebel against the divine justice, in the name of the paradoxical formula, 'evil as it may be, this is the best of all possible worlds'. Luzzatto states that God could have created an entire world without evil, 'and would thereby have refuted the people', in his words. However, 'He Himself refrained from doing so with his omnipotence,[2] in order to do as He

1. See my article, 'The Metaphysics of Luzzatto'.
2. See *Da'at Tevunot*, pp. 7-8. This is the place to note that two principal assumptions of King—(1) the impossibility of the omnipotent building a world as perfect as himself; (2) the assumption that evil is an inherent structural consequence

willed, in order to do absolute good'. This 'doing good' only has meaning if a will and a purpose exist, and if the good world is the product of his will and not of his omnipotence—and how much more so if we are not speaking of the flowing of the world from his own essence. One may therefore state that Luzzatto thereby emphasizes the primacy of ethics within creation, and that the purpose of man is to understand, 'in an apprehended and understood order',[1] that monism which lies beyond everything understood as dualism. Luzzatto presents these ideas under such headings as, 'His unity is clarified in the eyes of all'[2] and 'this is a great fundament for certain faith'.[3]

Against those who argue that God could have prevented the sin of Adam, King retorts that this is not only impossible, but also undesirable, as the prevention of the exercise of free choice opposes the law of nature! Using rather subtle logic, Luzzatto present a similar position. He admits that, were it not for the sin of Adam, being the recognition 'of two dominions or of any other evil opinions which the snake placed before him',[4] and had he remained firm in his 'belief in His unity', physical evil would not have been necessary—that is, evil

of the first axiom—were received with great admiration by Shadal (see above), who made use of these assumptions in order to attack Kabbalah, specifically because of its teaching, in his opinion, that the created and the creator are mono-substantial. He understands in this way the statement of the *Idra Zutta*: 'He is separated and distinct (*parish ve-itparish*) from all, yet He is not separated. . . for He Himself is the All'. Shadal argues that it is foolish to think that the position of the Kabbalist Joseph Ergas, author of the work *Shomer Emunim*, who argues that the doctrine of *zimzum* is not to be understood literally, can save the theistic position by stressing that it 'restricts the power of the Infinite to bring into existence beings which are not infinite'. Shadal says that all agreed that

> the Creator is unable to create another who would be equal to Himself, until an English sage, Samuel Clarke [a member of King's circle] developed in this wise a decisive answer to the complaints of the heretics concerning the existence of evil in the world: saying that evil was not *created*, but *came about* of necessity from the nature of created being, *because that which is created must of necessity be limited*, and all of its powers must have an end and limit, and that all evil in the world comes about only as a result of this. . . How profound is this secret, more so than all the secrets of the Kabbalah!

The author admits that 'he has not heard the like of this answer, to the great confusion born of the existence of evil'—*Vikuah 'al Hokhmat ha-Qabbalah*, pp. 74-75.

1. *Da'at Tevunot*, p. 22.
2. *Da'at Tevunot*, p. 12.
3. *Da'at Tevunot*, p. 13.
4. *Da'at Tevunot*, p. 28.

might have been a necessary element of the creation without being part of history or of human existence. However, following Adam's sin things are different—and such is the way of things.[1] *Ab initio*, Luzzatto does not assume that Adam was perfect prior to the sin: the state of perfection is incompatible with freedom of choice, which was born together with Adam, because the possibility of choosing sin existed from the very beginning![2] It is clear to King that the situation in the Garden of Eden was one of grace, but on the plane of nature his view certainly agreed with that of the Jew Luzzatto.

Luzzatto says the following: 'The Lord, blessed be He, did not ordain negation and loss for perfect beings, but for imperfect ones'.[3] This being so, the law of destruction and cessation of existence applies to those creatures which, from the beginning and by their very nature, could have been subject to this law! The positive laws given by God to man were intended to show him what is the good choice, and not to impose choices upon him; they are intended to protect us from the evils to which we are exposed by the very structure of our being. Thus, the evils or fundamental lacks conditioning our existence are a kind of gift to man, who enjoys the spiritual ability to choose between good and evil and is rewarded or punished in accordance with his ability to remain at that exalted place appointed to him in the chain of creation—namely, as a creature possessing the divine spirit. This is certainly an optimistic response to all those frustrated people of various sorts who complain against the supposed inability or lack of will or wickedness or powerlessness of God, who has abandoned the world to its sufferings. To this, the theodiceans would reply that God preferred an incomplete creation to the total lack of a creation altogether, and by his free will limited his own power, so that imperfection flowed from his infinite goodness. God does not take vengeance nor is there eternal punishment (a burning problem in those days), because that would imply the destruction of the universe; as is known, there is nothing more important to the theodicists than existence itself. In Luzzatto's writings as well, the promise that the world will not be destroyed by evil is repeatedly stressed. All this is based upon the condition that we understand the importance of the concept of unity

---

1. *Da'at Tevunot*, p. 30.
2. *Da'at Tevunot*, pp. 111-16.
3. *Da'at Tevunot*, p. 100.

which rules in the world; any other answer implies irrationality, arbitrariness, rebellion, heresy, and the like.

Sabbatianism as an Anti-Theodistic Tendency

We do not know in any clear or definite way the target to whom Luzzatto's remarks were addressed when he waged his battle on behalf of the dominance of unity and against dualism, as we do in connection with the European theodicists. A list of ideologies against which he polemicized would seem to correspond one to one to a theodistic formula,[1] although in practice I have found only one such, namely Sabbatianism, which contemporary scholarship tends to attribute to Luzzatto himself, in whom they see a hidden Sabbatian.[2] Clear echoes of my claim arise from two distinct sources. The first is a letter of Luzzatto to his teacher, R. Isaiah Bassan; the second, the theories found in his book, *Qin'at ha-Shem Zeva'ot* ('The Jealousy of the Lord of Hosts'),[3] which was explicitly written against Sabbatians, albeit it has been customary to read between the lines a different confession of its author.

The guiding line of the argument of this book is that any theory in which is recognized the independent rule of the Other Side (*sitra ahra*)—the name used for the powers of evil—is to be rejected. These remarks are primarily made with regard to the messiah, who is embodied in the *qelippot* (shells containing the lights of the broken

---

1. See *Da'at Tevunot*, pp. 13-19.

2. See I. Tishby, 'R. Moshe Hayyim Luzzatto's Attitude to Sabbatianism', in his *Netivei Emunha u-Minut* (Jerusalem, 1982), pp. 169-85 (Hebrew); the article was originally published in *Sefer ha-Yovel li-khevod Gershom Scholem* (Jerusalem, 1958), pp. 203-31.

3. This book was only published in part; in his article ('Attitude'), Tishby observed the existence of a more complete manuscript—Oxford 2237. H. Friedlander, who published that same MS, did not mention the fact that it was discovered by Tishby, and brought in the Introduction to his edition the information noted by Tishby on p. 167 n. 11-12. See Friedlander (ed.), *Sefer Ginzei Ramha''l* (B'nai Berak, 1984), pp. 68-70. The material published prior to Friedlander's edition is less than half of the total compass of the book; any analysis of Luzzatto's stance regarding Sabbatianism demands careful reading of the book as a whole, as well as of the rest of his writings. Tishby's interesting study leaves room for discussion and for renewed consideration concerning the relationship between messianism and Sabbatianism.

vessels), and the '*mizvah* which comes through a sin', which is a seemingly reasonable use of the necessity of evil in the service of the good. Luzzatto argues that activism of this tendency must be considered as heretical, entailing as it does recognition of the autonomous power of the *sitra ahra*. To use his more severe language: 'It is impossible for a transgression to become a *mizvah* [just as] repair can never become ruination!'[1] In the debate which he conducts with an opponent whom it is not difficult to identify, he elaborates that a transgression cannot be a *mizvah* save as a temporary measure (*hora'at sh'ah*)—and that, only where the temporary measure is itself perceived as a departure from the norm, but not as conveying the status of a new norm upon the ruling. He is doubtless arguing here with Nathan of Gaza, who defined *hor'at sha'ah* in one of the tractates which he sent to Sabbatai Zevi,[2] as a condition which may continue indefinitely, and he even attributed this anarchistic interpretation to Sabbatai Zevi himself.[3] Nathan of Gaza used this argument as an halakhic justification for Sabbatai Zevi's decision to convert to Islam![4]

In his principled defence of *hora'at sha'ah*, Nathan states that paradox is essentially as legitimate as any other form of logic. According to Luzzatto, who follows the classical interpretation—namely, that a *hora'at sha'ah* is introduced to serve the exigencies of a specific, unique situation, for which there is no other solution—paradox cannot serve as the foundation of the building, on an equal stature with non-paradoxical logic. For Luzzatto, the paradox lies at the borderline of the ethical, while for Nathan there is no ethical preference of one over another. Nathan of Gaza even undermined the ethical basis of the *tiqqun* itself by stressing the paradox involved in any system which is attached, *ab initio*, to the realm of the unclean. In Nathan's eyes, there is no reasonable answer to the connection between *tiqqun* and the persistence of impurity, and there is therefore no ethical answer at all to

1. *Qin'at Ha-Shem Zeva'ot*, in Friedlander (ed.), *Ginzei Ramha''l*, p. 95.

2. See G. Scholem, 'Nathan of Gaza's Letter on Sabbatai Zevi, and his Conversion', in his *Mehqarim u-meqorot le-Toldot ha-Shabta'ut ve-gilguleha* (Jerusalem, 1974), pp. 236-73 (Hebrew). The letter is entitled *Zot le-Moharan 'al malka meshiha*.

3. 'Nathan', p. 247.

4. I analyse this theological document, which is the most important of the ideological documents extant to date, in an unpublished article on 'Theology and Polemics in Sabbatian Thought'. I deal here only with the analysis of a few matters of principle.

the question, ' "Why was Bathsheba given to Uriah the Hittite?" And "Why was the Land of Israel given to the nations of Canaan?" To these questions we have no answers.' This being so, says Nathan, 'There is no difficulty [in the question] "Why does the King Messiah perform such acts as these?" ' Nathan would appear to have undergone a difficult theological crisis with regard to the theory of *tiqqun* based upon Lurianic Kabbalah, which he expressed by formulating the cardinal questions as to how sin can be repaired altogether by means of the enslavement in Egypt, by the descent into impurity, or by the profanation of the messiah among the nations, concluding that there is no answer for any of these questions beyond that of the paradox itself. The very fact of the paradox is therefore Nathan's religion, and he sought thereby to establish the legitimacy of the paradox within the framework of the halakhah. But even in his analysis of the logic of the doctrine of reincarnation and its connection to *tiqqun*, Nathan revealed an explicitly antinomian approach, which saw *tiqqun* as an eschatological concept, having the power to nullify the very concepts of commandment and transgression. I mention this here because of the radical difference between the path of Nathan and that followed by Luzzatto in his discussions of *tiqqun*, as we shall see presently. Luzzatto explains that there are limitations to the applicability of the concept of *hora'at sha'ah* and the possibilities of its use, but he is not prepared to interpret it as an anarchistic rule *per se*: the anarchistic use of this principle will be interpreted as the victory of the Other Side. In this, we have returned to his fundamental teaching that there is only one dominion in the world, namely, the rulership of the good which shall never pass to the hands of the *sitra ahra*. Luzzatto's doctrine is monolithic by nature. He believes that Sabbatianism is insufficiently strict in fixing the boundaries between sacred and profane, allowing room for the argument that the Other Side has vanquished the rule of the holy. Luzzatto adheres to an orthodox interpretation of the embodiment of the messiah and the righteous within the *qelippot*;[1] in his view, the suffering experienced by the messiah

1. There is no doubt that Luzzatto belongs within the boundaries of 'Sabbatian culture'; this indeed follows from Tishby's analysis ('Attitude'). At the same time, the anti-Sabbatian notes in Luzzatto's voice have not been heard properly, and his arguments must be understood in terms of his fundamental outlook. There may be room for a revision of the view of the scholarly community concerning the question of who is a Sabbatian or what is Sabbatianism.

and by the righteous within the *qelippot* consists in the fact that they cause them to suffer illnesses. They suffer for the sake of the redemption, and through their sufferings prevent the dominion of the *qelippot* and the destruction of the world which is under their rule. Luzzatto might agree with the formula, 'He is good within but his garments are painful', rather than, 'and his garments are evil'— adopted by the Sabbatians from the *Tiqqunei Zohar*. The problem of the sufferings of the messiah is therefore transferred to the area of 'the righteous to whom all evil befalls', which is a question of the ethical standing, and not the heretical one, of the righteous. Luzzatto concludes:

> But because they have free will, this matter [of being compelled to enter into the *qelippot*] is not possible for them, for one who becomes involved with the *Sitra Ahra* is not alive, but spoiling and impurity for the holiness will flee from him, and there will be no *tiqqun* at all![1]

The theory of the descent into the *qelippot* therefore contradicts the idea of free choice! On the other hand, Luzzatto explains that the words of the Sages, 'Great is transgression for its own sake', as alluding to a possible situation on the eve of the redemption, when the Other Side is at the pinnacle of its power and is liable to dominate the world of holiness if not given its rightful portion. At such times, we are subjected to temptation—such as that of the sin of Yael with Sisera—in order to prevent its dominance. But Luzzatto repeatedly emphasizes that there is a difference between such a sin as this, which is only performed as a temporary measure because the specific situation demands it, 'and not as a matter of ordering one's behaviour according to it, Heaven forbid'—that is, a change in the norms, meaning conscious submission to the domination of the forces of evil.

In a letter addressed to R. Isaiah Bassan dated Nissan (March–April) 1730,[2] Luzzatto repeatedly stresses the connection between his evaluation of Sabbatianism and the general tendency of justifying God. Thanks to this letter, we know with certainty that a number of the central theses forming the doctrine of *tiqqun* in *Sefer Da'at Tevunot*— written in 1734—were brought to strengthen the meaning of the closeness between Sabbatianism and theodicy. Unfortunately, Bassan did not understand Luzzatto's remarks, and the latter added that he

---

1. *Qin'at Ha-Shem Zeva'ot.*
2. *Iggerot*, pp. 110-17, 120-23.

failed to be fully understood by others to whom he wrote defending
himself against suspicions of dangerous intentions and the temptations
of the *sitra abra* because of the 'innovations' in his understanding of
Lurianic Kabbalah. The explanation of this matter, which I will
briefly cite below, extends over two letters—Letters 50 and 53 in his
Iggerot (Collected Correspondence)—whose logic it is in fact difficult
to understand fully without knowledge of his theory concerning the
question of *tiqqun* and the problem of 'the righteousness to whom
there befalls evil'. Moreover, in a sentence explaining his theodistic
motivations, he also states that Sabbatianism caused heretical pessimism because it established the date of final redemption, inevitably
leading to disappointment. Indeed, for his part—thus he argues—he
deals with *tiqqunim* as a necessary element in a general process, without determining any historical end.[1]

> Let the honor of his Torah know that the ways of the Lord are just, and
> the righteous shall walk in them and sinners shall stumble in them (Hos.
> 14.10). For this was in truth a place of danger to the stubborn of heart
> who pursue beauty, and their fellows who, in taking the matter according
> to the stubbornness of their evil heart, thought to permit every sin. And
> being evil, they did not understand that this is not said, Heaven forbid, so
> that one should violate the barriers, even concerning the smallest nuance
> of the scribes [*diqduqei sofrim*—i.e. minor rabbinical ordinances], but
> that in a deep way this secret is present to those who understand the truth,
> that God will not change or alter his law for ever; but he who changes it,
> even by the smallest thread—concerning him the Torah has already
> testified that one is not to listen to the words of that prophet. Now I will
> tell this to your honour of Torah, that I do not say this to justify my own
> soul, but I also need to justify God my Maker, and to my Maker I perform
> righteousness. For there are many among us who are pious according to
> their own lights, and when it does not yield the fruits which they had
> hoped from it—how many lying assumptions do they leave. Concerning
> the likes of these it says: 'The foolishness of man perverts his way, and
> his heart frets against the Lord' (Prov. 19.3). But they do not know or
> understand what piety is, to be pleasing before God.

Further on in this letter, Luzzatto explains the exact role of the
concept, 'those acquainted with disease', already made famous by
Sabbatianism, which applied to it Sabbatai Zevi himself, following

---

1. This motif already appears in *Ma'amar ha-Ge'ulah*, which is interesting for
understanding his approach, and for understanding the impact of the Lurianic doctrine of the soul upon the entire ideological framework of the 'Sabbatian culture'.

Isaiah 53 and its interpretation by the *Zohar*. Luzzatto explains this idea in light of *Tiqqunei Zohar*, refuting the view of those who claim that *tiqqun* must be historical, visible and involving open, face to face conflict of the *sitra ahra* with the *qelippot* themselves. Luzzatto attempts to maintain a concealed messianic tension, which will not harm any beliefs nor lead to disappointment or apostasy.

In *Sefer Da'at Tevunot*, Luzzatto explains his eschatological view within the context of divine justice and 'the way of behaviour'—that is, through examining the structure of the cosmos. His main thesis is that, in consideration of the fact that the source of evil is in the good and its purpose is good, every event has sufficient reason to serve the matter of the good, whether the thing appears good and just or not. This thing, 'in which it will be clearly seen, by whoever turns his heart to all that is born in the world, who will find that there is nothing which comes about, either for good or for evil, from which one cannot draw down benefit and good for the world'.[1]

Luzzatto recognizes eschatological time, in which there will be no gap between the visible world and its ontic 'source', as it is all a 'unity' without duality, without evil, but also without free choice. There also follows from this a question which is not purely theoretical, but which is required by the question of the relationship between moral, physical and natural evil: namely, on which of them does the weight of eschatological thought fall?

Luzzatto reserves an honourable place for man's role in performing *tiqqun*. The meaning of *tiqqun* is the abolition of duality, and the way thereto is what he calls 'the way of justice'—namely, bringing the world to a balanced situation by protecting those life arrangements which are just and correct. This is what we are taught by the Torah of Moses. This protection serves a double function: it prevents the suffering of human beings, and it broadens the preparation or field for intensified activity of the forces of good, who are constantly flowing towards *tiqqun*. Even terrible sufferings undergone by humanity, such as the Holocaust, can be interpreted in two different ways: either as a departure and deviation of human society from the norms which suit their commitment to 'lawful' ethical life,[2] in which case one must understand physical suffering as the direct consequence of moral evil, which could have been prevented by man by means of proper choice;

---

1. *Da'at Tevunot*, p. 188.
2. *Da'at Tevunot*, pp. 142-52.

or that things are understood within the messianic perspective of *tiqqun* over which we have no control, in which case the awful suffering is understood as a trial of withstanding on the eve of the redemption. In the second case, those who suffer are victims of the *tiqqun*, and not of sin;[1] they are victims of natural evil, in which upheavals of progress and of correction take place.[2] Those who suffer on the altar of *tiqqun* are called by Luzzatto 'those acquainted with diseases'; they are tormented people, the immediate cause of whose suffering is unknown, but the deeper reason for which is beyond doubt: they are 'the righteous to whom evil befalls'.[3] This is likewise the answer to those who complain 'until the heart is greatly tempestuous, because of the many thoughts and meditations within it'.[4] In any event, Luzzatto claims that, whether the cause of suffering is ethical or messianic, the structure of the universe is a sufficiently strong guarantee mitigating against the total destruction of the universe; there can be no destruction or non-existence of being because the structure protects itself, the universe. It will only change as the result of *tiqqun*, which will come about by itself through the inner workings of the processes which God wishes, but not as a result of the strengthening of evil. This is the justification of God in the eschatological realm. In *Da'at Tevunot*, Luzzatto explains at greater length something which he alluded to in his letter to his teacher a few years earlier concerning the two kinds of suffering and the *tiqqun* which he himself brings about. This *tiqqun*

1. Reward and punishment only apply to the commission of moral evil, not to natural evil. The recompense for the latter lies in the perfection of the world as a whole; therefore, the suffering of the righteous is for the sake of the *tiqqun* of the world. See *Da'at Tevunot*, pp. 184-90.

2. *Da'at Tevunot*, p. 194.

3. It was thus that Luzzatto explained to R. Benjamin b. Eliezer ha-Kohen Vitale of Reggio (R. Bassan's father-in-law) the great sufferings of the latter in his old age. R. Benjamin sent him a question about his suffering, and the matter became known to the opponents of Luzzatto, who reacted to it sarcastically. See *Iggerot*, pp. 46, 48, 111, 166. The concept, 'those acquainted with diseases', seems to have been a clearly defined and well-known one to the messianic world with whom Luzzatto held discourse. R. Benjamin himself is considered by scholars as a 'moderate Sabbatian', of the circle of R. Abraham Rovigo; see G. Scholem, *Halomotav shel ha-Shabbeta'i R. Mordekhai Ashkenazi* (Leipzig, 1938). It seems to me that, among all his correspondents, Luzzatto's closest connection was with him. On Nathan of Gaza being an authority to R. Benjamin as well, see Scholem, *Halomotav*, pp. 55, 63-68.

4. *Da'at Tevunot*, p. 192.

does not square with conscious involvement in impurity and the public declaration of the struggle with the *qelippah*; he sought a '*tiqqun* to gather light and power within his Exile', and not to go out high-handedly to destroy the Other Side! There is no truth in the accusation that 'I confirmed the words[1] of Nathan of Gaza, as you said, as Luzzatto calls bitterly toward his teacher—and it seems to me that he ought to be given credence'.

Luzzatto's struggle with pessimism is symptomatic. His battle with demonic thought is transparent, even though his imagination is fruitful and his energy charged with intense messianic tension. But the full scope of his thought can only be made clear through the presentation of his entire system of messianic Kabbalah, rooted in his commentary to the *Zohar*, and not necessarily in that of Lurianic Kabbalah.[2]

In conclusion, let me state that the power of structural vision which flowed from a neo-Platonic cultural development, the optimism that evil serves a positive practical purpose, the monistic belief that it is not to be denied from a metaphysical point of view, and the removal of the doubt arising about the relation of the world to the meta-physical plane: all these are among the characteristics of the theodistic literature of the end of the seventeenth and beginning of the eighteenth century. There can be no doubt that the Ramhal—R. Moses Hayyim Luzzatto—represented the voice of Judaism within this literature.

1. *Iggerot*, p. 114.
2. See also the testimony of R. Isaiah Bassan to the rabbis of Venice, in which he relates that he read Luzzatto's tractates pertaining to Lurianic Kabbalah, and did not find any Sabbatianism in them (although in fact they do not contain any messianic note either), and was very impressed by them (*Iggerot*, p. 60).

THEODICY AND ETHICS IN THE PROPHECY OF EZEKIEL*

Benjamin Uffenheimer

The present paper is intended as a modest contribution towards deciphering the complex personality of the prophet Ezekiel. The question I wish to explore is the relationship between his deterministic view of history and his conception of ethics, which is based on the presupposition of absolute freedom of human will. An additional question of interest is the evaluation of Ezekiel's place within the priestly and Deuteronomic tradition.

I

Let us turn first to Ezekiel's view of history, which is given especial expression in chs. 16, 20 and 23, and is touched on in chs. 11, 33 and 34 as well. He began his prophecy in the year 593 BCE (Ezek. 1.2) as a member of the exilic community in Tel Aviv on the river Chebar, five years after king Jehoiachin went into captivity. His last extant prophecy dates from the 27th year (of exile), 571 BCE (29.17). This circumstance makes it understandable that from the very first moment of his prophetic activity, he was pursued by the trauma of the feared destruction of Judah, which was closely associated with the problem of theodicy. His prophetic predecessors were eager to bring about a change in the behaviour of the people by their sharp reprimanding criticism, so as to shield them from divine anger. Yet from the very beginning, he proclaimed that the destruction of the temple and Jerusalem, the downfall of Judah and the exile of the few survivors

---

* Western transcriptions of this name vary in the wake of the Septuagint between Ezekiel, Ezechiel, Hesekiel and Hezekiel. For the English translation, I have chosen the standard name as it appears in *The Holy Scriptures. According to the Masoretic Text* (Philadelphia: The Jewish Publication Society of America, 1954). All biblical quotes in the text are likewise from this translation.

were the inevitable result of a definite, unalterable divine decision. True, the motif of destruction had been mentioned already decades before by Jeremiah, and almost a century earlier by Micah (Jer. 7.14; 26.6; Mic. 3.12). Yet these were 'mere' threats, as Jeremiah stressed in his apologia to his opponents; those threats could be rendered nugatory at any time as a result of a positive change in the lifestyles of the people (Jer. 26.13ff.).[1] But for Ezekiel, the destruction of Judah was an inevitable divine decree which nothing could alter.

Despite this insight, Ezekiel neither strikes out on the path of Job— who railed in fury against divine justice, only to be silenced at the end by God's reply from the whirlwind (Job 40)—nor does he tread the path of the psalmist in Psalm 73,[2] who struggled to find new faith after his despair (vv. 17-28). He also refrained from the reaction of the author of the book of Lamentations, whose initial heart-rending outcry amounted to criticism of divine justice, but gave way in the course of his speech to a rational evaluation of the events according to traditional norms of reward and retribution. Ezekiel never expressed even the slightest doubt about God's justice. On the contrary, he was committed to the total justification of the impending disaster.

In this way, he revealed himself to be the most stormy and radical critic of the society and history of Israel. He even went so far as to place the burden of the tragic events of his day upon all the generations of Israel, from the time of bondage in Egypt down to his own period. This radicalism was rooted in a deterministic anthropology of the people of Israel, whose stony heart was the main obstacle to repentance and improvement of its ways. This extreme charge of Israel's being totally depraved, which I will look at in greater detail below, is unparalleled in prophetic literature. Yet that was the only possibility for defending the belief in universal divine justice. Even Jeremiah, who had mentioned destruction as an eventuality, was convinced of the basically solid moral character of Israel. This is evident from the idealizing description of the desert generation and its loyalty to God (Jer. 2.1-3). His call for repentance and his hope for salvation (3.1-17; 4.1-4) were based on the faith that the purified remnant of Israel had already undergone this change of heart (chs. 30–31).

---

1. See my study, 'Jeremiah and the "False" Prophets', in *Neiger Memorial Volume* (Jerusalem: Israel Society for Bible Research, 1959), pp. 96-111 (Hebrew).

2. See my study, 'Religious Experience of the Psalmists and the Prophetic Mind', *Immanuel* 21 (1987), pp. 7-27.

Ezekiel thought differently. His prophecies of doom and his symbolic acts are nothing other than a vivid illustration of the approaching calamity. He intended to warn the exiles not to fall prey to illusions and to prepare them psychologically for the worst, including the fact that exile would continue for a long time to come, as Jeremiah had emphasized in his letter to the remnant of the elders of the captivity (Jer. 29). This attitude, which reflected the hopelessness of the situation before and after the destruction of Jerusalem as well as his personal depression, was suddenly transformed in his eschatology into a utopia rich with anticipation. That utopia was unparalleled in its hoped-for wondrous changes of human nature, history and the natural world: its high point was the envisioned resurrection of the dry bones of the dead. The realization of this utopia is not conceived as a one-time event, but rather as a drama whose first act is the destruction of the armies of the legendary king Gog from the land of Magog. This was tantamount to the destruction of the forces of evil in the end of days—a proof of God's greatness and holiness 'in the eyes of many nations' (chs. 38–39, esp. 38.23).

In this context, his ethics deserves mention in order to underscore the glaring contradictoriness and contrast with which his basic positions are imbued (3.16b-21; 18; 33.1-20). Here he appeals to man in his absolute freedom of will, and ventures to delineate the principles of divine justice in the fate of each individual. God judges the individual exclusively according to his moral status at the time of judgment, without taking his personal past or the behaviour of his fathers into consideration. That is, each person has the ever-present opportunity, untroubled by his past, to atone and return to God. This indeed is the polar contrast to his earlier mentioned historical and anthropological determinism, which can only be compared with the polarity between his extremely pessimistic consciousness of the present and the jubilant eschatological belief he nurtured in a wondrous future.

II

The profile just sketched will now be deepened and substantiated—and his contradictoriness perhaps made plausible—by means of an exegesis of the relevant sources. Let us begin with chs. 16, 20 and 23, which revolve around his historical concept, prefacing the analysis with a few comments on the current state of research dealing with the problem of the authenticity of these chapters.

It is laudable that scholarship has left the erroneous path pursued by Hölscher,[1] who portrayed Ezekiel as a free poet by denying that most of the prose passages were of his authorship, and venturing to transform the rest into poetry via diverse manipulations. Of particular importance is that trend in scholarship which stressed the traditional elements, adjusted and integrated within the writings of the classical prophets. That approach is represented in Zimmerli's monumental commentary on Ezekiel and H. Graf Reventlow's study,[2] as well as in the as yet only partially published commentary by M. Greenberg.[3] In the footsteps of Kaufmann,[4] who emphatically stressed that the priestly source was written and composed during the First Commonwealth, Greenberg pointed out that Ezekiel, having been brought up in this tradition, integrated and remoulded it in his speeches.

1. G. Hölscher, *Hesekiel, Der Dichter und das Buch* (BZAW, 39; Giessen: Töpelmann, 1924); A. Bertholet, *Hezekiel* (HAT; Tübingen: Mohr [Paul Siebeck], 1936); G.A. Cooke, *Ezekiel* (ICC; Edinburgh: T. & T. Clark, 1936); W. Eichrodt, *Der Prophet Hesekiel* (ATD, 22.1; Göttingen: Vandenhoeck & Ruprecht, 1959; 22.2, 1966); G. Fohrer, *Ezechiel* (HAT, 1.13: Tübingen: Mohr [Paul Siebeck], 1955).

2. W. Zimmerli, *Ezechiel* (BK 13; Neukirchen–Vluyn: Neukirchener Verlag, 2nd edn, 1959); H. Graf Reventlow, *Wächter über Israel* (Berlin: Töpelmann, 1962). Graf Reventlow strongly emphasizes Ezekiel's attachment to tradition, in particular to the priestly one, and to cult.

3. M. Greenberg, *Ezekiel, 1–20* (AB, 22; Garden City, NY: Doubleday, 1983); Reventlow, *Wächter über Israel*.

4. Y. Kaufmann, *Toldot ha-Emuna ha-Yisraelit*, I (Tel Aviv, 1937), pp. 113-84; II.2 (1948), pp. 52ff. Abridged English translation by M. Greenberg, *The Religion of Israel from its Beginnings to the Babylonian Exile* (Chicago, 1960). In Israeli research, there has been general acceptance of Kaufmann's dating of the priestly source. Cf. M. Haran, 'Biblical Studies—Ezechiel's Code (Ezek. XL–XLVIII) and its relation to the Priestly School', *Tarbiz* 44 (1974–75), pp. 30-53 (Hebrew); *idem*, *Temple and Temple Service in Ancient Israel* (Oxford: Clarendon Press, 1978); A. Hurvitz, *A Linguistic Study of the Relationship between the Priestly Source and the Book of Ezekiel* (Cahiers de la Révue Biblique, 20; Paris: Gabalda, 1982). The linguistically based proof by Hurvitz of the older origin of the priestly source vis-à-vis Ezekiel is of decisive importance for historical-critical research. In many points, Kaufmann's argumentation is indebted to David Hoffmann, whose works had little impact on German research; cf. D. Hoffmann, *Die wichtigsten Instanzen gegen die Graf-Wellhausensche Hypothese* (Berlin, 1904); *idem*, *Das Buch Leviticus* (Berlin, 1905–1906).

III

Before presenting my analysis of ch. 16, I would like to refer to Zimmerli's criticism, which is fairly representative of the scholarly consensus among the majority of scholars today. One of his aims, pursued energetically and systematically, was to extract the presumed Ezekielian core from each chapter, in order then to reconstruct the process of its further elaboration and handing down—be it those sections supposedly added by the Ezekielian school, or the presumed commentaries and glosses supplemented by later hands.

In respect of ch. 16, he comes to the conclusion that the core consists of vv. 13-15, 34, 37a, 39-40. Moreover, he contends that a larger portion of vv. 6-15 should be excluded as a later emendation. The original speech is assumed to have been written in an exalted narrative style using paratactically arranged short sentences.[1]

Its exclusive content focuses on the history of Jerusalem, its rise, fall and divine punishment. Jerusalem itself is portrayed as an abandoned foundling, saved by God, who surrounded her with loving care. Later on, when she had grown into a beautiful maiden, she was betrothed to God. But, the prophet asserts, Israel desecrated this marriage by her constant whoring after strange gods. According to Zimmerli, the objective of the narrator is the proclamation of judgment in vv. 37a, 39-40; the forces to which Israel demonstrated her licentious love will carry out the divine judgment in all its cruelty. This, in Zimmerli's view, is the Ezekielian core of the chapter.

Unfortunately, I must point out that Zimmerli's analysis strikes me as extremely arbitrary. His methodological approach imposes certain literary and content-related premises on the text that are totally alien to it. Nonetheless, he is preferable to those interpreters who were so bold as to simply reduce this chapter to a poem. But what is the origin of his equally venturous claim that the core is written in 'paratactically arranged short sentences'? After all, the broad style is precisely the hallmark of Ezekielian oratory. I find it necessary to reject his exclusion of supposed expansions in vv. 1-44 as inappropriate, especially since idolatry was performed in all its Egyptian, Canaanite, Assyrian and Babylonian variants, with the associated sexual cults and sacrifices.

---

1. See *Ezechiel*, pp. 362-63.

With regard to the motif of the sisters (44-58), excluded by Zimmerli, this should be seen as an intensification of Ezekiel's previous complaint, because Israel committed acts even worse than those of Sodom! Incomprehensibly, vv. 26-34 are also excluded by Zimmerli; here the motif of licentious love, exaggerated to the point of perversion, is given a political reinterpretation.

The closing section, which continues to develop the motif of the sisters, is viewed as a late addition, because it begins with the formula of divine speech. But it seems that it was mainly the comforting content which was felt to be disturbing, since in terms of the principles of classical criticism, speeches of scolding and abuse could only end with a judgment. Yet if one left out the verses of consolation, one would be guilty of falsifying a great many prophecies. Nothing is more natural than to introduce this drastic change for the better with such a formula.

I therefore feel obliged to reject Zimmerli's textual analysis, which reflects the predominant trend in current scholarship. It should be noted that Greenberg succeeds in reading the chapter as a rigidly structured, organic unity, although he does not overlook occasional scribal errors or expansions, all of secondary importance.

I must add that associative style elements, verbs or key words serve to strengthen the solid interlinking of the compositional elements, while the spontaneity and excitement of the speaker are vented in occasional outbursts and numerous repetitions, including the anticipation of the element of judgment.

The tripartite speech (3-43, 44-52, 53-63) contrasts Israel's sinfulness (3-43, 44-52) with God's favours (53-63). It reaches its dramatic high point in the second section with the motif of the sisters (44-52), which especially underscores Jerusalem's sinfulness in comparison to Samaria and Sodom, that paradigm of depravity. The eschatological conclusion, vv. 53-63, in which God assures his people that he will remain mindful of the covenant and preserve it for all eternity, is the emotional anti-climax of the angry speech of judgment. In actual fact, what is involved here is the notion of the reinstitution of the old covenant, elsewhere termed a new covenant (Jer. 31.30).

The literary structure of this and other prophecies—where blessing and curse, salvation and doom, destructive criticism of the present, and colourfully rich, comforting hope for the future are closely arrayed side by side—is reminiscent of Leviticus 26. In that chapter, initially there is a lengthy depiction of God's blessing, but in conclusion there is the divine curse, almost symmetrical in its length and ordering. Nonetheless, there is a great difference between Leviticus 26 and Ezekiel 16. In the former, blessing and curse are depicted as eventualities whose realization lies at all times in the hand of the people and of each individual in Israel; that is, Leviticus 26 emphasizes the ever open and available alternative between good and evil, the path of life and that of death, blessing and curse. Here in Ezekiel, this alternative no longer exists, because Israel's depravity from its earliest beginnings has finally acted to forfeit the blessing. Now Israel is hopelessly abandoned to the curse. Nonetheless, such a curse does not mean the destruction and downfall of the people, although it does imply the destruction of the temple, Jerusalem, Judah and the cruel slaughter of the majority of the population. The expectation of blessing, the 'Prinzip Hoffnung' (E. Bloch's 'principle of hope'), is pushed into the indefinite future, as already indicated in Isaiah (cf. Isa. 2.2). Indeed, prophecy of doom as an exclusive mission, as it has often been characterized since Wellhausen, Hölscher *et al.*, is a figment of scholarly imagination. Without the comforting content of eschatology, the judgment speeches would have been too great a burden to bear psychologically. That would transform classical prophecy, such as that of Ezekiel, into hopeless, insignificant pessimism. For this reason, I find it necessary to emphasize in the strongest terms by rejection of the customary trend in scholarship that attributes vv. 53-63 to later hands.

IV

Zimmerli's textual criticism takes a similar tack in approaching the structure of ch. 23, whose thematic content is most similar to that of ch. 16. In his view, the core consists of vv. 1-27. All other sections, contained in vv. 28-49, are categorized as later emendations and interpretations. But in order to single out the supposedly exalted narrative style in short sentences, he is forced to exclude a number of additional verses, namely 4b, 7b, 8, 9b, 10b, 12-14a, 18, 21, 23b, 25b and 26; that is, of 49 verses in the chapter, only 18 (!) are left which he concludes are attributable to Ezekiel. Eichrodt is somewhat more cautious, and attributes vv. 1-20, 22-27 and 31-34 to the basic core. One does have to assert that the chapter is not a closed unit.

Nonetheless, criticism here has been too much radical in approach, as I will explicate below.

The structure is as follows:

5-10	Oholah and her harlotry
11-21	Oholibah and her sin
22-31	the punishment of Oholibah
32-35	Oholibah's cup of punishment

The initial sections are descriptive (1-21), composed in the third person. The last two sections (22-35) are written in the second person; here the prophet proclaims the judgment to the sinful sister (22-31), and hands her the cup of sorrow and punishment (32-35). Verse 36 is a new beginning, that opens with a divine address to the prophet. Verses 36-44 report once again about the sins of the two sisters, and conclude with a description of their execution by stoning, the slaughter and the burning of their houses (46-49), after they had been found guilty of the sacrifice of children and the sin of adultery. Although this speech is separate, and is linked only thematically with the first part of the chapter, I fail to comprehend why this should be attributed to a later hand. Nothing justifies such a thesis, not even the questionable excuse that one of Ezekiel's pupils apparently tried his own hand here.

The sexual motif is the common link between chs. 16 and 23. In both chapters, idolatry and the changing policy of alliances of the states Israel and Judah with their neighbours are branded as harlotry. The motif of harlotry should be understood literally as well as metaphorically, as I will show below. The key word in both chapters is the root זנה (= 'to whore'), which reoccurs dozens of times in verb form and other combinations. Israel is called a harlot (זונה) and a whoring woman (אשה זונה, cf. 16.30, 31, 33, 36, 41). Israel's behaviour is designated harlotry. For that purpose, Ezekiel invents the intensive form תזנות, usually found here in the plural (תזנותיך תזנותיכם). It appears only in chs. 16 and 23, especially in phrases such as ותשפך תזנותיך על, in the sense of to 'pour out thy harlotries' (16.15; 23.9), ותרבה תזנותך 'and hast multiplied thy harlotry' (16.26, 29; cf. 23.19; etc.), and 'thou hast played the harlot with them, and yet thou wast not satisfied' (16.28). Similarly, in 16.36 he states:[1]

---

1. A. Geiger, *Urschrift und Übersetzung der Bibel* (2nd edn, 1928), pp. 391ff., emendates according to the LXX and T, חשפך = your nakedness, and reads ותגל,

יען השפך נחשתך ותגלה ערותך על מאהביך

because thy filthiness was poured out, and thy nakedness uncovered through thy harlotries with thy lovers (see also 16.38; 23.18).

In 16.16 he speaks about the 'high places decked with diverse colours' (במות טלאות), dedicated to harlotry. The outfitting of these cult sites (16.17-19) reminds one of the seductive description with which the harlot tempts the passer-by into her room (Prov. 7.8-20). Another description of the cult of high places marked by harlotry is given in 16.24: 'that thou hast built unto thee an eminent place, and hast made thee a lofty place in every street'. A verb that defines 'harlotry' more specifically is עגב (= 'to lust, dote'), as in 23.5, 7, 9: 'Wherefore I delivered her into the hands of her lovers. . . upon whom she doted'. The substantive form (עגבה) also appears: ותשחת עגבתה ממנה, 'she was more corrupt in her doting than her' (23.11).

The root נאף (= 'commit adultery') is used in its Pi'el form (16.32; 23.37). Israel is branded as an adulteress (נאפות, 16.38; 23.45). Her behaviour is adultery (נאופים. 23.43). The word זמה, 'lewdness' (16.27, 43, 58; 23.21, 27, 29, 35, 41, 44, 48) also belongs to this semantic field. The harlot's obscene behaviour is made concrete by reference to her uncovering her nakedness (16.36, 37; 23.18) and opening her feet to those who pass by ותפשקי את נגליך (16.25), or her 'bed of love' or 'her friendly intercourse', משכב דודים (23.17). He also does not forget the practice of the pressing and bruising of the breast, which Israel had accustomed itself to since early youth (23.3, 8, 21) שמה מעכו שדיהן ושם עשו דדי בתוליהן. The angry high point of his stormy condemnations is the declaration of the appropriate punishment:

And they shall deal with thee in hatred, and shall take away all thy labour, and shall leave thee naked and bare; and the nakedness of thy harlotries shall be uncovered, both thy lewdness and thy harlotries (23.29).

ועשו אותך בשנאה ולקחו כל יגיעך
ועזבוך עירם ועריה ונגלה ערות זנוניך וזמתך וזנותיך

Indeed, God discovered Israel as an abandoned, neglected found-ling, 'naked and bare' (16.7, 22): 'And when I passed by thee, and saw

arriving at 'you exposed your nether parts and uncovered your nakedness'. But following Driver (*Bib* 19 [1938], p. 65) and Greenberg, it seems to be a cognate of Akkadian naḫšati = 'morbid genital outflow (of a woman)', from nḫš = 'to be abundant, overflowing'.

thee wallowing in thy blood, I said unto thee: In thy blood, live. Yea, I said unto thee: In thy blood, live' (16.6). In the end, the adulterous wife is left to lie naked and uncovered by her lovers, that is, her enemies (16.32; 23.29). She is cast back into her primal state prior to divine lovingkindness.

These are a few examples from chs. 16 and 23 that depict Israel's faithlessness and judgment by use of the motif of the harlot. Ezekiel goes so far as to distort Israel to the point of non-recognizability, by portraying her as a perverse adulteress who gives her lovers gifts for their favours (16.32-34).

In this offensive style, which partly seems to imitate the base mode of street-walkers and harlots, he describes Israel as a person irrevocably enslaved to sin from early youth on; profligate sexual behaviour and child sacrifice are the accompanying phenomena of idolatry in this connection (16.20-21). This had started already in Egypt, where Israel whored with the thick-fleshed Egyptians (בשר גדלי)—an expression of offensive associations (16.26). Afterwards she did the same with the Assyrians (16.28-29; 23.5-10, 11-16), yet without growing satiated from such harlotry. Oholibah had 'friendly intercourse' with the Babylonians (23.17), 'whose flesh is as the flesh of asses, and whose issue is like the issue of horses' אשר בשר חמורים בשרם וזרמת סוסים זרמתם (23.20). In brief, in ch. 23, Ezekiel exceeds all the accusations ever heaped on Israel, and the final examples allude to the political element. Moreover, using the motif of the sisters borrowed from Jeremiah (Jer. 3.16-17), he multiplies the sin of Judah = Ohobilah's over against the northern kingdom = Ohola, since Judah did not learn the lesson from the fate of the northern kingdom, and had continued down the path of sin.

V

This obscene and plastic way of depiction reflects a profound crisis with regard to the tradition that attempts to introvert the relation of Israel to God by using intimate images of marital relations as a metaphor. In the ancient prose sources and in several poetic creations (Exod. 15; 19; 24; Num. 10.35-36; 23.22-24; 24.8-9; Deut. 32.8-12; 33.2-5; Judg. 5; etc.), Israel's relationship towards God is conceived of as a royal covenant, or more exactly as the contract of a vassal with his divine king. This contract is conceptualized in terms of the ancient Oriental vassal treaties, in particular those with their subordinate princes and kings. In other words in the oldest sources of the Pentateuch, the Sinai covenant is described in terms of the juridical genre of international law common at the time.[1] Buber appropriately called the covenant of Sinai a theopolitical event, in the course of which God was crowned as the king of Israel. But at the same time, a more intimate, familial version of the relationship of God to Israel was developing. This tradition occasionally refers to Israel as the firstborn or the son of God: 'And thou shalt say unto Pharaoh: Thus saith the Lord: Israel is my son, my firstborn. . . Let my son go, that he may serve me; and thou hast refused to let him go. Behold, I will slay thy son, thy firstborn' (Exod. 4.22-23; cf. also Jer. 31.8). Deut. 14.1 should also be understood in this sense, 'You are the children of the Lord your God'. God's special love for Israel and his oath to the fathers are depicted on several occasions there as the cause for her being saved from the house of bondage, and elected as God's people. In this connection, the verb אהב (= 'to love') is intensified by the root חשק ('to desire, crave'): 'The Lord did not set his love (אהב) upon you, nor choose you, because ye were more in number than any people—for ye were the fewest of all peoples—but because the Lord loved you (חשק), and because he would keep the oath which he swore onto your fathers' (Deut. 7.7-8; cf. also Deut. 23.6). He will persevere in this love if Israel follows the commandments of the covenant (Deut. 7.12-13).

Corresponding to God's love for Israel is the Deuteronomic commandment for Israel to love God (Deut. 5.9; 6.5; 7.9; 10.12; 11.13, 22; 13.4; 19.9; 30.6, 16, 20). Yet it does not state simply that 'you should love God', but rather 'thou shalt love the Lord thy God with all thy heart, and with all thy soul and with all thy might' (Deut. 6.5; cf. also 10.12; 11.13; 30.6)—a formulation which in essence represents an introverted version of the style of the vassal treaties.[2] To cite just one example, let us note the following paragraph in the contract between Hatushil III and Benteshina, king of Amurru, which parallels the above Deuteronomic triple formulation of the commandment to love God: 'If I, king of Hatti, depart for a campaign of booty, when

---

1. B. Uffenheimer, *Ancient Prophecy in Israel* (Jerusalem: Magnes, 2nd edn, 1984), pp. 70-107 (Hebrew).
2. See *Ancient Prophecy*, p. 83.

(then) Benteshima with his warriors (and) his chariots, and in his heart does not keep watch. . . '[1] The love of Israel for God is the fulfilment of his commandments (Deut. 11.13, 22), so that the phrase 'those who love me and keep my commandments' (אוהבי ושומרי מצותי) developed into a fixed formulation (Deut. 5.9; 7.9; cf. also 19.9; 30.16). Another verb that intensifies the commandment of love is דבק ('cleave'), as in, 'to love the Lord your God, to walk in all his ways, and to cleave unto him' (11.22; 30.20).

Indeed, the verb 'to love' and the familial vocabulary mentioned above also belongs to the semantic field of ancient Oriental state treaties. The designation of the vassal as a son or firstborn amounts to a legitimation of his throne by his sovereign, who calls himself father.[2] In Deuteronomy and the Deuteronomic tradition, these concepts are transformed into religious language, interiorizing the relations between Israel and God far beyond the confines of formal-juridical style. God's behaviour is the expression of his paternal love for Israel, while Israel, as the grateful son or firstborn, lovingly devotes himself to his father's service.

The prophets Hosea and Jeremiah venture a further step by penetrating into the erotic layer of family life in order to intensify Israel's relation with God. First a word about Hosea. As is evident from my earlier detailed study,[3] the point of departure for his prophecy was the adultery of his wife, or, more accurately, the discovery that his wife was a harlot. His disappointment, anger and pain combined in his consciousness with his abhorrence for the Canaanite sexual cults that were widespread in Israel. It suddenly became clear to him that this personal pain was basically identical with divine pathos,[4] that is, with

1. šumma Bente-šima iš-tu ṣabe-šu narkabati-šu ù i-na libbi-šu la-a i-na-ṣir. . . E.F. Weidner, *Politische Dokumente aus Kleinasien* (Leipzig, 1923), 9, line 3, p. 132. Cf. likewise the treaty between Mattiwaza and Šubbiluliuma, *Dokumente*, 2, lines 59-62, p. 56.

2. M. Weinfeld, *JAOS* 90 (1970), pp. 194-95.

3. B. Uffenheimer, 'Hosea's Marriage as a Prophetic Symbol', in *Shmuel Dim Memorial Volume* (Jerusalem: Israel Society for Biblical Research, 1958), pp. 269-79 (Hebrew); M.D. Cassuto, 'Hosea', *Entseklopedia Mikra'it*, II, pp. 802-806 (Hebrew).

4. A.J. Heschel, *Die Prophetie* (Krakow: Verlag der polnischen Akademie der Wissenschaften, 1936). In this book, Heschel developed for the first time the conception of prophecy as sympathy. In the American edition, *The Prophets* (Evanston: Harper & Row, 1962), there are minor changes in his general approach to

the disappointment and anger of the divine husband as a result of the adultery of his spouse Israel, who was enthralled to the sexual cults of the Canaanite deities. The traditional relationship of father and son between God and Israel changes here into a bond of marriage between the two, whose violation brands Israel as a harlot. The admonition (Hos. 2.4ff.) that gives expression to the rage and anguish of the deceived divine husband, also contains the divorce formula with which he casts aside his wife Israel, 'For she is not my wife, neither am I her husband', as explicated in my study.[1] There is no doubt that the general setting of this tragic internalization is the relationship between man and deity in Canaanite mythology, a body of myth replete with gods and goddesses, divine marriage, the sexual life of the gods, love and adultery, as reflected in the epic writings of Ugarit and the writings of Hellenistic historians.[2] The relationship of God with Israel, however, is devoid of any biological elements, because biblical monotheism repudiates the ontological foundations of the pagan man–God relation.[3] Indeed, the eschatological reinstitution of the covenant between God and Israel is depicted as a new marriage, the closing of a new nuptial union. The bridal gift of the divine husband is far removed from any associations of a biological or sexual nature. Rather, these are his intellectual, spiritual and moral attributes, realized her:

> And I will betroth thee unto me forever; Yea, I will betroth thee unto me in righteousness, and in justice, and in lovingkindness, and in compassion, and I will betroth thee unto me in faithfulness; And thou shalt know the Lord' (Hos. 2.21-22).

וארשתיך לי לעולם וארשתיך לי בצדק ובמשפט ובחסד וברחמים
וארשתיך לי באמונה וידעת את־ה

Indeed, these are the properties of God, enumerated by Moses in his

---

this phenomenon. See my critical discussion, 'Prophecy and Sympathy', *Immanuel* 16 (1983), pp. 7-24.

1. Cf. Uffenheimer, 'Hosea's Marriage', pp. 275-76.

2. C.H. Gordon, *Ugaritic Manual* (Rome, 1955); M.D. Cassuto, 'Ugarit', *Entseklopedia Mikra'it*, I, pp. 79-89 (in Hebrew); S.E. Loewenstamm, 'Philo of Byblos', in *Comparative Studies in Biblical and Ancient Oriental Literatures* (Neukirchen–Vluyn: Neukirchener Verlag, 1980), pp. 390-404.

3. B. Uffenheimer, 'Myth and Reality in Ancient Israel', in S.N. Eisenstadt (ed.), *The Origins and Diversity of Axial Age Civilizations* (SUNY Press, 1986), pp. 135-68, 505-10.

great prayer of supplication: 'The Lord, the Lord, a God merciful and gracious, slow to anger, and abounding in steadfast love and faithfulness' (Exod. 34.6) ה' ה' אל רהום וחנון ארך אפים ורב חסד ואמת. The contact between Hosea and the preceding passage refers to the major spiritual features of the Lord, his mercy (רחום, רחמים), lovingkindness (חסד) and faithfulness (אמת, אמונה). So there can be no doubt that the spiritual conception of Torah literature, including that of Deuteronomy, is the pre-stage leading to the image of the divine bridegroom and his bride Israel reflected in Hosea's prophecy.

Jeremiah seizes on that same image. However, his point of departure is not the disappointment and pain of personal experience, but rather the romantic longing for an idealized past of the people of Israel during their wanderings in the desert (Jer. 2.2-3):

> I will remember for thee the affection (חסד) of thy youth, the love (אהבה) of thine espousals; How thou wentest after me in the wilderness, in a land that was not sown. Israel is the Lord's hallowed portion, his first-fruits of the increase; All that devour him shall be held guilty, evil shall come upon them.

Yet it is this romantic backdrop that sheds an even harsher light on the present. In the following passage, Jeremiah saves no words in castigating the current transgression of Israel as harlotry (2.4-28, 29-37; 3.1-5). Despite the sharp and unqualified condemnation of the sexual excesses, perversions and bloodshed, closely bound up with the Canaanite cult, he is nonetheless convinced that Israel is capable of repentance. In the following section, he turns with heart-rending fervour to the exiles of the northern kingdom, calling on them to repent. In his spirit, he already hears the repentant tone of those returning, who answer his call (3.19-25). This dialogue closes with the prophet's promise that God will forgive repentant sinners. In ch. 31, it expands into a dramatic conversation in which God, those in exile and Rachel, Israel's mother, all take part. This anticipation of the opined return at the end of days closes with a new covenant between God and his people (31.31-34). That is a covenant whose commandments are not inscribed on stone tablets, but rather are written in the heart of each individual. Jeremiah's hopeful joy reaches its culmination here. Yet it should be noted that the erotic image of marriage between Israel and God has been replaced by that of the mother of the people, Rachel, who weeps for her children before God. Her supplication is also being heeded when God calls Ephraim his dear son, his darling (31.14-19).

VI

Let us now turn again to Ezekiel. The great difference between him and Jeremiah consists in his deterministic–pessimistic outlook both with regard to the history of Israel and the character of the people. Jeremiah still believed in Israel's basic moral nature that had been polluted in the present, but that would assert itself once more via those who would return purified from exile. Employing the image of the good figs, he emphasizes the moral superiority of those in exile (ch. 24). In the parable of the potter (18.1-12), he gives the people and each individual the free choice of turning away calamity; he is convinced that there is a genuine chance for this to occur. In contrast, Ezekiel is convinced that the impending catastrophe cannot be averted, because Israel's harlotry, idolatry, bloodshed of child sacrifice and inconstant foreign policy[1] are evidence of its total depravity and abandonment to sin—in Ezekelian language, the stony heart (2.4; 11.13, 21; 36.26) that renders nought any prospect for return and betterment. Ezekiel's deterministic pessimism leads here to an unreserved theodicy that does not permit any doubts about divine justice. In his eyes, the fall of Jerusalem is already a visionary reality. In the vision contained in chs. 8–11, the divine chariot leaves the court and rises into the heavens. At the same time, a torch is hurled into the city of Jerusalem, and six destroyers are mentioned—the beginning of catastrophe. Ezekiel cries out in great anguish to the Lord: 'Ah Lord God! Wilt thou destroy all the residue of Israel in thy pouring out of thy fury upon Jerusalem?' (9.8). Yet earlier, in his vision of the temple inner sanctum, he 'discovered' the elders of Jerusalem secretly practising idolatrous, disgusting cults, whose concrete meaning remains a riddle for scholarship down to the present day. Neither Jeremiah, who knew the situation in Jerusalem on the basis of his daily experience, or the author of Second Kings, or even the book of Lamentations, give the slightest hint of the presence of such scandalous cults. I thus cannot avoid assuming, together with Kaufmann, that it was Ezekiel's pathological need to justify God at any cost, despite the terrible events,

---

1. Ezek. 16.26; 17.1-24; 23.3, 12, 17, 23ff.; cf. 2 Kgs 17.4; Hos. 5.13; 7.11; 8.9; 12.2.

which induced him to such abstruse inventions. In chs. 16 and 23, his use of obscene harlot language closes the path for any return to the motif of the family, especially in its erotic character. The adulterous misuse by Israel of divine intimacy caused him to completely abandon any familial sketches of the relationship between God and Israel in his later prophecies—in order to describe the ideal future in terms of the image of the shepherd, who watches over his flock with love and care, leading them to drink (ch. 34).

VII

Let us now return to ch. 20, which represents the complement to chs. 16 and 23. According to its title, this speech is from the year 591 BCE, in which the prophecy of Hananiah, energetically opposed by Jeremiah, was supposed to be fulfilled (Jer. 28.2-4).[1] Ezekiel's words are directed to the elders of Israel, who asked him for the word of God, as in 8.1 and 14.1. However, the concrete reason for their request is not mentioned. This speech lacks the metaphorical element determining the character of chs. 16 and 23; it is a prophecy of doom, written in the matter-of-factness of the priestly tradition. The first part, which is especially concerned with the fate of Judah, concludes with v. 31. The second part, which most scholars do not believe was written by Ezekiel, concerns the fate of those in exile. However, Greenberg's stylistic study[2] demonstrates that vv. 32-44 are a clear continuation of vv. 1-31, that is, there is no reason to deny Ezekiel's authorship.

As vv. 3 and 31 emphasize, this speech is not meant as God's reply to the inquiry of the elders, because God refuses to reveal himself to them (cf. 14.3). This is a speech that brands Israel's behaviour since its beginnings as rebelliousness. Thrice he repeats, 'But they rebelled against me' (8, 13, 21). This had begun already during their slavery in Egypt, when they refused to forswear Egyptian idolatry, although God had revealed himself to them there (v. 5; cf. Exod. 6.2-8). The same thing occurred in the desert (vv. 13, 21) and after their settlement in Canaan (v. 28), when they practised the cult of high places. On all hills and beneath each tree with heavy foliage (28), they sacrificed to the Canaanite deities. This behaviour, that revolves

1. See my 'Jeremiah'.
2. See *Ezekiel*, pp. 376-88.

around the concept of high altars so much castigated by the author of Deuteronomy (Deut. 12), along with the desecration of the sabbath (vv. 20, 21, 24), is emphasized here as a cardinal sin. This so thoroughgoing damnation of the cult sites, the *bamoth*, prompted some scholars to assume that the delegation of elders intended to win Ezekiel over to the idea of introducing sacrifices in Babylon, just as we learn from the Elephantine papyri.[1] Emphasis on the illegality of the *bamoth* supposedly contained the prophet's negative answer. Later on we shall return to this intriguing assumption, which, however, cannot be substantiated by the plain text.

In his response, the prophet emphasizes two major arguments: first, the assertion that Israel has been enthralled to idolatry since its early beginnings in Egypt, that is, that it is thoroughly depraved. Secondly, that God, enraged by Israel's rebellious behaviour, had decided already, during their wandering in the desert, to disperse them among the nations (v. 23; cf. Ps. 106.26-27), but waited with punishment until the cup was full. Ezekiel's deterministic pessimism, especially as regards Judah, reaches its culmination here. It is true that the threat of dispersing Israel among the nations is already present, and in the same style, in the priestly tradition (Lev. 26.33-46). Exile is also mentioned in Deut. 4.25-28; 28.36ff.; according to these passages, Israel would be compelled there to serve wood and stone. But by speaking in terms of an inevitable, final decision, Ezekiel goes far beyond that tradition, where this disaster is alluded to only as an eventuality.

The second section of his speech, especially formulated for those in exile (vv. 32-44), contains a broad and consoling eschatological conclusion. Paradoxically, however, it is cast in the spirit and language of the preceding speech of judgment, because the cause behind salvation is neither the compassion of the Lord for the remainder of Israel nor the repentance of the sinners, as in Jeremiah 3 and 31. No, it is only God's concern for his name—that it not be desecrated among the nations. In other words, it is the theocentric motif which shaped the eschatology and historical views of Ezekiel. Accordingly, the fear of God that his name could be desecrated among the nations is the only factor keeping him from pouring out his wrath upon the rebellious

---

1. A. Menes, 'Tempel und Synagoge', *ZAW* 50 (1932), pp. 268-76; J.A. Bewer, 'Beiträge zur Exegese des Buches Ezechiel', *ZAW* 63 (1951), pp. 193-201; G. Fohrer, *Ezechiel, ad loc.*; Zimmerli, *Ezechiel*, p. 441; S.E. Loewenstamm, 'Datam shel Yehudei Yev.', *Entseklopedia Mikra'it*, III, pp. 439-44.

generation of the desert (20.23). This is the extension of one of the arguments advanced by Moses in his plea after the affair with the golden calf. 'Wherefore should the Egyptians speak, saying: For evil[1] did he bring them forth, to slay them in the mountains, and to consume them from the face of the earth?' (Exod. 32.12). This demonizing interpretation of divine action would be a desecration of his name, that is, a pagan distortion of his nature. A similar argument appears in the request by Moses after the affair with the spies in Num. 14.15-16. The punishment of Israel in the desert would be a sign of God's impotence in the eyes of the Gentile nations. 'Because the lord was not able to bring this people into the land which he swore unto them, therefore he hath slain them in the wilderness' (Num. 14.16). These traditions, in general assigned to the priestly source, appear to have been available to Ezekiel, because the argument of the desecration of the divine name is only a further elaboration of it. It follows that according to Ezekiel, Israel's mission in history is the consecration of God's name by the exemplary fulfilment of his commandments. The opposite, namely Israel's transgressions against God, is interpreted as a desecration of his name.

The theocentric conception of history, including the eschatology that is usually hidden behind the formula 'and they shall know that I am God', is particularly emphasized with great pathos at the end of ch. 38 (v. 23): 'Thus will I magnify myself, and sanctify myself, and I will make myself known in the eyes of many nations; and they shall know that I am the Lord'. The destruction of the armies of the legendary king Gog from the land of Magog is conceived as a world-historical event of central importance; it is the proof of God's power before the whole of mankind. That approach is formulated in even clearer contours in 36.22-24:

> I do not this for your sake, O house of Israel, but for my holy name, which ye have profaned among the nations, whither ye came. And I will sanctify my great name, which hath been profaned among the nations, which ye have profaned in the midst of them; and the nations shall know that I am the Lord. . . when I shall be sanctified in you before their eyes. For I will take you from among the nations, and gather you out of all the countries, and will bring you into your own land.

Thus, Israel's redemption is completely independent of her own

---

1. That is, with an evil intent.

actions. Nor is it an expression of God's grace, love or mercy, as emphasized by Hosea or Jeremiah. On the contrary, it is an angry judgment by God against his people:

> And I will bring you into the wilderness of the peoples, and there will I plead with you face to face. Like as I pleaded with your fathers in the wilderness of the land of Egypt, so will I plead with you, saith the Lord God. And I will cause you to pass under the rod, and I will bring you into the bond of the covenant. And I will purge out from among you the rebels, and them that transgress against me; and I will bring them forth out of the land where they sojourn, but they shall not enter into the land of Israel; and ye shall know that I am the Lord (20.35-38).

The desert in biblical literature, that wilderness in which the surly desert generation was to wander and perish after God had denied them entry into the Promised Land due to their sinfulness—that desert is transformed in Ezekiel's imagination into the wilderness of the peoples (cf. Hos. 2.16ff.), that is, into the situation of scattering and dispersion, Diaspora, exile. There the sinners shall die, and will not experience the return to the land.

VIII

Who then are these sinners and rebels? The answer is contained in 20.32-34:

> And that which cometh into your mind shall not be at all; in that ye say: We will be as the nations, as the families of the countries, to serve wood and stone. As I live, saith the Lord God, surely with a mighty hand, and with an outstretched arm, and with fury poured out, will I be king over you; and I will bring you out from the peoples, and will gather you out of the countries wherein ye are scattered.

Here those in exile are specifically accused of having assimilatory tendencies. This is not the total and entire accusation and complaint that he raises against the inhabitants of Judah. But he is far from the idealizing perspective of a Jeremiah, who compares the Diaspora to the good figs (Jer. 24). Certain circles are mentioned here which, due to their weariness to make a forceful stand against a foreign culture, wish to join in worship of the idols of the nations. That must have been a large proportion of those in exile. Otherwise, the description of exile as a sieve, and the Deuteronomic expression 'with a mighty hand, and with an outstretched arm', which is meant there to designate the superior power of God against Egypt (Deut. 4.34; 5.14; 26.8; 1 Kgs 8.42), and is intensified here by the addition of 'fury poured out' (vv. 8, 13, 21; cf. 7.8; 9.8; 14.19; 22.22; 36.18; Jer. 21.5; Lam. 2.4), would indeed have been inappropriate. A second motif, that links the beginning of the speech with its end, revolves around the key word 'land'. The contrast is emphasized here between the 'land of Egypt' (8,10) or the 'wilderness of the land of Egypt' (36), the lands of dispersion (6, 15, 23, 34, 41), in plural form, on the one hand, and the 'land flowing with milk and honey', the 'beauty of all lands' (6, 15), 'the land, which I lifted up my hand to give unto them' (28), on the other.

The second group of expressions is intensified at the end with parallel designations: 'For in my holy mountain, in the mountain of the height of Israel. . . there shall all the house of Israel, all of them, serve me in the land; there will I accept them, and there will I require your heave-offerings. . . ' (v. 40). And in conclusion: 'when I shall bring you into the land of Israel, into the country which I lifted up my hand to give unto your fathers' (v. 42). This emphasis on the land in connection with offerings and sacrifice can be interpreted as an answer directed to the elders, who may have wished to inform themselves about the legitimacy of the cult of sacrifice outside the land of Israel.

To summarize the common denominator of chs. 16, 20 and 23, it consists in the deterministic pessimism regarding the character of the people, which stamps the downfall of Judah as the unavoidable will and judgment of God.

IX

The major problem deriving from this state of affairs is the prophet's repeated call for repentance (3.17-21; 18; 33.7-20), which is associated twice with his calling as a watchman over Israel. In connection with ch. 14, he develops a rigorously individual ethics that makes each individual alone responsible for his moral situation at the time of divine judgment, even disregarding his personal past—this in contradistinction to the traditional belief in the mutual responsibility of the generations (Exod. 20.4-5; Deut. 5.8-9). On the other hand, in so doing he robs even the most just, such as Noah, Job or Daniel (known from Ugaritic epic as a just king), of the possibility, at the time of a general judgment, to save anyone except himself—not even his own children (14.12-23, esp. 14ff.). Indeed, Ezekiel opens the doors and gates of repentance for each individual, no matter what his personal past. At the same time, the concept of sin is freed from any magic notions. As I mentioned above in discussing Zimmerli, we must understand his speech from the living context, as it seems that he tried to persuade his contemporaries in public discussions. His point of departure is the common proverb or, more accurately, the common reproach: 'The fathers have eaten sour grapes, and the children's teeth are set on edge?' (18.2; cf. Jer. 31.28). Or another argument that was common currency: 'Our transgressions and our sins are upon us, and we pine away in them; how then can we live?' (33.10). In the area of penal law, the author of Deuteronomy had already emphasized (25.16) 'The fathers shall not be put to death for the children, neither shall the children be put to death for the fathers; every man shall be put to death for his own sin'. But as far as divine judgment was concerned, the belief in the mutual responsibility of generations was still prevalent.

Ezekiel enters the discussion at this point. But his astonished audience apparently challenged him several times, shouting 'The way of the Lord is not fair' (18.25, 29; 33.17), meaning that this could not really be God's way.[1] So he felt compelled to defend a new ethics, and did so using two arguments. With regard to personal responsibility, the argument was as follows: 'Behold, all souls are mine; as the soul of the father, so also the soul of the son is mine; the soul that sinneth, it shall die' (18.4). In other words, each must account personally for himself before God, because God is the owner of all souls. For that reason, no one is called to account, whether a son or a father, for the deeds of the other.

The second argument concerns the reckoning of the individual before the throne of God's judgment. This means that 'just man' and 'sinner' are not concepts that can be calculated in quantitative terms, and in which the past either acts as a burden weighing down upon the present, or serves to relieve it. No, what is decisive in this regard,

---

1. לא יתכן דרך ה' The root תכן in qal (Prov. 16.2) and pi'el (Isa. 40.13) means 'to determine the measure, content or character of something'. The ancient versions (Septuagint, Targum, Syriac peshitta) render 'not right', 'not fair', i.e., not adjusted to standard norms, erratic, arbitrary. The way of the Lord is arbitrary; it does not conform to the traditional concept.

solely and exclusively, is the present of the given individual, his current moral status. 'Have I any pleasure at all that the wicked should die? saith the Lord God; and not rather that he should return from his ways, and live?' (18.23). That is, God, the creator and owner of all life, wants to preserve life. The conclusion to be drawn is:

> Cast away from you all your transgressions, wherein ye have transgressed; and make you a new heart and a new spirit; for why will ye die, O house of Israel? For I have no pleasure in the death of him that dieth, said the Lord God; wherefore turn yourselves, and live (18.31-32).

How is this ethics compatible with Ezekiel's conception of history, according to which the judgment of death has been handed down, irrevocably, over all of Jerusalem—a judgment to which all must fall prey, without exception, men, women and children? Indeed, his anthropological determinism of the stony heart makes any call for turning and repentance an impossibility (11.19; 36.26). I believe that it is impossible to bridge the tensions between these two poles by any kind of harmonizing exegesis, no matter how well-intentioned. At the same time, I must warn against any tampering with the text that would attempt to attribute the individualistic ethics, even 3.16b-21, to the so-called Hezekelian school, or perhaps to an unknown emendator or scribe, as is common practice, even today.[1]

---

1. F. Herrmann (*Ezechiel übersetzt und erklärt* [KAT 11; Leipzig: Deichertsche Verlagsbuchhandlung, 1924], *ad loc.*) excludes 26–29 as a parallel text; Zimmerli, however, rejects the exclusion of 33.10-20 (*Ezechiel*, p. 396). He adds that the vocabulary of this chapter moves within the 'range of a schoolroom explanation'. Yet this is certainly not sufficient reason to deny Ezekiel's authorship of the chapter, especially since it has been definitely established that he stood within this priestly tradition. The crucial point that indicates Ezekiel's hand is the radically individualistic ethics of this disputational passage. As to 3.16-21, many critics (Cooke, Zimmerli, Wevers, etc.) regard this passage as secondarily inserted here, while the original version is that of 33.1-20. But the fact is that these sections are completely different in nature: this section is a personal warning to the prophet to speak out. Verse 15 tells us that he was sitting for seven days, 'desolate', i.e., mute, silent, unable to speak, among the exiles. This silence was evidently the result of his shocking experience, when he was appointed as prophet of downfall, destruction and slaughter of the inhabitants of Judah (2.1–3.15). Now he was warned by God that his duty is to speak out in order to save at least those few backsliding righteous men who would revert to good under his influence. On the other hand, the kernel of 33.1-20 is a public speech, nay a public discussion, in the course of which he refuted the despairing fatalistic interjections of the audience (10, 17; cf. also 18.2, 19, 25, 29).

Nonetheless, I believe that that tension is acceptable and can be made plausible if one keeps in mind that Ezekiel's concrete sphere of action and activity was indeed the community of exiles in Babylon. His devastating judgment on Jerusalem was intended for their ears—in order to prepare them for the worst. At the same time, he was interested in keeping alive the hope for redemption among this community and in calling on each individual to ward off the divine wrath of God from himself and the community as his strength and abilities permitted. In other words, Ezekiel called on each person to take his own fate and that of the community in hand and act—by leading an exemplary life in accordance with traditional norms. As can be gathered from 8.1, 14.1 and 20.1, he was often asked by the elders for advice and about the word of God. Likewise, 33.30-33 indicates that his orations enjoyed great sympathy and popularity. It is true that he complains that his words for them are 'as a love song of one that hath a pleasant voice, and can play well on an instrument; so they hear thy words, but they do them not' (33.32). But it seems that his prophecies were cherished by the exiles. Even his admonitions give evidence that it was not just a small number of individuals who came to listen to his words. No, it was the whole people: they 'come unto thee as the people cometh, and sit before thee as my people, and hear thy words, but do them not' (v. 31). Yet despite this harsh criticism, it appears that he enjoyed great influence and an excellent reputation. In Jerusalem, he would have encountered stormy opposition, as illustrated by the fate of Jeremiah. I believe that his influence reached wide circles especially after the fall of Jerusalem. His individualistic ethics fell on fertile soil specifically after the fall of the city. That was the moral backbone of all those who had not given up hope in returning; this seems to have been the majority.[1]

Yet despite his pessimism, he saw himself compelled to struggle against the voices of despair and the bitter sarcasm of the critics in Babylon and in Jerusalem itself. Particularly before the fall, it was the voices that filtered through from Jerusalem—voices of resignation and desperation. Thus we hear from Jerusalem, 'Indeed, shortly houses will be built![2] This city is the cauldron, and we are the flesh' (11.3).

---

1. This dominant trend is manifested in Deutero-Isaiah's prophecy.

2. The text is uncertain. My reading is הלא בקרוב בנות בתים; this is not a negative statement, as appears from the M text, but a reassuring confirmation. Fohrer explains the sentence as a negation: the inhabitants of Jerusalem who took over the abandoned

In other words, our generation has suffered much, we are being boiled, as it were, like meat in a cauldron—but that cauldron, the city, will continue to exist and shall be rebuilt.

A word of self-consolation is contained in 12.22: 'Son of man, what is that proverb that ye have in the land of Israel, saying: The days are prolonged, and every vision faileth?' That is, in the course of time, all vision will prove to be nugatory. Another statement directed against the exile community is,

> Son of man, as for thy brethren, even thy brethren, the men of thy kindred, and all the house of Israel, all of them, concerning whom the inhabitants of Jerusalem have said: Get you far from the Lord! unto us is this land given for a possession (11.15).

That is, the inhabitants of Jerusalem wish to disown the exiles, because they believe they are the elite of Israel that has steadfastly adhered to the land.

If we follow these citations, it becomes clear that Ezekiel had to struggle against the influence of his opponents from Jerusalem, whose argumentation was a mixture of derision, consoling self-deception and arrogance. But voices of despair also penetrated out into the Diaspora. Thus, it is noted that the elders tried to justify their proclivity for idolatry with the lame excuse, 'The Lord seeth us not, the Lord hath forsaken the land' (8.12; 9.9). Another voice of despair that Jeremiah (31.28-29) had already alluded to stated, 'The fathers have eaten sour grapes, and the children's teeth are set on edge?' (18.2).

This is the critical point of departure for Ezekiel's individualistic ethics. As already mentioned, that ethics is the comforting answer of Ezekiel to the hopelessness of the situation before and after the fall of Jerusalem; it was designed to enhance the courage to go on living and the morale of those in exile after the war. In brief, each individual is, in ethical terms, a *tabula rasa*; each has the possibility, free from the shackles of the past, to realize his ethical personality. The mutual responsibility of the generations, a concept that dominated the old ethics (Exod. 20.5-6; Deut. 5.9-10), has been abrogated.

This new position is presented in two variations. One is contained in 18.31, where each is called upon to make a new heart and a new

homes of those who went into exile consoled themselves with the thought that they would thus not have to build homes in the near future. Yet such a questionable joy was not the intention here.

spirit. The other predicts this change as something eschatological: God, in his creative freedom, will create a new heart and spirit for each individual, instead of the stony heart of flesh. He will put his spirit in their hearts (36.26-27). In the vision of the resurrection of the dry bones, Ezekiel beholds this event as an eschatological drama.

X

In summary, I would like to emphasize the following:

1. The point of departure of Ezekiel's prophecy was the knowledge of the irrevocable nature of the catastrophe, the fall of Jerusalem (2.1–3.7).

2. On his search for the total justification of this divine decision, he sketched the history of Israel from its earliest beginnings as a witness to the faithlessness of Israel (16; 20; 23).

3. That adulterous faithlessness had been a hereditary burden for generations, because Israel's father was an Amorite and his mother a Hittite (16.23).[1] His ineradicable and abiding primal trait is his stony heart (3.7; 11.13; 36.16-36).

4. Ezekiel is in contradiction here to Hosea and Jeremiah, who attribute the depravity to the influence of the Canaanite vegetation cults, while they depict the pristine period of Israel in Egypt and in the desert as a testimony of the moral qualities and the intimate relationship between the desert generation and God. Ezekiel's conception should be evaluated as a radicalization of the Torah traditions of the surly generation in the desert.

5. Ezekiel's plastic presentation of Israel's faithlessness in obscene descriptions, which partially make use of the style of harlots, took the erotic intimization of the theology of the covenant, as developed in Hosea and Jeremiah, *ad absurdum*. When, after the catastrophe, Ezekiel made a new beginning aimed at demonstrating this emotional internalization, he chose the traditional image of the caring shepherd (ch. 34).

6. Ezekiel's historical and anthropological determinism, marking his prophecies of doom, is in flagrant contradiction to his individualistic ethics, according to which each person and generation is

---

1. The question as to whether this is in keeping with the historical facts is of no importance in our connection, since what interests us is Ezekiel's consciousness as it is given expression here. Cf. Zimmerli's remarks, *Ezechiel*, pp. 347-48.

responsible only for his or its own deeds. Additionally, he emphasizes that the personal responsibility of the individual before the chair of divine judgment can only refer to his own concrete and individual moral situation, leaving aside his personal past. In this way, he liberates his generation from the consciousness of having to do penance for the sins of the fathers, and opens up for each individual the possibility—despite the transgressions committed even in his personal past—to strike out on a new beginning. On the other hand, he warns against the moral placidity of those who boast about their past achievements or those of their forbears, and try to elude responsibility in this way for their concrete behaviour in the present. This position, that was designed to rescue the generation of exile from the profound despair into which it had been plummeted by the catastrophe, was the spiritual precondition for the great movement of renaissance that had its beginnings in the Babylonian exile—its culmination is the sermons of the unknown prophet, whom we call Deutero-Isaiah. Both Ezekiel's prophecies of doom, in which he wished to convince the exile community of the inexorable nature of the catastrophe, and to justify its occurrence, as well as his new ethics, based on a quite different foundation, were meant to save the exilic community spiritually and psychologically, and to lay the intellectual foundations for the future community.

7. We arrive at Ezekiel's eschatology. While the new ethics was directed in particular to the exile community, in order that they might liberate themselves from their moral crisis, in his eschatology he mentions the creative activity of God, who will replace the stony heart with one of flesh, who revives the dead and pours out his spirit upon them (11.19; 36.16-36; 37; 38–39) in order to gather them again in the land of Israel and to renew his kingdom. The new people that he fashions in his creative freedom will come to know him. This will be the great proof of God's mightiness before the peoples of the world. Ezekiel here gives special emphasis to the theocentric aspect of his conception of history. The sole objective of the redemption of Israel is the sanctification of the Lord's name, so that all shall know and recognize him. Hence, the process of redemption will encompass all the people of Israel. He will lead back those who are scattered among the peoples, 'with an outstretched arm. . . with fury poured out'. The main motif of his eschatology is not pity for the remainder of Israel but rather the 'interest' that God has in the sanctification and

recognition of his name in Israel in the cloak of the Deuteronomic tradition, but mainly in that of the priestly one.

Yet his attempts to persuade his contemporaries in open, public discussions led him far beyond these traditions, as we have stated above. Eschatology for him is not an abstract theory whose realization lies in a distant future. Chapters 40–48, the visionary transportion to the future Jerusalem with its temple and sacrifices, is the present utopian fulfilment, so to speak, of these hopes. This anticipation was designed to shape the concrete present. It is here that eschatology exerts a formative influence on contemporary consciousness—in order at a given hour to shape the concrete course of events. In actuality, it was the utopian elements of this eschatology—and not the real conditions of existence in the Babylonian exile—that moulded the consciousness of the exile community. Thanks to its living faith, Israel was able to overcome the tragedy, to recover and return to new life after two generations. These, then, are but a few characteristic traits of Ezekiel's prophecy.

The image of the prophet that emerges from this analysis is far removed from that of an outstanding and exemplary writer,[1] or of a poet, 'with his dazzling, imaginative and passionate rhetoric',[2] that of a curer of souls and lawgiver,[3] a 'priest in the cloak of a prophet',[4] as Wellhausen asserted in his embarrassment, or even that of a phil–osopher.[5] All attempts to grasp his personality with preconceived schematic conceptions are doomed to failure, since the tragic situation, unparalleled in world history, demanded a personality that, in its uniqueness, could contribute to efforts to confront and stand up to its dangers. Naturally, Ezekiel was a writer and poet; in a certain sense, he was also a curer of souls and law-giver, closely associated with the priestly tradition. Yet I believe that the dominant feature of this man was his vital connection with his people, a man able to listen to the voice of that people and to persuade his contemporaries in living discussion. He drew his inner strength from his visions, given to him in

---

1. H. Ewald, *Die Propheten des Alten Bundes* (Stuttgart, 1840), p. 327.

2. Hölscher, *Hesekiel*, pp. 5-6.

3. R. Smend, *Der Prophet Ezechiel* (KeH, 8; Leipzig: S. Hirzel, 2nd edn, 1880), p. vi.

4. J. Wellhausen, *Prolegomena zur Geschichte Israels* (Berlin: Georg Reimer, 6th edn, 1905), p. 59.

5. K. Koch, *The Prophets*, I (London: SCM Press, 1982).

all their pictorial vividness by the glory of God. Yet this self-realization was not exhausted in the seclusion and isolation of the visionary, but rather in his involvement with the problems, sorrows and hopes of the community. The living dialogue of the priestly messenger of God with his contemporaries, always listening, reprimanding, consoling and encouraging—this is one of the outstanding features of Ezekiel.

'JUSTICE AND RIGHTEOUSNESS'—משפט וצדקה—
THE EXPRESSION AND ITS MEANING

Moshe Weinfeld

The concept of social justice was expressed in ancient Israel and in the ancient Near East by means of a hendiadys.[1] The most common word-pair to serve this function in the Bible is משפט וצדקה,[2] 'justice and righteousness', or צדקה ומשפט, 'righteousness and justice'. However, alongside this expression, we find צדק ומישור or צדק ומישרים, 'righteousness and equity', word-pairs which are found in poetic passages, and therefore appear primarily in parallelism (see Isa. 11.4; 33.15; 45.19; Ps. 9.9; 58.2; 98.9; and compare Prov. 1; 3; 2.9). The pair צדק משר is found in the list of gods from Ugarit,[3] and was later preserved among the Phoenicians as well, as attested by Philo of Byblos.[4] The terms צדק/ישר, 'righteous and upright', are found as well in the Ugaritic literature[5] and in Phoenician inscriptions,[6] and the

---

1. For hendiadys in biblical literature, see E.Z. Melamed, 'Hendiadys in the Bible', *Tarbiz* 16 (1945), pp. 173ff. (Hebrew); *idem*, *M. Segal Vol.* (Israel Bible Society, 1965), pp. 188ff. [Hebrew]. On hendiadys in the treaty terminology of the ancient Near East, see my article 'Covenant Terminology in the Ancient Near East', *JAOS* 93 (1973), pp. 190-99.

2. See Y. Avishur, *The Construct State of Synonyms in Biblical Rhetoric* (Jerusalem: Kiryat Sepher, 1977), pp. 31-32, 95 n. 176 (Hebrew).

3. RS 24.271, A:14, *Ugaritica* V, p. 585. See J.C. de Moor, 'The Semitic Pantheon of Ugarit', *UF* 2 (1970), pp. 187-228, 196, 225.

4. *Zydk Mišor* in the writings of Philo of Byblos are hypostases of the principles of righteousness, as are *ṣdq mšr* in the list of gods from Ugarit. See S.E. Loewenstamm, 'Philo of Byblos', *Perakim* 2 (Yearbook of the Shochen Institute for Jewish Research of the Jewish Theological Seminary, ed. E.S. Rosenthal) (1971), p. 319 (Hebrew).

5. *'tt ṣdqh / mtrht yšrh* (Keret, *CTA* 14, pp. 12-13).

6. Yehimilk inscription: *kmlk ṣdq wmlk yšr lpn 'l gbl*, 'as a righteous (*ṣdq*) and upright (*yšr*) king before the gods of Byblos' (KAI 4:6-7). For a recent discussion of

word-pair thus predates Israelite literature. Similarly, we find the word-pair צדק/אמונה or אמת, 'righteousness and truth' (1 Kgs 3.6; Isa. 11.5; 59.4; Ps. 85.12; 66.13; Zech. 8.8) which is similar in meaning to the Akkadian word-pair *kittum u mīšarum*, literally 'truth and equity'.[1]

Word-pairs similar to the above but less comprehensive in meaning are *kidinnum kubussûm*, 'protection and righteousness', or in Elam, *ṣullum kubussûm*, 'protection and righteousness'.[2] The Egyptian term *ḥwi mki* apparently belongs to this class as well.[3]

---

the pair צדק/ישר in Phoenician Hebrew, see Y. Avishur, *Phoenician Inscriptions and the Bible*, I (Jerusalem: Rubenstein, 1979), pp. 51-53 (Hebrew). For the terms צדק, ישר and משר, and the royal ideology connected with them, see H. Cazelles, 'De l'ideologie royale', *JANESCU* 5 (1973), pp. 59. He also explains the substitution of משפט in biblical Hebrew for Ugaritic *mšr*. The phrase 'righteousness and equity' entered the lexicon of ancient Greece. Hesiod, in *Works and Days*, calls upon kings to establish righteousness, and in this context he says that they should judge the cause of the stranger and citizen, and not violate the principles of 'equity and justice (ἰθὺς καὶ δίκη) (1.226). See below, pp. 234-35 n. 4.

1. See the entry *kittum* in *CAD*, VIII, p. 470b 2'. These, too, appear in the form of gods; see p. 471, 4'. *kittum* (Sumerian *níg-gi-na*), which is derived from the verb *kânu* ('to be established'), means honesty, or truth. For the connection between the Hebrew verbs כון and אמן (from which Hebrew אמת, 'truth' is derived) see Deut. 13.15, 'and behold the matter is true (אמת) and confirmed (נכאן)', and see M. Weinfeld, *Deuteronomy and the Deuteronomic School* (Oxford: Clarendon Press, 1972), p. 93. *mīšarum*, from the root *ešēru*, 'to go straight', equals biblical מינור or מישרים, 'equity', but it is the semantic equivalent of צדק/צדקה, 'righteousness'. Cf. 1 Kgs 3.6: באמה ובצדקה ובישרת לבב. For the semantic equivalent of *kittum u mīšarum* with אמת וצדקה in Hebrew see E.A. Speiser, 'Cuneiform Law and the History of Civilization', *Proceedings of the American Philosophical Society* 107 (1963), pp. 536-41.

2. P. Koschaker, 'Göttliches und weltliches Recht nach den Urkunden aus Susa', *Orientalia* ns 4 (1935), pp. 45; W.F. Leemans, 'Kidinnu', in *Symbolae J.C. van Oven* (1946), pp. 48-49. *kiddinu* is the symbol of divine protection, which grants special rights, and thus it is synonymous with *ṣullu*, '(sheltering) shadow'. Cf. the Sargon documents: 'The King spread his shadow over Harran and wrote for her the bill of rights' (H. Winckler, *Die Keil-Schrifttexte Sargons* (2 vols.; Leipzig, 1889), 146, pp. 9ff.). For *kiddinu* in the Mesopotamian cities in later periods see H. Reviv, 'kiddinu', *Shnaton* 2 (1977), pp. 205ff. (Hebrew).

3. The term *hwi-mki*, 'protection and shelter', is connected with the grant of freedom in Egypt. See recently, A. Theodorides, 'Dekret', *Lexikon der Ägyptologie*, II, fasc. 7 (1974), pp. 1040f. It is very close in meaning to the Elamite *ṣullu kubussû*. See below regarding Egyptian proclamations of liberty, p. 235.

I shall try to ascertain the meanings of the Hebrew משפט וצדקה,
'justice and righteousness', and its Mesopotamian parallel, *kittum u
mīšarum*. They can be defined more precisely in context, as we shall
see below.

The term משפט וצדקה can refer to a character trait granted by God
to the king: 'O God, endow the king with your justice (משפטיך), the
king's son with your righteousness (צדקתי); that he may judge your
people rightly (בצדק) your lowly (poor) ones, justly (במשפט)' (Ps.
72.1-2). God thus is said to grant the king justice and righteousness,[1]
that is, a sense of justice with which to judge justly the people and the
poor. Likewise *kittum u mīšarum* means a sense of justice, that is, a
characteristic endowed by the gods. For example, it is said of
Hammurabi that Shamash gave him truth (*kinātum*),[2] while it is said
of Shamash himself that *kittum u mīšarum* are his gifts.[3]
Ashurbanipal writes in one of his letters that the gods have granted
him *kittu mīšaru*, 'truth and equity'.[4]

Justice and righteousness are considered a sublime, divine ideal in

---

1. The pair משפט וצדקה is here divided among the two hemistiches for the sake of
parallelism. See Melamed, 'Hendiadys', p. 183.

2. G.R. Driver and J.C. Miles, *The Babylonian Laws*, II (Oxford, 1955), xxvb:
97 (p. 98).

3. *ša mēšerum isiqšuma, kinātum* and *šeriktim šarkasum* in the long inscription of
Yahdunlim, king of Mari. Cf. *Sources for Early Biblical History: The Second
Millennium B.C.* (trans. and ed. A. Malamat; Jerusalem: Akademon, 1977), p. 10,
lines 4-5 (Hebrew). *kittum u mīšarum* are the son and daughter of the god Shamash
and his courtiers (= *sukallu*; the An-Anu god list, M.A. Deimel, *Pantheon Babyl.*
124 p. 196, no. 2387. Cf. for Mari, G. Disson, 'Un "pantheon" d'Ur III a Mari',
RA 61 (1967), pp. 100; for Ugarit: *Ugaritica* V, p. 220, l. 166). Misor and Zydkyk
in the works of Philo of Byblos are related to the sun gods (see recently A.I.
Baumgarten, *The Phoenician History of Philo of Byblos: A Commentary* [Leiden:
Brill, 1981]). He describes Zydyk as the father of Asclepius, god of healing, who is
identical wtih Esmun. See E. Lipiński, 'Eshmun "Healer"', *Annali dell' Instituto
Orientale di Napoli* 33 (1973), pp. 161-83. For Eshmun as the god of healing, cf.
his title *b'l mrp'*, 'master of healing', in *CIS*, I.41, p. 3, and see the trilingual Punic
inscription (Punic, Latin and Greek), *KAI* 66: 'To the lord, to Eshmun. . . who
donated, he heard his voice and healed him'. The connection between the sun,
righteousness, and healing is seen in Mal. 3.20: 'The sun of righteousness, with
healing in its wings' (שמש צדקה ומרפא בכנפיה).

4. L. Waterman, *Royal Correspondence of the Assyrian Empire* (Ann Arbor,
1930–36), no. 926:14. Cf. R. Borger, *Esarhaddon*, p. 106, iii:32: *kittu u mīšaru
išrukuinni*.

Ps. 33.5: God is said to love righteousness and justice. (Cf. the tenth blessing in the Eighteen Benedictions of Jewish daily prayer: 'Blessed are you, O Lord, the king who loves justice and righteousness', אוהב צדקה ומשפט). The Mesopotamian goddess Ishtar is likewise said to love *mīšarum*,[1] and Nebuchadnezzar, king of Babylon, is said to be a lover of truth and righteousness, *ra'im kittu u mīšaru*.[2] Similarly, the Assyrian king, Ashurbanipal, is proud that he loves *kidinnūtu*,[3] liberty (lit. 'the rights of protection'), granted to the residents of holy cities (see below).

In another biblical verse, we find an explicit parallel between משפט וצדקה, 'justice and righteousness', on the one hand, and 'equity', on the other: 'it was you who established equity (מישרים), you who performed "justice and righteousness" (משפט וצדקה) in Jacob' (Ps. 99.4). From this verse we can also learn of the royal aspect of justice and righteousness. Like the Mesopotamian *mīšarum*, which takes effect at the king's enthronement, here, too, God is said to establish justice and righteousness and equity in Jacob after he begins his reign and is exalted over all the peoples (vv. 1-2). Just as the enactment of the Mesopotamian *mīšarum* is bound up with promulgation of a series of regulations, here, too, the establishment of equity, justice and righteousness is followed by the giving of decrees and laws through Moses and Aaron (v. 7).

משפט וצדקה and *kittum u mīšarum* are considered a social ideal, along the lines of mercy and kindness. Thus, for example, in Isa. 16.5 the establishment of the Davidic throne with kindness and truth is connected with the demand for justice and righteousness: 'A throne shall be established with *kindness* (חסד) and on it shall sit in *truth* (אמת) a ruler that seeks *justice* (משפט) and is zealous for *righteousness* (צדק) in the tent of David.'[4] Elsewhere, the prophet says that King David's throne was established with justice and righteousness (9.6).

1. See W. von Soden, 'Zwie Königsgebete', *AfO* 25 (1974–77), p. 83:10.
2. S. Langdon, *Neubabylonische Königsinschriften* (VAB 4; Leipzig, 1912), p. 100 no. 12:5. Cf. p. 192 no. I:9.
3. T. Bauer, *Das Inschriftenwerk Assurbanipals*, II (Leipzig, 1933), p. 40 l. 8.
4. The pairs חסד ואמת and משפט וצדקה were each separated here for the sake of parallelism. The verse means, 'A throne shall be established with חסד ואמת, and a devoted judge, who seeks משפט וצדקה, shall sit upon it in the tent of David'. See Melamed, 'Hendiadys', pp. 180, 182-83. Melamed dealt with Isa. 16.5 in his supplement to the above article, also in Hebrew, in *The 'Tarbiz' Anthology* (תרביץ לקופי) I (1977), p. 218.

The fact that the establishment of a throne with *justice and righteousness* is synonymous with its establishment with *mercy and kindness* can be derived from the book of Proverbs as well. In 20.28 a throne is said to be maintained with חסד, kindness, while elsewhere the throne is established with צדק, righteousness (25.5; cf. 16.12). A similar synonymity is found regarding God's throne: 'צדק ומשפט are the base of your throne; חסד ואמת stand before you' (Ps. 89.15).

Kindness and truth, חסד ואמת, are found often in the Bible in conjunction with justice or with righteousness (Ps. 33.5; 89.15; Jer. 9.23; Hos. 2.21; 12.7; Mic. 6.8). I show elsewhere[1] that the social reforms which are the fruit of משפט וצדקה are in fact rooted in the king's kindness and goodwill towards the people. In the Hellenistic period these reforms, such as remission of debts, etc., were named τὰ φιλάνθρωπα, that is, philanthropy.

kittum mīšarum in Mesopotamia is also linked to acts of kindness. In the Epilogue to his Code, Hammurabi says that by giving laws he led his people in the way of truth and the path of kindness.[2] Elsewhere he says that he set *kittum u mīšarum* in the land, and dealt kindly with people (col. V, 2.20-24). Ashurbanipal says that the gods gave him preordained kindness (*šīmat damiqtim*), and created him with *kittum u mīšarum*.[3]

The practical application of משפט וצדקה accords with the usage of the term in an ideal sense: it refers to just dealing in the social sphere, particularly when the pair משפט וצדקה is found in conjunction with the concept of דרך, 'way' of life. Indeed, in the first instance of biblical use of the term צדקה ומשפט (Gen. 18.19), we find the term in conjunction with the word דרך: 'So that they keep the way (דרך) of YHWH by dealing with righteousness and justice'. This verse, which is predicated upon the sins of Sodom (Gen. 18.20-21), emphasizes the Israelite mission of social justice, in contrast to the Sodomites[4] who

---

1. In a forthcoming study.

2. *mātam, ūsam kīnam rīdam damgam, ušaṣbitu* (*Babylonian Laws*, xxiv b: 6-8). See below regarding the 'way'.

3. M. Streck, *Assurbanipal und die letaten assyrischee Könige bis zum Untergang Niniveh's* (VAB, 2; Leipzig, 1916), II, p. 30, iii:98. Cf. a Babylonian prayer '*mišaru* is on your right, kindness (*dumqu*) is on your left' (E. Ebeling, *Die Akkadische Gebetsserie 'Handerhebung'* [Berlin: 1953], p. 60; 71).

4. See Ehrlich's comment in *Miqra Kifshuto* (Berlin, 1899), to the preceding verse: 'This is the meaning of the verses: Will I not reveal to Abraham. . . he must know that I am destroying Sodom because of the cry that reaches me, in order that he

'did not support the poor and the needy' (Ezek. 16.49).

Other verses also speak of the way, or path, of justice and righteousness:

> guarding the *paths* (אחות) of justice, protecting the way (דרך) of those loyal to him. You will then understand what is just (צדק), righteous (משפט), and equitable (מישרים), every good course (מעגל) (Prov. 8.20).

> The path of equity (מישרים) for the righteous man; O just one, you make smooth the course (מעגל) of the righteous (Isa. 26.7).

> They do not care for the *way* of integrity, there is no justice in their course (במעגלוהם). They make their *paths* crooked, no one who walks in them care for integrity. That is why justice (משפט) is far from us, and righteousness does not reach us (צדקה) (Isa. 59.8-9).

'He leads me in the paths of righteousness' (Ps. 23.3) is parallel to the phrase from the Code of Hammurabi cited above: 'He led his people in the way of truth'. In fact, the Mesopotamian concept of *kittum u mīšarum* is itself related to the word 'way'. Thus we find often in Mesopotamia the phrase *ḥarran/uruḥ kitti u mīšari*,[1] 'the road/way of truth and equity'. The connection between law or custom and the concept of 'way' is implicit in the Elamite term *kubussûm* mentioned above, and it is likewise reflected in the term *kibsum*, which also means 'road'.[2] Both are derived from the verb *kabāsu*, 'to tread' (cf. Heb. כבש, and late Heb. כְּבִישׁ, 'road'), and like the term *halakhah*, derived from Heb. הלך, 'to walk', they refer to a way of life bound with the observance of just laws.[3]

---

command his sons to do צדקה and משפט. I believe that a contrast is indicated here between the cry (זעקה/צעקה) of Sodom (vv. 20, 21) and the destiny of צדקה for Abraham and his descendants. The contrast between צדקה and צעקה ('cry') reminds us of Isa. 5.7. It is interesting to note that in the same passage of Hesiod's *Works and Days* mentioned above, in which equity and justice are mentioned (ἰθὺς καὶ δίκη), we read of an entire city and nations that are destroyed because they subvert justice, and of immortal gods who walk among men in order to learn of subversions of justice, which remind us of the destruction of Sodom, and the mission of the angels there. For the last matter, cf. also *Odyssey* 17.485-487; Ovid, *Metamorphoses*, 8.611-712.

1. *CAD* 8 K, p. 471 d. See also Borger, *Esarhaddon*, p. 2, i:36: *ḥarran kitti u mīšari*.

2. *CAD* 8 K, p. 338.

3. See Koschaker, 'Recht', p. 39, and S.N. Kramer and M. Weinfeld, 'Sumerian Literature and Psalms', *Bet Miqra* 57 (1974), p. 157 n. 7 (Hebrew), for

Dealing justly is referred to explicitly in the Epilogue of the Code of Hammurabi as 'walking on the good path', in the section referred to above: *dīnāt mīšarim ša Hammurabi šarrum lēûm ukinnuma mātam ūsam kīnam rīdam damqam ušaṣbitu*, 'the equitable laws[1] which were established by the mighty king Hammurabi, who led[2] the land in the way of truth and the road of kindness'.

Similarly, Hammurabi says that the stela upon which he inscribed the laws will show his royal successor '*the way* in which to perform law and justice' (*kibsam ridam*,[3] 41.75-85). The justice and righteousness which a god performs toward his creatures is also referred to as

---

the connection with *ūsu* and *rīdu*, and there, too, for the meaning of the term *halakhah*. Cf. too, I. Tzvi Abush, 'Alaktu and Halakhah, Oracular Decision, Divine Revelation', *HTR* 80 (1987), pp. 15-42. P. Artzi has recognized in Ebla du-tum = *alaktum* as law or custom; see his article 'Ten Years of Ebla Research; Retrospective Notes on Ebla as a "Western" Precursor', in *Ebla 1975–1978* (ed. L. Cagni; Napoli: Istituto Universitario Orientale, 1987), pp. 409-17, 415. For דרך in the sense of law or custom, see Jer. 5.4-5: 'They did not know the way of the Lord, the law (משפט of their God'. Cf. also 2 Kgs 17.33, 34. The משפט of the Samaritans, 'who follow their former משפט (2 Kgs 17.40; see also 17.34) or 'the משפט of the nations' (17.33), should be understood as a custom or normative practice (i.e. a 'halakhah'). For משפט in this sense see 1 Sam. 2.13; 27.11. In the Aramaic Targums משפט is translated *halakhah*; see Ps. 72.1, 2. The ὁδός, 'way', of *Acts* is likewise to be understood as normative practice. Thus Paul justifies himself before the governor by saying that he worships 'according to the way (ὁδός), which they call a sect (αἵρεσις)', i.e. according to the 'halakhah' of the Christian sect (24.14; cf. 9.2; 19.9, 23; 22.4; 24.22). דרך is used in this sense in the Qumran scrolls as well. Cf. 'These are the norms of the way (דרך) for the משכיל' (*Manual of Discipline* (9.21; cf. 4.22; 8.10, 18, 21; 9.5, 9; 11.11; *War of the Sons of Light* 14.7; *Hodayot* 1.36). See the discussion of A. Fitzmyer, *Essays on the Semitic Background of the NT* (London: Chapman, 1971), pp. 281-83. The Pharisees called the Essene halakhah 'the other way'. See S. Lieberman, 'Light on the Cave Scrolls from Rabbinic Sources', *PAAJR* 20 (1951), pp. 395ff. For normative practice referred to as a 'way' compare the Arabic *shari'ah*.

1. Cf. 'righteous laws and statutes', חקים ומשפטים צדיקים, Deut. 4.8. For the relationship between this phrase and *dīnāt mīšarim*, see Weinfeld, *Deuteronomy*, pp. 150-51.

2. *harānam ṣabātu*, literally 'to hold the way', means to walk on the way, and the causative verb *šuṣbutu* means 'to lead', or 'guide'.

3. Literally, 'way course', a pleonasm common in biblical Hebrew (see Isa. 3.12; Job 6.18), for which see Y. Avishur, *The Construct State of Synonyms in Biblical Rhetoric* (Jerusalem: Kiryat Seter, 1977 [Hebrew]), and my note in *Shnaton* 1 (1976), p. 90 n. 9 (Hebrew)].

showing them the *way*. Thus in a Mesopotamian hymn to Ishtar[1]: 'You judge the people with *kittu u mīšaru*; You regard the oppressed and beaten, and lead them daily with equity (*tušteššeri*)' (ll. 25-26). Afterwards the supplicant requests: 'Grant liberty (*šubarrû*), straighten my path (*šutešri kibsi*)' (ll. 83-84).

Similarly, we find in the prayer of Nabonidus, king of Babylon, 'Day and night they grant me kindness. . . the way of peace and equity, the road of *kittu u mīšari* they place at my feet' (cf. Mal. 2.6: 'Truthful instruction was in his mouth. . . in peace and equity [מישור] he walked with me'). The verb *ešēru*, which is the root of the word *mīšarum*, means primarily to proceed along a straight path,[2] a concept which accords with the conception of justice and equity as a path upon which one should travel. The Akkadian term *andurārum/ durārum*, 'liberty', likewise means to proceed without obstruction. The same applies to the concept *šubarrû*, borrowed from the Sumerian *šu-bar*, which means to open the seizing hand, that is, to let go (= *wuššuru*).[3]

Social justice and equality are bound up with personal freedom, and liberating a man means allowing him to follow his own path without stopping him or binding him. In Egypt, too, the concept of liberty is expressed with the word *wstn*, which means 'to walk unbound'[4] and it is thus parallel to the Akkadian *ešēru*. It is surprising that even the Greek term for freedom, ἐλευθερία, which in Hellenistic times was the term for a proclamation of liberty, is connected with 'walking': ἐλεύσομαι being the future form of ἔρχομαι, 'to go'.

Performing mīšarum *in Mesopotamia and* משפט וצדקה *in Israel: The Concrete Meaning of the Concepts*

Walking in the path of *kittum mīšarum* means, as we shall see, the establishment of social equity, that is, improving the status of the poor and the weak in society through a series of regulations which prevent oppression. As we shall see, doing משפט וצדקה is likewise bound up

1. Ebeling, 'Handerhebung', pp. 130-31.
2. Langdon, *Königsinschriften*, 260: 31-32.
3. Compare Latin *manumittere* (= *manus* + *mittere*). The Sumerian opposite *šu-dù/du* means to seize with the hand, which equals Latin *mancipium* (= *manus capeo*); cf. P. Steinkeller, *ZA* 75 (1985), p. 43 n. 8.
4. A. Theorides, *Lexikon der Ägyptologie*, II, pp. 298ff., 'Freiheit'.

with actions on behalf of the poor and the oppressed. In this light, I shall analyse the concept of משפט וצדקה in the Bible.

First, one must distinguish between משפט צדק, 'a righteous judgment' (lit. a judgment of righteousness, adjective = צדק), and משפט וצדקה, 'justice and righteousness'. Although the same word, משפט, is used in both phrases, in the first it signifies a correct *judgment*, as can be seen in Deut. 16.18, משפט צדק, ושפטו את העם משפט צדק, 'they shall judge the people with true justice' (cf. Lev. 19.15, בצדק תשפט עמיתך, 'you shall judge your neighbour truly'), while in the second it is part of a hendiadys, the whole phrase signifying the concept of social justice.

In general, צדק refers to the abstract principle of righteousness, while צדקה refers to the concrete act.[1] צדק as an abstract ideal is thus personified; it is said to 'look out from heaven' (Ps. 85.12; cf. Isa. 45.8); peace and צדק are said to kiss one another (Ps. 85.11); צדק ומשפט are considered the foundation of God's throne (Ps. 89.15; 97.6); and God betroths Israel with צדק and משפט (Hos. 2.21). By contrast, צדקה is bound up with actions (see Isa. 56.1; 58.2; עשה צדקה, 'did צדקה', i.e. acted righteously), and later it became the Hebrew word for giving alms to the poor (Dan. 4.24).[2]

The rabbis and the traditional commentators connected משפט וצדקה with the proper execution of justice, that is, correct judicial decisions. However, they were not unaware of the problematic nature of the double term. Thus in regard to 2 Sam. 8.15, 'David performed משפט וצדקה', the rabbis asked: 'If there is משפט ('strict justice'), how can there be צדקה ('charity'), and if there is צדקה, how can there be משפט?', and they answered: 'Which judgment (משפט) involves charity (צדקה)? Compromise (a settlement between the two litigants)' (*b. Sanh.* 6b; cf. TJ *Sanh.* 1.8, 18b).

The rabbinic deliberations on this issue are expressed in *Abot deRabbi Nathan*:

1. For this distinction see Y. Licht, '*ṣdq, ṣdqh, ṣdyq*', *Encyklopedia Migrait*, VI, p. 681 (Hebrew); A. Jepsen, 'צדק und צדקה im AT', *Gottes Wort und Gottes Land. Festschrift H.W. Hertzberg* (Göttingen: Vandenhoeck & Ruprecht, 1965), pp. 78-89; Bo Johnson, 'Der Bedentungs unterschied zwischen *sädaq* und *ṣedaqa*', *ASTI* 11 (1977–78), pp. 31-39; F. Crüsemann, 'Jahwes Gerichtigkeit (*ṣedaqah* und *ṣaedaeq*) im AT', *EvT* 36 (1976), p. 431.
2. Y.F. Rosenthal, 'Sedakah, Charity', *HUCA* 23 (1950), pp. 411-30. See also A. Hurwitz, 'The Biblical Roots of Talmudic Term: The Early History of the Concept צדקה (= charity, alms)', *Language Studies*, II-III (ed. M. Bar-Asher; 1987), pp. 155-60.

Abraham performed צדקה first, and then משפט, as it is written 'For I have singled him out, that he may instruct his children and his posterity to keep the way of YHWH by performing צדקה and משפט' (Gen. 18.19). Whenever two litigants came before Abraham, our father, for judgement, and one said that the other owed him a mineh, Abraham would take out a mineh of his own and give it to him, and only then say 'present your cases before me'. But David did not do this; he did משפט before צדקה, as it is written, 'David performed משפט and צדקה for all his people' (II Sam. 8.15). Whenever two litigants came before the king he would say, 'Present your cases'. If in fact one owed the other a mineh, he would then take out his own mineh and give it to him.[1]

The rabbis understood משפט as judgment, while צדקה was understood to refer to an act of charity performed within the framework of the judicial process. Needless to say, this has nothing to do with the original meaning of the text.

When the prophets speak of משפט וצדקה, they certainly are not referring to a settlement between the parties, or acts of charity associated with the judicial process, and they certainly do not mean merely *just* judicial decisions. When we survey the verses that refer to משפט וצדקה in the prophetic literature and the Psalms, we find that the meaning of the concept is not confined to the judicial process. On the contrary, the concept refers primarily to the improvement of the conditions of the poor, which is undoubtedly accomplished through regulations issued by the king and his officials, and not by offering legal assistance to the poor man in his litigation with his oppressor. The term משפט, which was originally connected to the concept of administration (cf. Ugaritic *tpt*, and see below regarding the verb *špt*), later acquired a specifically juridical connotation, and this caused confusion regarding the meaning of משפט וצדקה. Instead of the biblical term משפט וצדקה, rabbinic Hebrew uses the hendiadys צדקה והסד, 'righteousness and kindness', or גמילות הסדים, 'performing kind acts'. In fact, the term משפט וצדקה implicitly refers to kindness and mercy as well, as we shall see below, and the word משפט in this word-pair should not be understood in the juridical sense.

I shall now attempt to offer support for this view. The establishment of a throne with משפט and צדקה is synonymous with its establishment with חסד, 'kindness', or חסד and אמת, 'kindness and truth' (Isa. 16.5; Prov. 20.28). Similarly, we find חסד in conjunction with

---

1. *ARN*, first version 33, ed. Schechter, p. 94.

משפט and צדקה or in parallelism with them; for example, 'He loves צדקה and משפט, the חסד of YHWH fills the earth (Ps. 33.5); 'צדק and משפט are the foundation of your throne, חסד and אמת go before you' (Ps. 89.15); 'He performs חסד, משפט and צדקה in the land' (Jer. 9.23); 'to do משפט and love חסד (Mic. 6.8; cf. Hos. 12.7; Ps. 101.1): 'And I shall betroth you unto me with צדק and משפט, חסד and רחמים (mercy)' (Hos. 2.21); 'He who pursues צדקה and חסד' (Prov. 21.21).

חסד, 'kindness', is identical with goodness and mercy. It is not a *character* that is congruous with strict justice, since if it were to be applied in court it would otherwise interfere with the execution of justice, which must be untempered by partiality. We must therefore conclude that the word משפט, and especially the phrase משפט וצדקה, does not refer to the proper execution of justice, but rather expresses, in a general sense, social justice and equity, which is bound up with kindness and mercy.

This understanding of the term משפט וצדקה is implicit in the prophetic exhortations. When Micah presents the demands of the divine ideal and says, 'He has told you, man, what is good. And what does the Lord demand of you? Only to do משפט and love חסד, and walk humbly with your God', he is not referring to the proper execution of justice, since (1) the demand is made of every 'man', and not every man is a judge of who is responsible for legal rulings, and (2) the last two demands of loving חסד and walking humbly imply that the demands are general and moral in nature, referring to good deeds, and thus doing משפט refers to actions of social justice. In a similar vein, Amos asks that 'משפט well up like water, צדקה like a mighty stream' (5.24).

If we look for exactly what it was that the prophets opposed, we see that the main wrongdoing is not the perversion of the judicial process, but oppression perpetrated by the rich landowners and the ruling circles who control the socioeconomic order. Amos rebukes those who 'store up lawlessness and rapine in their fortresses' (3.10), the women who 'rob the needy' (4.1), those who 'exact a levy of grain' from the poor, but live in 'houses of hewn stone' (5.11), those who 'use an ephah too small and a shekel too big', who 'buy the poor for silver, and the needy for a pair of sandals' (8.5-6). The last verse refers to those who are enslaved for non-payment of debts.

This concept of משפט וצדקה is clearly expressed by Isaiah. After the parable of the vineyard, which ends 'he hoped for justice (משפט); for equity (צדקה, lit. 'righteousness'), but behold, iniquity (צעקה, lit. 'crying out')' (5.7),[1] we find an indictment of landowners who enlarge their estates: 'Ah, those who add house to house and join field to field, till there is room for no one but you to dwell in the land' (5.8). This undoubtedly refers to those who foreclose the mortgages of the poor who cannot repay their debts, and turn their fields into their own personal property. Elsewhere Isaiah rebukes those who 'enact laws of injustice and compose (ומכתבים) iniquitous decrees', that is, those responsible for enacting laws and regulations (Isa. 10.1).[2] By making unjust laws, they subvert the cause of the poor, rob the rights of the needy, despoil the widows and make orphans their booty (10.2). Subverting justice here does not refer to abusing the judicial system *per se*, but rather to the enactment of unjust laws.

These unjust laws are apparently the cause of the foreclosures referred to in Isa. 5.8. An echo of the situation described in Isa. 5.8-24 and 10.1-4 is found in Psalm 94. The poet turns to the divine judge, and asks him to wreak vengeance on the evil, haughty men who oppress God's people and his inheritance (vv. 5, 14). He decries the evil men who act unjustly (v. 4), who commit crimes against widows and orphans (v. 6) and the righteous man (v. 21), and he prays that 'judgement (משפט) shall once again accord with righteousness (צדק)' (v. 15). All this is done by those who 'frame mischief through statutes (עמל עלי חק)' (v. 20), which reminds us of Isa. 10.1. The beginning of Psalm 94, 'give the haughty their deserts' (v. 2) reminds us of Isa. 5.15-16: 'Yea, man is bowed, and mortal brought low; brought low is the pride of the haughty. And YHWH of Hosts is exalted by משפט, the Holy God proved holy by צדקה'. According to these verses, God, the judge who performs משפט and צדקה, is exalted by bringing down the haughty.

The same type of condemnation of those who disregard משפט and

---

1. The 'cry' here is the cry of the oppressed and their complaint (cf. Exod. 22.26; 1 Kgs 8.5); compare 'the cry of the poor', Ps. 9.13 and Job 34.28, and the cry of the people and their enslaved wives in Neh. 5.1. See above, p. 232, regarding the cry of Sodom in Gen. 18.20, 21; 19.13.

2. This verse teaches us that laws were presented in writings, as in Greece. Whoever sponsored a new bill in Athens was required to present it in writing (see D.M. MacDowell, 'Law-making at Athens in the Fourth Century B.C.', *JHS* 95 [1975], pp. 62ff.). In Athens, where lawmaking was a democratic process, it was necessary to present the bill for approval of the Assembly, while in the East the law was presented to a small council.

צדקה is found in the prophecies of Micah against those who oppress a man and his house, a person and his inheritance (2.2). Since they dispossess the poor people of their inheritance they will not get any land when allotment of territory will take place in the community (2.5). As A. Alt has shown,[1] Micah here predicts that in the future allotment, or reallocation of territory by lot (which was customary in the 'community of YHWH', קהל יהוה), landowners who oppress their fellow men will not be allotted territory. Fields were allotted at the time of 'proclamation of liberty', a practice which was also quite common in social reforms in Greece (ἀναδασμὸς γῆς). The prophet therefore prophesies paradoxically that those who were responsible for צדקה and משפט, that is, alloting land to farmers, will not even be allowed to receive their own territory when the reforms are instituted within the framework of the community of YHWH.

Similarly, the prophet condemns those who drive women away from their homes (2.9), apparently because their husbands had been taken captive in war (v. 8). This is similar to the situation we encounter in the Middle Assyrian laws,[2] according to which the estate of a man who died in battle, or an estate abandoned by its owner, can be given away by the king to whomever he chooses. This was also the case in Israel. Witness the case of the Shunamite women in 2 Kgs 8.1-6. When she returns to the land after a seven-year absence due to

---

1. A. Alt, 'Micha 2,1-5, ΓΗΣ ΑΝΑΔΑΣΜΟΣ in Juda', in *Kleine Schriften*, III, pp. 373-81. The prophecy which denies a portion in the allotment of field is preceded by a prophecy which sees the enemy dividing the land. See Amos 7.17, 'Your land will be divided with a measuring line', and see the inscription of Idrimi of Alalakh, l. 95: 'His kingdom and land will be measured out to him with a measuring line' (*ebla limdudushišu*); see N. Naaman and A. Kempinski, 'The Inscription of Idrimi of Alalakh', in *Excavations and Studies Presented to Prof. S. Yeivin* (Archaeological Institute, Tel Aviv University, 1973), p. 215 (Hebrew). The translation proposed by E. Greenstein and D. Marcus ('The Akkadian Inscription of Idrimi', *JANESCU* 8 [1976], pp. 94-95) and their criticism of the above translation which was also proposed by M. Tsevat (*HUCA* 29 [1958], pp. 94-95) are untenable, especially since they depend upon an emendation. However, the pronoun attached to *limdudu* is in fact problematic, as Greenstein and Marcus have pointed out.

2. G.R. Driver and J. Miles, *The Assyrian Laws* (1934), A & 45 (vi: 85-88); cf. G. Cardascia, *Les lois assyriennes* (Paris: Cerf, 1969), pp. 218, 226; J.N. Postgate, 'Land Tenure in the Middle Assyrian Period', *BSOAS* 34 (1971), pp. 496-520.

famine, her house, field and estate are denied her, and she cries out to the king. He commands his eunuch to restore all her property, including the yield of her field.

Those who 'detest משפט', and 'make crooked all that is straight' (Mic. 3.9) are those who 'build Zion[1] with crime, Jerusalem with iniquity' (v. 10). Jeremiah specifies precisely how they do so: 'Ha! He who builds his house without righteousness (צדק) and his upper chambers with injustice (בלא משפט) who makes his fellow work without pay and does not give him his wage' (Jer. 22.13), which means they used enforced, unpaid labour. This is in contrast to the way of Josiah, who 'dispensed משפט וצדקה and upheld the rights (דן דין, lit. 'judged the case') of the poor and needy' (vv. 15-16). The phrase דן דין or שפט משפט occurs in Jer. 5.28 as well: 'They do not uphold the rights (דן, דין lit. 'judge the case') of the orphan... nor uphold the cause (שפט משפט, lit. 'judge the case') of the needy'. There, too, the meaning of the terms is to act on behalf of the poor and orphan. Josiah upheld משפט and צדקה and the rights of the poor, unlike his son Jehoiakim, who oppressed them. This brings us to the analysis of the terms שפט דן דין/משפט.

שפט משפט / דן דין

The phrase 'to do משפט וצדקה' is not the only one which refers to the establishment of social justice and equality. The phrases דן דין or שפט משפט (lit. 'judge the case') or שפט בצדק (lit. 'judge with righteousness') also refer to the concept of social justice. This has already been pointed out by I.L. Seeligmann,[2] who saw that the original meaning of שפט is to save the oppressed from the hands of the oppressor, or the enslaved from his enslaver. This can be done through the judicial process, through active intervention, by proclamation of an edict from on high, or through battle and struggle, cf. 'judges', שפטים, in the book of Judges, who wage war in order to save the Israelites from oppression.

We are concerned here with social oppression, and in that light we read of the king who judges (שפט) the poor and the needy (Isa. 11.4;

---

1. Read נבי ציון with LXX, Peshitta and the Targum.
2. See I.L. Seeligmann, 'Zur Terminologie fur das Gerichtsverfahren im Wortschatz des biblischen Hebraisch', *Hebraeische Worforschung, Festschrift W. Baumgartner* (SVT, 16; Leiden: Brill, 1967), pp. 251-78, 273-78.

Ps. 72.2, 4; Prov. 29.14), or judges the case (דן דין) of the poor and
needy (Jer. 22.15-16). This means that he saves them and acts on their
behalf, as can be clearly seen from Ps. 72.4: 'He will judge (= uphold)
the cause (ישפט) of the poor of the people, he will *save* the needy and
will suppress the oppressor'. Similarly we find that the divine king is
'שופט the orphan and downtrodden' (Ps. 10.18), and the word שופט
here is correctly translated in the NJPS version 'champion'. The term
שפט, 'to judge', even when applied to God, the judge of all nations of
the earth (Ps. 9.9; 67.5; 82.8; 96.10-13; cf. 98.9), refers to salvation,
and not necessarily to the pronouncement of judgment from the judicial bench. This is especially striking in Ps. 67.5: 'You judge (תשפט)
the peoples with equity (מישר), you guide the nations of the earth'.
Guidance here refers to leading people on the path of righteousness
(see above p. 233), and in this light the verb תשפט should also be
understood. The entire world rejoices when God appears for this
'judgment' (96.11-12; 98.7-8), and thus it is apparent that שפט here
refers to salvation, not a judicial process. Cf. also Ps. 76.10, 'as God
rose to משפט, to save all the lowly of the earth'.

Similar terms are applied to judges and officers. Isaiah, when he
asks for an end to evil, says, 'שפטו (lit. 'judge') the orphan, plead the
cause of the widow' (1.17). He certainly did not mean that the judicial
process should deal only with the cases of the poor and fatherless,
neglecting the cases of the upper classes. Rather, he meant that the
poor and weak should be saved in their struggle with the mighty, as
can be seen from the first half of the verse: 'Learn to do good, seek
משפט, aid the wronged'. Thus, too, should we understand Ps. 82.3-4:
'שפטו the wretched and the orphan, vindicate the lowly and the poor,
rescue the wretched and the needy; save them from the hand of the
wicked'. We should understand in a similar vein the phrases 'דן דין of
the poor and the needy', 'דן דין of the orphan', 'שפט משפט of the needy'
in Jer. 5.28, 22.15-16, and Prov. 31.9. In Gen. 49.16, 'Dan shall
judge (ידין) his people' means he shall save his people, and this is also
the meaning of God's 'judgment' of his people in Deut. 32.36 and Ps.
54.3.

This usage is especially common in the Israelite and Mesopotamian
psalm literature, in the context of pleas for salvation. Thus we read in
Ps. 43.1, 'Save me (שפטני, lit. 'judge me'), O God, and champion my
cause against faithless people; rescue me from the treacherous, dishonest man'. As in Ps. 82.3-4, cited above, here, too, שפט refers to

rescue from a faithless people and a dishonest man. The rescue is done by God the judge, who decides in favour of the good man, and thus saves him from the bad man. In these circumstances the righteous man is prepared to be tested in the divine court, in order to prove his innocence. Thus the supplicant in Psalm 26 declares that he walked in innocence, and therefore God should judge him, try him and test him, so that his innocence and righteousness may be made manifest:

> Judge me (נפטני), YHWH, for I have walked in innocence;
> I have trusted in YHWH; I have not faltered.
> Probe me, O YHWH, and try me, test my heart and mind,
> for my eyes are on your kindness; I have walked in your truth
> . . . I walk in my innocence. Redeem me. Have mercy on me! (Ps.
> 26.1-3, 11)

Similarly, we find in Psalm 7 a request for the divine שופט, apparently in the context of a political conflict,[1] in which the supplicant asks God to judge him (שפטני) according to his righteousness and innocence (v. 9), and in this context he mentions God's probing of heart and mind (v. 10). One should mention here also Psalm 35, which begins, 'Plead, O YHWH, my cause and fight my battle' and ends with a request for the divine שופט, 'for my cause, O my God and my Lord! Judge me (שפטני), YHWH my God, as you are beneficent. . . ' (vv. 23-24).

In each of these cases we are dealing with divine salvation, presented as a divine court decision. The same metaphor is found in Mesopotamian psalm literature. There as well, the supplicant asks for divine assistance, using juridical terms,[2] for example: *dīni dīn, purussâya purus / dīni dīn alakti limad / ina dīnika mīšarūtu lullik* ('judge my judgment, decree my decree / judge my judgment, learn my ways / in your judgment I will go in equity'). Not only in Mesopotamian psalm literature do we find *dīni dīn* ('judge my judgment') in the sense of 'save me'; the phrase is quite common precisely in the area with which we are dealing, the field of social justice. Thus, in issuing a series of proclamations for the good of his people

---

1. See J.H. Tigay, 'Psalm 7.5 and Ancient Near Eastern Treaties', *JBL* 89 (1970), pp. 178-86.
2. See W. Mayer, *Untersuchungen zur Formensprache der Babylonischen 'Gebetbeschwörungen', Studia Pohl—Series Maior* (Rome: Biblical Institute Press, 1976), pp. 221ff., and references there to various texts.

'Hammurabi "judges" the land',[1] that is, he deals justly with the widow and orphan (1.61) and the oppressed (1.74), and ensures that the weak will not be given over to the strong (11.59-60). We often hear in Mesopotamia of 'judging the judgment of the weak and oppressed', that is, intervention on their behalf.[2]

Especially revealing is the following passage, taken from a neo-Babylonian work, entitled by its editor 'Nebuchadnezzar King of Justice'.[3]

> He did not neglect the justice of *kittu u mīšari* (truth and equity), judgment and decision, acceptable to Marduk the Great Lord, and established for the good of all men and the settlement of the land of Akkad, he wrote with counsel and wisdom. He enacted the laws of the city for good. He established the laws of the kingdom for all generations (ll. 22-27).

Truth and justice/equity are thus given expression by means of law-making that benefits the population.

The role of the king in dealing justly with the orphan and widow is especially stressed in the Ugaritic texts. The true king is characterized as one who will 'uphold the cause of the widow, will do justice to the orphan/the wretched'.[4]

Doing שופט in the sense of doing good for the poor and the weak is especially stressed in the prophetic literature, and Zechariah's prophecy (7.9-10) is especially instructive. In listing the idealistic demands of the earlier prophets,[5] the prophet says, 'Execute true justice (משפט אמת שעטו); deal kindly and mercifully with one another, do not defraud the widow, the orphan, the stranger, and the poor; and

---

1. *dīn mātim ana dânim*, in the Epilogue of the Code of Hammurabi (Driver and Miles, *Babylonian Laws*, xl:70). For the meaning of *dīnam dânum* in the Code of Hammurabi see F.R. Kraus, 'Ein zentrales Problem des altmesopotamischen Rechts: Was ist der CH?', *Geneva*, Musée d'art d'histoire, ns 8 (1960), pp. 284f.

2. *dânu dīn ša enšiu habli*. For the meaning of *enšu*, see my article, 'זרמים תיאלרגיים בספרותהתולה', *Bet Migra* 42 (1971), p. 16 n. 4 (Hebrew). For references see *CAD* vol. 3D, s.v. *dânu* 4' (p. 103).

3. W.G. Lambert, 'Nebuchadnezzar King of Justice', *Iraq* 27 (1965), pp. 1ff. According to H. Tadmor, this work refers to Nabonidus, not Nebuchadnezzar (personal communication).

4. *ydn dn 'lmnt ttpṭ ṭpṭ ytm* (Aqhat = Herdner, *CTA* 19, i:23-25; 17, v:7-8); *l' tdn dn 'lmnt i' ttpṭ ṭpṭ qṣr npš* (Keret = *CTA* 16, v:33ff., 45ff.).

5. 'The message that the Lord proclaimed through the earlier prophets' (v. 7). Verse 8 interrupts the flow of v. 7 into v. 9 and is a textual error. See commentaries.

do not plot evil against one another in your hearts.'

There is an apparent contradiction here: true justice ought by right to be free of compassion and mercy.[1] However, Zechariah here is not referring to the correct execution of justice in court, but rather to the establishment of social justice, and the restoration of equilibrium to society by aiding the needy: the stranger, widow and orphan. Zechariah is apparently influenced here by Jer. 7.5-6: 'if you execute justice between one man and another, if you do not oppress the stranger, orphan and widow. . . .'.

This also is the meaning of Zech. 8.16: 'Render truth and peaceful (or perfect) justice in your gates' (אמת ומשפט שלום שפטו בשעריכם). Here, too, the rabbis asked how one can have the 'truth' and 'peaceful justice' together, and they answered, as above, that this verse refers to compromise, or a settlement between the parties (TJ *Sanh.* 1.5, 18b).[2] However, the plain meaning of the verse is that 'truth and peaceful justice' refers to social justice, and not to correct judicial rulings.

Thus when the prophets refer to משפט and צדקה, they do not mean merely that the judges should judge accurately. They mean primarily that the officials[3] and landowners should act on behalf of the poor. In Job 29.14-17 as well, doing צדק and משפט mean helping the needy: 'I clothed myself in צדק and it robed me; my משפט was my cloak and turban. I was eyes to the blind and feet to the lame. I was a father to the needy. . . .'.

Divine משפט and צדקה are likewise help for the poor and oppressed, for the stranger, orphan and widow: 'He does the משפט of the orphan and the widow, and loves the stranger, giving him bread and clothing' (Deut. 10.18); 'YHWH performs righteous acts (צדקות) and just acts (משפטים) for all the oppressed' (Ps. 103.6); 'He does justice (משפט) for the oppressed; he gives bread to the hungry' (Ps. 146.7).

In conclusion, some clarification is necessary. My interpretation of 'justice and righteousness' does not exclude the juridical sense of the

---

1.   David Kimhi, the mediaeval commentator, saw the problem in the verse and tried to solve it harmonistically: 'When you judge a man and his fellow, let the judgement be true, and if it be necessary to act toward anyone with kindness and mercy, which are beyond the law, do so.'

2.   See E.E. Urbach, 'The Quest for Truth as a Religious Obligation', in *Hamiqra Veanahnu* (ed. U. Simon; Ramat Gan, 1977), pp. 18-19 (Hebrew).

3.   On officers/judges with judicial and executive authority, see my article 'Judge and Officer in Ancient Israel and the Ancient Near East', *IOS* 7 (1977), pp. 65-88.

expression. The judge, although subject to legal rules, cannot overlook considerations of fairness and equity, thus bringing about 'true judgment'.[1] My contention, however, is that 'justice and righteousness' is not a concept that belongs to the jury alone, but is much more relevant for the social-political leaders who create the laws and care for their execution.

---

1. See J. Bazak, 'The Meaning of the Term "Justice and Righteousness" in the Bible', *The Jewish Law Annual*, VIII, pp. 5-13.

This panel discussion took place at the close of the symposium on 21 June 1990 and the participants were Professors Amir, Falk, Frey, Graf Reventlow, and Uffenheimer.

Reventlow: We are now beginning our panel discussion: 'Biblical Justice Today?' The question mark shall be a stimulus for our discussion.

Uffenheimer: First I want to thank Professor Frey cordially for his instructive contribution. His rich remarks were so profound that I want to concentrate my reaction on the close study of the wording of his paper. I just want to stress one point: we biblical scholars are always slaves of historical details, and we, not just we, but all historians believe that God dwells in the detail, whereas very few biblical scholars find their way when thrown into the realm of philosophy, because they simply have no philosophical, theological education. Therefore, I mean to say, contacts between both sides, between theology and historians, are stimulating.

My thoughts were directed upon sociological aspects, but I wanted to mark the starting point as the *hic et nunc*, namely the present situation: are the biblical principles of justice still valid for us? The difficulty lies in the manifoldness of the biblical material and in the fact that the Bible does not contain any methodical philosophy of justice. We have to find out the basic position of the Bible from occasional remarks and from the argumentative parts of some law passages and edicts. In the present context I want to understand justice and righteousness in the sense of social righteousness, but the starting point has to be, as I remarked, our present situation which can be characterized as post-communist. Before our eyes Soviet communism is breaking down as a sociopolitical system. But it has to be stressed that the communist system in spite of all errors, confusions and crimes was founded upon principally moral axioms, because it took in earnest the economic sense of the watchword *égalité*, though at the expense of *liberté*. Why did this project fail, which has taken the breath of the world for 70 years? It seems to me first, that it was founded on the erroneous assumption that human society even at the end of the twentieth, technological century could not only be suppressed by terror and brutal means, but also formed by those means. Officially the means of power were used in the service of the idea, but the interests of the tyrannical minority distorted and falsified the idea, so that in a short time out of the equalized, terrorized masses a minority crystallized which was equipped with economic prerogatives. Its brutal conduct did not stop before any law. Secondly, it became evident that the motivation of the working classes, which were deprived by forced collectivization of the fruit of their endeavours, was reduced to nothing. The undifferentiated, low payment and recompense which did not consider the individual achievements and efforts undermined the working morale so that the Soviet Union after 70 years of communism has fallen back to its economic starting point. Enormous parts of the population, especially in the Asiatic republics, are living on a very low level which has no parallel in the West. The irony of fate lies in the fact that the movement which proclaimed historical materialism as its religion had no understanding at all of the daily material needs and endeavours of the individuum. But the breakdown of communism does not at all mean a justification or the victory of capitalism, as the illness that communism intended to heal grows on at the present day. Its name is poverty, hunger and social backwardness of millions of people. Doubtless free competition in the liberal form of economy which incites and rewards the diligence and inventiveness of the individual is the irreplaceable psychological basis for the high standard of living in the Western countries. A standard of living which the centralistic system of communism, burdened by an endless bureaucracy, never can and never will reach. The nightmare of Franz Kafka's novel *The Process* (especially the last chapter 'In Front of the Law' which was published at first separately) seems to contain a presentiment of communist totalitarianism without expediency. But on the other hand, there exists the danger that the free, liberal economy which promotes brutal greed for gain, might deliver the economic resources of our planet into the hands of a small minority, a minority facing the impoverished, passive, sweated and hungry masses of South America, Asia and Africa. The unlimited freedom of capitalism, the political frame of which is democracy, might provoke dangerous situations which might prepare the way to power for the satanic elements of the human soul.

What has the Bible to say to this situation? Can it say anything? I believe yes. But not in the sense of a concrete social or political programme, but as a storehouse of important principles that have to be transposed or translated into the reality of the modern world. Here I can but indicate; as a classical example I want to mention the agrarian legislation of the Bible, in which the following principles are expressed:

1. Society needs a plan. In the legislation a cycle of seven and of nine years is spoken of. Without planning every economic action is chaotic.

2. This plan has to include all, men and beasts, and that means also the ecological element which modern socialist ideologists completely neglect.

3. Here we are dealing above all with the third cycle, which was treated by my colleague Amit, the year of jubilee. It regulates the restitution of the land, a reparation of distortions of the possession of land during a certain period and the realization of the principles of freedom. That means equality and freedom; equality not in a mechanical sense, but in the sense of pushing back poverty. The Bible is realistic, it knows that poverty will never disappear. Therefore it believes that even this grand programme will never be sufficient.

4. Hence comes the turn to the single individuum to realize this programme, in our context especially the landowner who has to concede special rights to the poor, but rights which he can decide about himself. I mean Lev. 19.9. These are the subjects I wanted to hint at. Perhaps we shall treat them later on in more detail.

Reventlow: I want to include that you have tried on one side to describe the situation of our world in a very global way. This part of your remarks I understand as an interpretation of the 'today'. The other side which you touched upon is: how far can biblical foundations of our acts help us on a global, but also on a local level—as we have to add—to contribute to a solution of the problems which embrace the world today more and more globally. For we recognize that it is no more possible to manage a special territory, even the whole of Europe, separated from the rest of the other continents and their differentiated problems or to cope with these problems.

Falk: I would like to say something about the topic 'Biblical justice today'. It includes four problems. I think the problems are the following: the social conflicts we heard about in a detailed way, international conflicts, religious conflicts and theological problems. The topic 'Biblical justice today' I see in the context of these four problems. Because already much has been said about the social conflicts, I want briefly to indicate something on the other matters:

Regarding international conflicts I want to say, the question arises whether the biblical idea of justice only knows the messianic solution, will say, as with Isaiah and Micah that world peace and peaceful settlements of all conflicts is postponed to the future, or if there exists a model in biblical thinking for the settlement of conflicts. I think this is a very important problem. Just to give an impression of what I mean: I am thinking for example of 1 Kgs 20.31. There it is said about the kings of Israel, that they are known as מלכי חסד—the term 'mercy' relating to international conduct. But that would be a theme for a separate symposium, as has been remarked.

Now to religious conflicts. In my opinion I see the main conflict to be between the individual and the religious establishment. Also here I want to mention one idea only: according to Jewish, rabbinical understanding the decalogue is defined as an address to the individual, so that everybody is addressed personally. That goes to say that for the rabbis there exists a picture of a God who speaks to everybody in his own language, in different forms speaks to different people. This picture is dramatized and illuminated by the following metaphor: imagine a dabicon, that is a Greek Orthodox church in which the icon is in the dome. Everybody who looks upon the icon feels himself looked upon by the icon directly, the icon is looking just upon him. In the same way God addresses the people of Israel; not 'who brought you out of the land of Egypt', but 'I am God, thy God who brought thee out of Egypt'. Everybody is addressed. This possibility has been developed by Franz Rosenzweig who distinguishes between the law, which is common, and the command, which is directed to each person personally. I think that is a central problem in the religious situation of today. Justice demands that one think more differentiatedly, meet the individual halfway and take the interests and the needs of the individual more into consideration than the religious establishments did in former times.

Now I am coming to the theological problems. Here also I want to articulate just some problems which I observe in connection with 'Biblical justice today'.

The first problem for a Jew is in my opinion the problem of theodicy. When we speak about biblical justice today we cannot pass over the question of theodicy. I think that this question has no answer, and we should not try to give any answer. The only answer is the one given by Job (13.15): הן יקטלני לו איחל—'Even if he gives me the death-blow, I will wait upon him'. That means, for the religious man God is the only possibility for life. Thereby he can overcome the problem of theodicy. But the problem does exist, and there is no sense in trying to evade it.

Secondly, I think that the question of biblical justice is connected with the term 'sin' or the repudiation of righteousness by works. According to Jewish tradition we express that in the prayer:

אבינו מלכנו חננו ועננו כי אין בנו מעשים
עשה עמנו צדקה וחסד והושיענו:

Our father, our king, give us grace and answer us, for we have no works, do with us צדקה (what transcends that which one can expect) and grace, and help us!

The third I have already indicated: pluralism. I think that pluralism belongs to biblical justice, a pluralistic understanding of society. Pluralism is expressed in the word מישרים. In the Talmud Eretz Jisrael in connection with the explanation of the Torah which is many-sided and manifold, the word in the Canticle of Canticles (1.4) מישרים אהבוך (מישרים is justice) is thereby explained that everything, however as straight as it may appear, is to be put into the plural. You can look upon justice from different sides. Therefore מישרים and not מישור. At other places you find מישור, but מישרים is in the plural, meaning: What to one appears straight and rightful whatsoever, to the other it does not appear so. Therefore the Torah has to be interpreted in different ways, in a dialectical manner, only thereby it can become effective.

Finally the idea which I already spoke of before: justice means also criticism of every authority, including religious authority. In our daily prayer we have a special blessing, in which we criticize the existing authority. It is the blessing:

Restore our judges as they were before and our counsellors as they were in the beginning, and make us free from the evil and from injury. Rule yourself over us, only thou, with grace and mercy, and make as just by the law. Praised beest thou, God, the king who loves justice and the law as well.

Frey: Your actual scripture-exegesis always makes me very thoughtful, because I have asked already in what actuality consists. For it is obviously not dead exegesis of the letter, but an attempt to speak into the problems of life.

Therefore, I want to thank you, Professor Falk, for your pointing to theodicy. I think that Christianity has still more to learn there, and also from Jewry, for it has from time to time rather triumphalist traits, as if the justice of God were already definitely revealed. I think we could learn from the not yet definitely solved question of theodicy the following.

It seems to be a temptation for many religions to establish cosmic interrelationships, to make the present life-condition depend on actions in the past. The most rational of all religions would then be Hinduism by its theory of re-incarnation which in fact places one's life-condition and acting into a world-wide connection, exceeding the personal existence of a single individual. If one thinks over the full consequences of that, such a religion could not have compassion for other people; this one has to define otherwise, if one wants to have it at all, because we are dealing with a complete connection of balance. But wherever the question of the justice of God has not yet found a definite answer, there passion is real passion, because it cannot be placed into a theoretical connection. I think Christianity should learn with all energy exactly this contribution of the book of Job and stick to it, because thereby we would actually give reasons for what in modern times is but postulated, an ethics of compassion. Schopenhauer and Albert Schweitzer merely postulated it, but they were never able to give a real reason why we should begin with compassion. The reason, however, consists in the fact that the world does not resemble a complete invoice in which the justice of God had already broken through as a total calculation. That is seemingly one of the most important contributions of Judaism and Israel also for Christianity, at this place. Only starting from there can we also speak about human rights and the fulfilment of their needs independently from their merit. Here basic human rights are first founded and inaugurated.

Now I would like to come to two matters. The first is the agrarian vision. I am told how things are running nowadays in Israel: that whoever is an orthodox law-observing Jew farms out his land to a foreigner, a non-Jew, in the seventh year, so that one can escape *de facto* from the law. I see in that a challenge to consider what are the fundamentals of participation in a particular society. In an agrarian society it is doubtless land propriety. In the present one has to think about social insurance, about social security, about the inequality of women and their treatment. On this field the intention of the agrarian legislation of Israel comes back. Similarly I would see the situation of the מלכי חסד (1 Kgs 20.31).

In Christianity this model has sometimes been repristinated rather thoughtlessly. Whenever Luther did not know how to get on, he thought about David or the great ruler who would solve everything—in his time a well-founded expectation. But if one transposes this model into the times of a state that is at least in rough measure a democratic one—where everybody's responsibility is asked for—the projection of responsibility onto one person who bears it as a representative and completely alone becomes dangerous. That means that here one has actually to ask, can the members of a democracy, in such a responsible way and avoiding the schematisms of justice, altogether become such מלכי חסד, forming a society of people living together which does not distribute opportunities according to extreme liberal rules of competition, letting some perish, and others win? This seems to me the main requirement.

Amir: Of the theme of this panel discussion I have looked above all upon the question mark at its end. That is what engages me most. 'Biblical justice today?'—What is biblical justice? It has often been said, by people who are more competent than I, that the Bible did not construct a system. In spite of that I believe one can characterize with one word what biblical justice is, when I look upon the ethos in the context of which this biblical postulate of justice is valid. There I must come back upon the agrarian legislation which has already been mentioned several times. The whole legislation there is based upon two verses of the respective chapter which Ya'ira Amit has also mentioned, two verses which are adapted to one another and have a close mutual assonance. The first says, כי־לי הארץ 'Because the land is mine' (Lev. 25.23) and the other, formulated in a parallel fashion, כי־לי בני־ישראל עבדים עבדי הם 'For mine are the children of Israel my servants' (Lev. 25.55). Out of this pair, 'Mine are. . . ', 'They belong to me' the whole effective ethos of this legislation comes into being. Then I have to ask: what can that mean, 'Biblical justice today'? 'Today' means in a secularized society. Can this postulate, that has its deepest existence in the ל 'mine', gain a chance of influence in a secularized society? If we do not want to have to do with mere postulations, how a legislation which is nourished from the Bible should look or the order of a society, then this ethos, if it is going to be understandable, if it is going to reach humankind to which it is directed, must be secularized. Otherwise it will not be understandable. Then comes the question which is paramount for all of us: can something like this be secularized without losing what is peculiar to it? This secularization is as impossible as unavoidable. Therefore in the theme, the question mark is decisive for me. How can what the Bible has to say to humankind be expressed in a language for the humankind of today? No doubt, the solution to this problem has already been spoken about; a way of secularization has been Karl Marx. What has come out of this is visible nowadays. But in spite of that we know that, in some way one has to try over and over again to translate something which, as all of us, Christians and Jews, know by heart, cannot be formulated in a secular language completely, as far as possible into a language that is understandable and accessible to the mankind of today. If this concept 'Biblical justice today' is to have a chance it seems in my opinion to depend on this nearly desperate task. We have said over and over again, secularization means ruin, or it means profanization. But nevertheless we know that without an attempt at a translation into a language which is accessible to the humankind of today all that we are saying today here, sitting at a table together, can make an impression only to a certain circle of convinced people, but can alter nothing of what moves the minds of men. Besides we know—not only the most recent experience, but actually the whole history of mankind speaks for that—that in the name of God and in the name of religion over and over again the most incredible things have happened and have been justified, that therefore this secularization is something urgently dangerous. But nevertheless we know that, if what we want to say here is not to die away in an empty room, we must seek what actually is nearly impossible to reach, a responsible form of uttering in a secular way what we want together here. Something that is motivated for us in a religious sphere, which shall nevertheless somehow remain expressible to all who do not understand this basic secretum of our language.

Uffenheimer: I want to continue on the theme of my neighbour. In the year 1940, Buber published his book *Trails in Utopia*. At that time he described the kibbutz as a not yet miscarried attempt to realize justice.

Amir: It was you who added 'not yet'!

Uffenheimer: Not miscarried..., pardon. But that was not meant ironically, but quite in earnest, because all attempts since Adam Riese until now have miscarried. But I believe that the realization of this principle has a chance even in a secular society. Here I simply want to mention the new forms of settlement which have developed in Israel, the collective settlement, the kibbutz, and the moshav, the cooperative settlement and most recently the communal settlement. In these three variations the attempt is made to realize justice in differentiated forms which are perhaps adapted to the psychology of the different groups of people. Here the first attempt is made to combine equality with freedom. But I don't believe that secularization is necessary, as we have also the kibbutz dati, a religious kibbutz, the motivation of which is religious, so that we have here a practical starting point. This starting point can be confirmed by the study of those pioneers who invented this idea, pioneers who are not known in the West, Buber excepted. I just want to mention some pioneers who were realizers: Aaron David Gordon (1856–1922) who postulated the organic connection of man with nature by the creative power of labour. Another is Jizchaq Kabenkin. He was a Marxist, but Marxism one can leave aside here. A third is Leiv Japhet who wanted to motivate the moshav, the cooperative settlement. That is what I wanted to say.

Reventlow: Now I want to speak myself, against the sequence. I wanted to say that I believe, it would be wrong simply to assume a biblical model, a model of society, and to transpose it to the present time. I want to give two extreme examples in order to show how absurd that would be. In the sixteenth century it was common use to prove absolute monarchy out of the Bible on the model of David and other just kings. There exists a literature on it, even sermons and laudations. It was a usual model then. A modern model is the segmentary society, which is connected with the name of Kippenberg who tried to explain early Israel as a society of total equality without rulers and subjects. But in the meantime also this model has become untenable, because the idea of a society without rulers does not fit even for the

earliest conditions in Israel, before the monarchy, as Lemche and
others have shown, in my opinion, convincingly. It is impossible
simply to take patterns from the Bible as a model. The approach has
to be started otherwise.

Falk: I wanted to reply to the things we have heard from Professor
Amir with the following: as regards secularization I want to remind
you of Dietrich Bonhoeffer's 'Christianity without Religion'. I would
say, from a Jewish viewpoint this is something quite usual. I would
connect it with the verse in Jeremiah:

על־מה אבדה הארץ ויאמר יהוה על־עזבם את־תורתי

Why has the land been destroyed?. . . God speaks: Because they have
left my tora (Jer. 9.11-12).

This moves the sages to develop it in the following way: 'God says: I
would like them to keep my commandments, even when they have left
me, because the light lying in the commandments would lead them
back'. This is an absolute ethical definition in that it does not aim at
the authority standing behind the commandments, but at the content of
these commandments. Therefore I think that an application of biblical
ideas should be possible which does not start from the theological
basis and hope for a theological insight as the result of a process of
education, but which lies in the commandments themselves. Therefore
I mean that in fact the question of secularization and the reaction of
secularized society is very basic for Judaism and Christianity and for
the religions at all, and that we must find ways to make the thought of
the Bible about justice fruitful, without the theological fundamentals
being a *conditio sine qua non* for its understanding.

Frey: You have taken the words out of my mouth! I believe every
religion concedes that reason can rule also outside of it. At least I see
this in the Old Testament. I must remind myself of Bileam, who, I
think, was no Israelite, but did in this case what was human and reasonable. But there are other figures. What about Ruth and Boas, and
so on? Also Christianity must over and over again let itself be
reminded that its God is greater than what it proclaims and what it
believes about him, that he is therefore not in the story of theologians.
The task of translation is so important! Therefore I want to ask: how
are things running in modern Israel? I would like to learn about this
legislation, how biblical impulses, British law and whatever social
systems interact. What does really happen there?

Amir: One could answer that, having just heard Professor Reventlow saying that to assume the model is evidently not a sufficient way for doing justice to the task of translation. Of course one has tried to assume models in building up Palestine. The legislation of Keren Kajemet, the National Foundation, was strictly directed upon a not-absolute possession of ground. The principle of 'mine is the ground' was there replaced by 'the ground is national', meaning after a certain time of tenure the ground has to be given back to the national institution, in order to prevent the individual possession of the ground, to prevent ground-speculation and so on. How that has been developed, how that has been evaded and so on, is a very complicated question, about which Professor Falk could say more than I could.

Falk: For this, we wait upon another invitation, for another symposium.

Reventlow: As Professor Falk is just mentioning this key word, I would like to end by expressing my wish that our dialogue which began in Tel Aviv and is now continued in Bochum, can be continued at the next opportunity. We have seen how many questions and also answers are common to us and how we learn in this way that we are placed into a common task. We observe that we go our different ways while coming from the same Bible. I want to thank all who have contributed not only to this discussion, but also with lectures, by taking part in the dialogues and by offering helping hands in different services for the success of our symposium, also all who only listened. I hope all of us will take something of it home with us.

Uffenheimer: At the end allow me to express my thanks for your hospitality, for our friendly reception. I believe and I hope that this dialogue can and must be continued to a mutual enrichment. As I have already indicated in my opening words, the centre of the Christian world is the theological interest, which is not yet developed with us in the same degree. I spoke about the interest in details, because the return to our land has made us interested in each part of the Bible and its concrete meanings in such a way that a 'Theology of the Bible' has not yet been written. Except if one takes Kaufmann's great book *Toledot Ha-Emuna Jisraelit*, which, however, is something totally other than theology in the Western sense. Secondly, I want to thank all my colleagues of Bochum for their contributions. Thirdly, the student hearers who showed their lively interest by their intent listening.

So I hope that we did not just inspect biblical models. We did not want to realize biblical models, but only principles according to which we can build new models. I hope that we will not just meet in Tel Aviv, but in Jerusalem:

בשנה הבאה בירושלם

JOURNAL FOR THE STUDY OF THE OLD TESTAMENT

Supplement Series